THE
MILLENNIAL
MAZE

Sorting Out Evangelical Options

STANLEY J. GRENZ

INTERVARSITY PRESS
DOWNERS GROVE, ILLINOIS 60515

InterVarsity Press is the book-publishing division of InterVarsity Christian Fellowship, a student movement active on campus at hundreds of universities, colleges and schools of nursing in the United States of America, and a member movement of the International Fellowship of Evangelical Students. For information about local and regional activities, write Public Relations Dept., InterVarsity Christian Fellowship, 6400 Schroeder Rd., P.O. Box 7895, Madison, WI 53707-7895.

Cover illustration: Roberta Polfus
ISBN 0-8308-1757-3

Printed in the United States of America ∞

Library of Congress Cataloging-in-Publication Data
Grenz, Stanley, 1950-
    The millennial maze: sorting out evangelical options/Stanley J.
Grenz.
      p.   cm.
    Includes bibliographical references.
    ISBN 0-8308-1757-3 (alk. paper)
    1. Millennialism.   2. Dispensationalism.   3. Eschatology.
   4. Evangelicalism.   I. Title.
   BT891.G74   1992
   236'.9—dc20
                                         92-14865
                                            CIP

16	15	14	13	12	11	10	9	8	7	6	5	4	3	2
04	03	02	01	00	99	98	97	96	95	94	93			

To Al Parmenter,
seminary schoolmate,
who raised for me
the question
of the millennium

98848

Preface

For as long as I can remember I have been interested in eschatology. I can still vividly recall viewing *The Thief in the Night* and other significant evangelical films depicting the Second Coming during Sunday-evening gatherings in the churches where my father served as pastor. And I remember as well being the kid confronting his fellow elementary school students with the necessity of becoming Christians before it was too late— before the horrors of the tribulation came upon the inhabitants of the earth.

Although as a seminary student in the 1930s my father had been instructed in the postmillennialism of A. H. Strong, early in his ministry he had become an ardent dispensationalist. It was therefore quite in keeping with the sincere piety of my childhood home that when I graduated from high school in 1968 my parents presented me with a leather-bound New Scofield Reference Bible.

When I entered Denver Seminary in 1973, I learned firsthand that not all evangelicals are dispensationalists. My New Testament professor, Kermit Ecklebarger, was a promoter of "historic premillennialism" with its focus on the posttribulation rapture. Although this raised in my mind the question of the time of the rapture, the basic premillennial chronology that I had inherited as a child remained intact. As I progressed from junior to middler status and prepared to enter systematic theology classes, I offered a cavalier remark about the matter to Al Parmenter, a Denver seminarian who, being a year ahead of me, was in the midst of determining his own view. I told him that for me the millennium was not even an issue, but that only the rapture question remained open. Al's struggle with amillennialism, however, soon infected me. As a consequence of my studies, despite the tutelage of an avowed dispensationalist theology professor, I graduated from a staunch premillennial seminary as an amillennialist.

In addition to raising for me the question of the millennium, my education at Denver Seminary introduced me to the newer thinking about eschatology. Of special importance were the young German scholars connected with the "theology of hope," especially Wolfhart Pannenberg. Subsequent doctoral work with Pannenberg in Munich, Germany, resulted in my coming to see a deeper significance to eschatology beyond the mere question of the time and nature of the thousand years spoken of by John in Revelation 20:1-8. Eschatology shapes our attitude as the people of God in the world.

Such reflection led me to conclude that classical amillennialism does not offer the final answer to this deeper dimension of the millennial debate. Rather, there are also important truths articulated by premillennialism and even by the all-too-readily-dismissed view known as postmillennialism.

My theological odyssey, therefore, is not dissimilar to that traversed by many other evangelicals. It has led me out of the older dispensationalism, through historic premillennialism, into an amillennialism sympathetic to postmillennialism. In the end, the "end times chronology" I have come to accept resembles that of amillennialism. But I find the traditional amillennial understandings of the thousand years unsatisfying. In contrast to the "unearthly" emphasis on a spiritual realm, characteristic of many classical amillennialists, I believe that the biblical vision demands that we focus our attention on a transformed creation as our final abode. In this task of making sense of who we are to be—and to become—as the people of God in the world, I find helpful theological insights in all the millennial positions.

In one sense, then, I have left the dispensationalism bequeathed to me by my father and childhood church community. At the same time, I retain great respect for this tradition and for the positive contribution dispensationalism has made and continues to make to evangelicalism.

In the era of transition in which we are living, evangelical thinkers—whether they be among the so-called laity or vocational pastors—must understand the various currents of eschatology that have shaped the movement in which we participate. But we dare not leave the discussion of the millennium at its current impasse nor dismiss the entire matter as if it had no importance. Rather, because there are deeper issues at stake in this debate, we must strive to see clearly the world view represented by each of the major positions. And having done so, we can then listen intently to what the Spirit is saying to the church through each.

It is to this end—that the discussion might be advanced and that the voice of the Spirit might be heard—that this book is offered to the church.

I owe a word of gratitude to several persons who provided valuable assistance in the process of seeing these pages to print—to the support staff at Carey Theological College, Beverley Norgren and Lois Thompson; to my teaching assistants, Gerald Deguire and Jane Rowland; and of course to Jim Hoover of InterVarsity Press. Above all, I thank Professor Bruce Ware of Trinity Evangelical Divinity School who graciously offered crucial suggestions to the entire work, but especially to the treatment of dispensationalism.

May the Sovereign Lord of history be pleased to employ our efforts in the expansion of his reign. To him alone be glory in the church.

Stanley J. Grenz
Holy Week 1992

Introduction

> And I saw the souls of those who had been beheaded because of their
> testimony for Jesus and because of the word of God. . . . They came to
> life and reigned with Christ a thousand years. (Rev 20:4)

In April 1981, James McCullough, a successful Arizona surgeon, terminated his medical practice, his wife sold her Nevada boutique, and they parted with their Porsche in anticipation of the Second Coming. They, together with the other members of the Lighthouse Gospel Tract Foundation of Tucson, Arizona, were preparing to be lifted to heaven on the date predicted by their leader, Bill Maupin—June 28, 1981. On earth would follow the tribulation and the rule of the antichrist until Christ's return to set up his millennial kingdom, which Maupin calculated to be set for May 14, 1988. Fellow church member Bub Bowman noted, "We're ready for the rapture. My little one sort of wants a three-wheeler before it happens, but we're ready to go."[1]

About the same time a totally fallacious news item was being reprinted in several Christian publications concerning a purported incident involving the United States Internal Revenue Service.[2] Supposedly the IRS had sent out a number of social security checks that the banks were instructed not to cash unless the bearer had the proper identification—a "mark in the right hand or forehead." The fallacious news story then added that when contacted IRS officials said the checks had been erroneously circulated prior to their intended effective date—1984.

Declarations of the impending end of the age do not always come on the heels of apparent setbacks in world affairs. For example, the fall of the Iron Curtain, the defeat of Iraq, the arrival in Israel of Ethiopian and Soviet Jews and the new burst of democracy in the world led the ultra-orthodox Jewish Lubavitch movement to announce in the summer of 1991 the imminent arrival of the Messiah. In fact, some members believe that the sect's spiritual leader, Rabbi Schneerson of Brooklyn, New York, may be the long-expected Messiah.[3]

Maupin's date setting, the "news" item concerning the coming mark of the beast and the Lubavitch announcement are only three among a rash of incidents in recent decades related to heightened expectations concerning the return of the Messiah to inaugurate the thousand-year kingdom. Interest in the sequence of events that must transpire in the "end times" and after the coming of the King, however, is not merely a late-twentieth-century phenomenon. Even before his ascension Christ's followers asked, "Will you now restore the kingdom to Israel?" Repeatedly church history has witnessed times of increased speculation concerning the end and the advent of a golden age on earth. The approach of the year A.D. 1000, for example, caused a great stir of expectations. When both that year and A.D. 1033 (a thousand years after Christ's death) passed, interest turned to A.D. 1065, for in that year Good Friday coincided with the Day of the Annunciation. Multitudes journeyed to Jerusalem to await the Lord's return, some arriving already during the previous year and waiting in the Holy City until after Easter.[4]

In the United States, the nineteenth century brought continuous waves of interest in end-times predictions, especially among those who looked for an earthly reign of Christ following that grand day. Historian Ernest Sandeen notes that from 1843 to 1848 and again from 1867 to 1870, "prophetic calculation and civil unrest coincided to bring expectations to a boil."

He adds, "Some prophetic scholars seemed to possess an indestructible faith in their ability to predict the time of the next great fulfillment of prophecy; no sooner had their hopes for one date been dashed by the passing of time than they rushed into print with another prediction."[5] The rise of communism, two world wars, the rebirth of the state of Israel and the conflicts and tensions in the Middle East provided sufficient fodder for a repeat of end times and millennial speculation throughout the twentieth century.

Times of increased anticipation of the imminent end of the age and the dawn of the thousand-year reign gave birth to a multitude of religious groups, each of which originally sought to advance a specific teaching concerning the chronology and nearness of these events. Many sought as well to prepare themselves and the world for the Second Coming and the kingdom era that it would inaugurate. The list of such groups ranges from the Montanists of the patristic era to the Seventh-day Adventists in the nineteenth century, not to mention the numbers of small sects oriented toward the end-time theme that have populated the religious landscape of the twentieth century.

Incidents of speculation and date setting throughout church history indicate that the question of the time and nature of the return of Jesus Christ, especially when coupled with specific understandings concerning the earthly kingdom era that supposedly lies beyond that event, holds continual fascination for Christians. Indeed, our Lord did instruct his disciples to be prepared for the coming of the Son of man at the end of the age. And repeatedly the New Testament writers admonish believers to live in the light of that glorious day.

Above any other text of Scripture, John's vision of the thousand-year reign of those martyred for the cause of Christ—and not passages that center more closely on the rapture and the question of *when* the Lord will return—has captured the imagination of Christians throughout the centuries. This verse has been the focus of interest for believers who have sought to dispel the mystery of God's action and anticipate the flow of history until it climaxes in the consummation of the age. Consequently, this verse—Revelation 20:4—stands at the heart of the differing expectations concerning the Second Coming of Jesus and the events that surround that glorious occasion.

The biblical teaching concerning Christ's return and the proper expectations of the church concerning the future are among the topics systematic theologians discuss under the broader category of eschatology (or the doctrine of last things). This focus is indicated by the term itself. The word "eschatology" arises from two Greek terms, *eschatos,* an adjective that means "farthest" or "last," and *logos,* a noun meaning "word" or "study." Eschatology, therefore, is the word concerning, or the study of, what is ultimate or last, that is, what is final in the program of God.

Taken as a whole, eschatology speaks concerning several dimensions of what is final in God's program, as well as the inaugurated aspects of that grand purpose. It focuses on what lies beyond for individual human life; hence, it treats death and life after death. Eschatology also focuses on what is final for corporate human history; consequently it seeks to delineate how God will bring human history to its climax and how that goal is already at work in the present. Finally, the doctrine of last things addresses what is final with respect to the cosmos in its entirety; therefore, it speaks of the way in which God's entire activity in the universe is being moved toward its intended goal in the eternal reality that lies beyond the flow of history. In short, within the context of Christian doctrine the topic of eschatology provides an overarching vision of the faith. It seeks to set forth what is the ultimate goal toward which God's work in the world is directed, how that work will be consummated and in what manner that goal is already in the process of being realized.

One issue of eschatology with which many Christians have struggled throughout church history and that forms a crucial topic for many today focuses on the actual chronology of the events that lie before us. What will be the sequence of happenings that will lead up to and then immediately follow Jesus' return to the earth? Foundational to this question, however, is a more focused query: What is the relation of the golden age anticipated by the prophets, and more specifically the thousand-year period envisioned by the seer in Revelation 20:1-8, to the return of Christ?

This more significant question concerning the millennium prophesied in the Bible is the main focus of the following chapters. Because the millennial question is its primary focus, this book is a volume on eschatology. It is not, however, a treatment of the doctrine of the last things in its entirety. Rather, it speaks to only one of several crucial issues addressed by the broader doctrine. Its goal is to assist the process of bringing a degree of clarity to that central eschatological issue: How are we to understand the vision of the thousand-year reign of the blessed followers of Christ with their Lord?

1

THE NEARNESS
OF THE END

The Millennium Question in the Bible & in the Present

A s the twentieth century approaches its end," notes culture commentator Christopher Lasch, "the conviction grows that many other things are ending too. Storm warnings, portents, hints of catastrophe haunt our times. The 'sense of ending,' which has given shape to so much of twentieth century literature, now pervades the popular imagination as well."[1] What Lasch perceives concerning the prevailing popular conviction was evidenced in a comment purportedly voiced in the fall of 1983 by President Ronald Reagan to the executive director of the American-Israeli Public Affairs Committee:

You know, I turn back to your ancient prophecies in the Old Testament and the signs foretelling Armageddon and I find myself wondering if we're the generation that is going to see that come about. I don't know if you've noted any of those prophecies lately, but, believe me, they certainly describe the times we're going through.[2]

Lasch has put his finger on what appears to be a profound permanent result produced by the monumental changes accompanying the breakdown of the modern era. The mood widespread in our society poses a grave danger to the future of the world. At the same time, its presence offers a crucial opportunity for the church as we seek to proclaim the good news of the soon return of the risen Lord Jesus Christ.

The Mood of Society and the Contemporary Church

The last several decades have witnessed the shattering of many of the illusions that dominated the ethos of previous generations. One of the most tenacious of these was the unbridled optimism that lay at the heart of the world view of the modern era, the unfaltering belief in the inevitability of progress that had been a cardinal doctrine of the faith of Western culture since the Enlightenment. It was self-evident to the previous generation that careful application of the scientific method could only result in a continuous advancement in knowledge. And as knowledge increased and was disseminated, the orthodox doctrine of modernity believed, humankind could take increasing control of the realm of nature and thereby surmount the social ills humans faced. In keeping with this attitude, "progressive" became the code word of the modern era, the criterion for all activity and the chief acclamation for what was perceived to be good and righteous.[3]

The heyday of the modern era came in the nineteenth century. The mood of Western culture at that point in history was one of optimism and progress. People looked forward to expansion and development in the coming days. No obstacle seemed sufficiently tenacious that it could not be overcome by the onslaught of the forces of human advancement. The mood of optimism and progress characteristic of the nineteenth century fostered a flourishing of various types of utopianism. Christian progressivism suggested that the advancing spread of the gospel throughout the world would result in the triumph of the Christian faith and the advent of a better day. Its heretical cousin, Marxist utopianism, offered a secularized alternative. It anticipated the victory of the proletariat as the climax to the class struggle.

As a consequence of the widespread optimism and utopianism little thought was given to the possibility of the world coming to a catastrophic end. The future was bright. No ominous clouds had yet gathered to darken the horizon of expectation.

A significant reversal in expectations for the future soon emerged, however. In contrast to the optimism of the nineteenth century, the mood since the mid-twentieth century has been generally one of pessimism. This phenomenal shift in attitude began in Europe at about the time of the First World War and slowly spread to North America. Its onward march was abetted by the Second World War, major conflicts in Korea and Viet Nam, and skirmishes in many parts of the world. The German Old Testament scholar Klaus Koch notes the importance of World War 2 to the rise of pessimism in Europe. After the outbreak of this war, "nearly all discerning Christians had finally lost faith in a divinely willed progress in history," so much so that "longing for the speedy approach of the kingdom of God in time became suspect."[4] By century's end pessimism had become the dominant motif not only on the European continent but throughout the Western world.

In addition to the succession of military conflicts in our century, another cause of the contemporary pessimism was an increased awareness that profound problems threaten not only our lives but even the existence of life itself on earth. Our generation was raised knowing the threat of nuclear war, the possibility of worldwide famine and the dire problems related to overpopulation. The last decades have been marked by energy crises, financial crises, health crises and now, most ominous of all, ecological crises. Not only do these menacing realities have the potential to undermine the fabric of stable society in the present, they also cast a foreboding shadow across the very future of humankind and the earth as a whole.

Widespread awareness of the crucial problems of our day, facilitated by the broad access to information characteristic of our technologically advanced age, has meant that people today are faced with the definite possibility of a cosmic catastrophe—the world could indeed come to an end.[5] The crisis in the contemporary Zeitgeist that this realization produced is profound. It means that the central dictum on which the modern world was founded—progress through ever-increasing technological and social advancement—is now being questioned. The well-ordered world view that has sustained Western society for decades is now collapsing around us.

As a result of these phenomenal changes in world view, the biblical vision of an end to history no longer seems as far-fetched as the modern mentality once perceived it to be. At the close of the twentieth century, the message of the doomsday preachers—once the brunt of jokes and the laughingstock of "enlightened" citizens of the modern world—has become in the minds of many people a serious possibility and a genuine concern in a way unparalleled in prior decades. For the first time in recent history, we sense that our civilization is tottering on the edge of a precipice peering into the abyss of self-destruction and chaos.

Ours is not the first generation to be gripped by a sense of the imminent end of the world, nor is ours the first age of pessimism the world has known. Other generations have passed through a "crisis of faith" precipitated by a loss of hope for the future. What is unique now is the depth of the crisis and the way people today conduct life on the brink of disaster. Unlike similar periods in the past, the current crisis of faith is the product of the growing awareness that technology is becoming increasingly capable of bringing about the kind of ghastly scenario that people at various times in history have feared. As a consequence of this lost faith in the future many people in our generation resign the world to its fate—possible imminent annihilation—and turn their gaze to their present, private worlds. This move is typified by the commonly expressed hesitancy to bring children into "this world," an attitude in which Robert Lifton finds an indication that the traditional modes of immortality (such as the desire to live on in one's children) have lost their power.[6]

Accompanying the sense of despair in the face of the future is a loss of the past. In contrast to earlier ages, people today are no longer driven by a sense of historical continuity, an awareness that they belong to a succession of generations uniting past, present and future.

Christopher Lasch has termed the turn to the self spawned by the prevailing mood of hopelessness "the culture of narcissism." He writes:

> People today hunger not for personal salvation, let alone for the restoration of an earlier golden age, but for the feeling, the momentary illusion, of personal well-being, health, and psychic security. To live for the moment is the prevailing passion—to live for yourself, not for your predecessors or posterity.[7]

The current reawakening of our society to the possibility of the end of the world as we know it and the despair that this awareness has provoked in contemporary society offers a grave challenge to the people of God. Throughout its history, the church has proclaimed that the curtain of history will be brought down by nothing less than the glorious return of the risen and exalted Lord Jesus Christ. This event, which a mere generation ago secularists held up to ridicule on the basis of the prevailing belief in optimism and progress, is the only genuine hope possible in a world despairing of the future and disconnected from the past.

In the midst of the current climate of uncertainty, however, Christians who have earnestly sought to remain true to the great doctrines of biblical and historic Christianity find themselves unable to articulate with one voice a message of hope for our world. Among the areas dividing the Christian ranks, few have been as explosive as those surrounding the doctrine of "last things," or eschatology.

One central point of disagreement involves the meaning of the thousand-year reign of Christ found in the vision of Revelation 20 and hence the expectation of a future millennial kingdom. Since the breakdown of the evangelical consensus in the nineteenth century, evangelicals have held to differing views on this question. Differences over eschatology have not merely been confined to groups on the fringe of the movement but have found their way into mainstream evangelicalism as well. Unfortunately, such differences have fostered divisions—at times even the breaking of fellowship—among believers who otherwise share broad agreement concerning the central doctrines of the faith.

Christians who are committed to the proclamation of the return of their Lord as the only final hope for the world must seize the opportunity the current mood offers the church. To do so, however, they will need to move beyond the divisions in their ranks caused by differences over the millennial issue. Such divisions only serve to hinder the cause of the gospel in the world and are a source of confusion to people both in the church and in the world.

The healing of the current divisions among evangelical Christians will not be accomplished by a simple exoneration of one or another of the protagonists in the contemporary discussion of eschatology. It is most probably not the case that one view is solely correct and biblical, whereas the others are totally false. Consequently, true progress toward a consensus on the question of the millennium is possible only as we come to see the strengths and weaknesses of each of the various systems. Then we will be in a position to move the entire question to a deeper level, from which we are able to discover and utilize the valid theological point each participant in the discussion is seeking to make.

Major Contemporary Options in the Millennial Debate

Over the course of the last hundred years, evangelicals have differed with each other concerning the events surrounding the return of Christ, especially as they focus on the question of the thousand-year reign of the saints with their Lord. More specifically, the debate focuses on two issues, the nature of the millennial reign and the relationship between the visible return of Christ and the thousand-year period.

Although each view contains differences of detail, three basic positions, the most popular of which may be delineated into two basic varieties, subsume the parameters of the current discussion within evangelicalism. The nomenclature popularly used to delineate these basic positions arises from the answer given by each to the second question, namely, the time of the return of Christ relative to the millennium.

A first position represented among evangelicals carries the label "post-millennialism." As the name suggests, adherents of this view antici-pate that the physical return of Christ will occur *after* an earthly golden age, the era of peace and righteousness that the vision in Revelation 20:1-6 pictures in terms of a thousand-year reign of Christ. Hence, the Second Coming is "postmillennial." This viewpoint emphasizes the conti-nuity between the current era and the golden age. The thousand years will be a period of time much like our own, but with a heightened expe-rience of goodness, due to the pervasive influence of Christian principles throughout the world. Postmillennialism also emphasizes human involve-ment in the advent of the millennium. Although the golden age comes as the work of the Holy Spirit, God employs human efforts in advancing its coming.

Other Christians adhere to a second viewpoint, commonly termed "amil-lennialism." The word itself means literally "no millennium." Its propo-nents do not anticipate a literal one-thousand-year golden age sometime in the future but find some other significance to the symbol in Revelation 20. Some amillennialists interpret the figure as referring to a specific period of time in the past during which Christ held sway in his church. Or it could symbolize the church age in its entirety, so that the reign mentioned is either one dimension of the experience of the church as a whole or of the individual believer. Others interpret the thousand years as the reign of departed saints in the heavenly realm during this age. Or the chapter may be a vision of the eternal kingdom of God. In any case, all amillennialists anticipate that the Second Coming of Christ will mark the beginning of eternity without an intervening interregnum.

Advocates of a third position, commonly called "premillennialism," ex-pect the return of the Lord prior to the thousand-year period mentioned in Revelation 20. Thus, Christ's coming is "premillennial," that is, before the millennium. Contemporary adherents of this viewpoint anticipate that Jesus will be physically present on the earth to exercise world dominion during his thousand-year reign. This period of time will be marked by goodness and a relative absence of evil, insofar as Satan will be restrained from exercising influence over human affairs until the age comes to a close. In contrast to postmillennialism, this view emphasizes the discontinuity between the current age and the thousand years. This discontinuity means that human agency plays no role in the coming of the golden age. Rather, the millennium arrives solely as the gift of divine grace and only after a catastrophic act of God that brings the present eon to a close.

Adherents of premillennialism among evangelicals fall into two distinct groups, historical premillennialists and dispensational premillennialists. The "historic" in the name "historic premillennialism" arises from the claim of proponents that this variety of premillennialism has been present in the church since the patristic era. Its defenders anticipate a time of tribulation directed against the church, climaxed by Christ's coming to rescue the community of his disciples from the forces of evil. The millennium, in turn, is a time for God to bless Christ's faithful followers.

The term "dispensational" in "dispensational premillennialism" is derived from the tendency of its adherents to divide human history into distinct periods of time or "dispensations." Beyond this emphasis, dispensationalists differ from their historic premillennialist cousins on the basis of their understanding of which people will be the focus of God's attention in the tribulation and the millennial era. Rather than view the future tribulation and millennium in terms of God's program for the New Testament church, dispensationalism tends to find the significance of these eras in God's intention for national Israel.

During the tribulation God will be preparing Israel to accept their Messiah. Consequently, the majority of dispensationalists hold to the pretribulational rapture, although there are some who anticipate the rapture either at the midpoint of the tribulation or at its close. The teaching of a pretribulation rapture asserts that the church will be removed from the earth prior to this awful period. Further, just as the tribulation is the time of "Jacob's trouble," so also the millennium will be the time during which God will pour out unparalleled blessings on Israel. Thus, national Israel, not the New Testament church, is prominent in the dispensationalist understanding of the vision of the thousand years.

Corporate Eschatology and the Biblical Message

The contemporary discussion of eschatology among evangelicals, fueled as it is by questions surrounding the significance of the vision of Revelation 20, ought not to be dismissed as being of no consequence to the Christian faith. On the contrary, by considering the question of millennialism, evangelicals are engaged in a debate concerning the climax of human history, understood in terms of God's intention for creation. In so doing, the parties to the discussion are probing a theme crucial to the biblical message, the *euangelion* (gospel), the proclamation of which evangelicals have always seen as central to the Christian mandate in the world.

The anticipation of a climax to human history—a corporate eschatology—and the resultant question concerning the millennium as a specific stage in that climax cannot be relegated to the fringes of the biblical proclamation. On the contrary, it belongs to the heart of what the Bible intends to teach.

The Scriptures as a whole assert that God's program is directed to the bringing about of a redeemed people living within a redeemed creation. The Bible presents history as meaningful, in that it is directed toward a goal— namely, the reign of God or the presence of the will of God throughout the earth. This goal forms the central petition of the Lord's Prayer: "Your kingdom come, your will be done on earth as it is in heaven" (Mt 6:10).

The Bible, therefore, presents history in the form of a narrative, the recounting of the acts of the Sovereign Lord of history accomplishing his goal. This biblical story reaches its climax with the grand vision of the new heaven and new earth anticipated by certain Old Testament prophets, such as Isaiah, and developed more fully by the closing chapters of the book of Revelation.

John, the inspired seer who wrote the Revelation, looked to an eon beyond the present that will mark the completion of the divine program in human history. The future new order will be characterized by reconciliation and harmony. Its citizens will live in fellowship with each other, with creation and most importantly with God.

The seer pictured the new order as a human society, a city, the new

Jerusalem (Rev 21:9-21). In that city, nature will again fulfill its purpose of providing nourishment for its inhabitants (Rev 22:1-4). Most glorious of all, however, God will dwell with humans on the new earth:

> And I heard a loud voice from the throne saying, "Now the dwelling of God is with men, and he will live with them. They will be his people, and God himself will be with them and be their God. . . ."
>
> The throne of God and of the Lamb will be in the city, and his servants will serve him. They will see his face, and his name will be on their foreheads. (Rev 21:3; 22:3-4)

John's vision forms the climax to a long history of prophetic promise that stretches back to the Garden of Eden. God's intent from the beginning was to be *with* his people. The central focus of this divine promise, of course, lies in the coming of Immanuel—God with us (Mt 1:22-23). The final reality, the ultimate fulfillment of the promise, is the dwelling of God with humankind in the new heaven and new earth, which thereby brings to completion God's ultimate design for creation.

The centrality of John's vision of a future eon characterized by a new order of reconciliation and harmony indicates that what theologians call "corporate eschatology"—the consummation of human history—lies at the heart of the concern of the Bible, when understood from the perspective of the whole. God's ultimate intention is not directed to a transpositioning of the individual believer to an isolated, individual realm of unending "eternal life" beyond the world and time. Rather, God's program focuses on the corporate human story and therefore on humans as potential participants in a new society in the coming eon.

The Apocalyptic Background of Millennialism

The concepts of a corporate eschatology and a climax to human history so important to millennialism are central to the biblical message. Yet these expectations, especially as they incorporate a conception of a millennial rule, are the product of a specific trajectory in the development of the biblical outlook. This trajectory reached its height in what is generally called "the apocalyptic movement."

Over the last hundred years biblical scholars have come to understand the importance of apocalyptic as a special category or genre of writing.[8] Although its roots lay earlier in Old Testament history, this style flourished between 200 B.C. and A.D. 100 among Jewish and Jewish-Christian circles. Most of the apocalyptic writings were not included in either the Hebrew or the Christian canons. Nevertheless, the genre is represented to some extent in the biblical books of Daniel and Revelation, and possibly in sections of other canonical writings, including Isaiah, Zechariah and the synoptic Gospels.

Biblical scholars have pinpointed several characteristics typical of apocalyptic writings.[9] Central to this literary style is the use of visions as a means whereby a heavenly messenger reveals to the seer knowledge concerning decisively important aspects of the human destiny that had to this point been hidden in heaven but would soon transpire on earth. The seer often describes the spiritual turmoils these visions produced in the visionary's own countenance and then draws conclusions from the visions for the seer's community, including an "eschatological ethic," a call issued to the faithful to endure under persecution. The visionary generally employs rich, at times even bizarre, symbols to convey the heavenly message to the faithful community. The use of symbols is advantageous, as they serve to hide the meaning of the vision from the uninitiated eye while communicating clearly to members of the seer's own community.

Not only do the apocalyptic writings display certain common characteristics, they also set forth certain common themes.[10] Apocalypticists emphasized world history as the stage on which a cosmic drama is being played out. This drama pits God and the hosts of heaven in a fight to the death with Satan and the forces of evil. Consequently, the goal of world history is the replacement of all earthly empires, which are in the service of Satan, with the eternal kingdom of God.[11]

Presently the outcome of this conflict may appear to be in doubt, but according to the apocalypticists it is not. The transformation from the world kingdoms to the kingdom of God transpires when God ascends to his throne and asserts his sovereignty. Hence, the belief that ultimately

God is in control of history lies behind the apocalyptic vision.[12]

Although the kingdom of God is a future reality, it is nevertheless present, albeit in concealed form, as a hidden power currently at work in bringing the end to pass. Further, en route to the final goal, world history divides itself into distinctive time segments. The major content or characteristics of each of these ages was determined from the days of creation;[13] thereby the eons all give evidence of the underlying sovereignty of God.

Perhaps the most central and yet most radical characteristic of apocalyptic literature concerns its expectation of the soon overthrow of current earthly conditions, that is, the imminent, catastrophic end of the world. In fact, what sets the apocalyptic vision apart from other expectations of the consummation of history is the catastrophic nature of the event it anticipates; to the seers, the end comes as a grand cosmic event. This event will be preceded by the dominion of evil, a time of unprecedented persecution for the righteous, but also of widespread disaster and human suffering.[14]

From the expectation of an imminent catastrophe characteristic of this literature, Bible scholars have concluded that in the minds of the apocalypticists the anticipated future forms a contradiction to, rather than a continuation of, the present. Although he may have overstated the difference, H. H. Rowley capsulizes the situation: "Speaking generally, the prophets foretold the future that should arise out of the present, while the apocalyptists foretold the future that should break into the present."[15]

The players in this end-time scenario are not only humans but also armies of angels and demons who belong to the cosmic drama now being worked out on the earthly stage. Also of immense importance is a mediator figure, a person with royal and juristic functions, who is God's agent in the accomplishing of the final redemption and judgment.

The apocalypticists, therefore, were able to draw back the curtain that separates the heavenly from the earthly realm, so that the distinction between human and cosmic history evaporates. In the climactic event, the divine glory and the divine power over the spiritual hosts and over world history is revealed. Then, in the new eon lying beyond the catastrophic end of the age, this curtain remains open. The faithful saints of God participate with the good angels in the eternal divine kingdom, sharing thereby in the glory of that eon.

The point of the catastrophic scenario described by the apocalypticists, however, goes beyond the transmission of knowledge of future events and of the current situation in the light of the future. It has a definite ethical import for the present. The coming of God's power in judgment and salvation, according to the apocalyptic message, means that a line will be drawn between people. For the Jewish apocalypticists, this line not merely elevates Israel as God's chosen above the gentile nations. Rather, it also cuts through Israel itself. The righteous in Israel will be divided from the ungodly and apostate. Only the remnant will experience the salvation of God.

Consequently, the apocalyptic writings contain a note of urgency.[16] Their message is in part directed toward the people who name the name of God. The faithful are encouraged to remain firm to the end, to endure persecution during the short season of Satanic sway, in view of the glory to follow. The apostate in Israel and the ungodly nations are warned of their impending doom, which is sure to transpire when God assumes the cosmic throne and the kingdom of God replaces the kingdoms of the world.

The Old Testament Roots of Apocalypticism
The apocalyptic outlook reflected the world view of the Jewish people during the intertestamental period. But its development lay deeper in Hebrew history.

Earlier in our century scholars looked to influences outside of Israel, especially to Persia during the time of the exile, for the genesis of the rise of apocalyptic. However, recent scholarship has rejected this thesis in favor of sources within the Old Testament itself.[17] Some now argue that the phenomenon developed as an outgrowth of the wisdom literature after Judah no longer had its own king.[18] Jonathan Z. Smith, for example, articulates this theory: "Apocalypticism is Wisdom lacking a royal court and patron and therefore it surfaces during the period of Late Antiquity not as a response to religious persecution but as an expression of the trauma of the cessation of native kingship."[19]

Most scholars, however, look to the prophetic movement as the source of apocalypticism,[20] although holding out the possibility of its subsequent enrichment from wisdom traditions.[21] The trajectory of thought, they argue, moved from prophecy to apocalyptic.

The prophetic outlook was present in the early stages of Israelite history. With the establishment of the monarchy, however, prophets took on new roles, roles that were both political and religious.[22] During this era, God called certain prophets to confront royalty with the will of Yahweh and thereby to hold the king accountable to the divine ideal for the office of earthly rulership. Central to the prophetic message was the proclamation of Yahweh's desire for justice, the theme that eventually led to the expectations of a catastrophic in-breaking of God to establish salvation and mete out judgment, so characteristic of the apocalyptic literature.

The quest for justice was embedded in the Hebrew psyche from the beginning of nationhood. Through much of its history, Israel was an oppressed people. Deliverance from Egyptian bondage and immigration to the "Promised Land" did not bring the enjoyment of complete justice. Both internal and external factors contributed to the problem. Israel did not live in complete accordance with the law and the covenant with God. And Israel was continually buffeted by neighboring and indigenous peoples. Consequently, many looked to the inauguration of the kingship as the vehicle through which the situation would be rectified. However, in the face of repeated military pressure from powerful neighbors and falling prey to the temptation to use political position for selfish gain, Israel's kings were either unable or unwilling to establish justice in the land.

In the midst of this growing discontent and then subsequently as Israel came under the dominance of Assyria and Babylonia, the prophets increasingly directed the hopes of the faithful in Israel away from the present rulers and toward the future. A king would one day come in the name and power of Yahweh to bring justice to the nation. In this way Yahweh would vindicate his name and establish his glory.

This great event, however, would not be God's act alone; the people also had a role to play. The establishment of justice could come only after the people had prepared themselves for it. The prophets, therefore, came to view their task as including the proclamation of the divine call that Israel repent from their past covenant unfaithfulness and live righteously in view of the great deed that God would accomplish in the future.

The later prophets knew as well that God's act of self-vindication could not be an isolated, national event alone. In fact, from the foundation of the Hebrews as a people—as early as the call of Abraham—God had promised that this nation would be the vehicle of blessing to the entire world (Gen 12:1-3). Consequently, the demonstration of the divine glory must occur in the presence of all nations. This was only right, in that the oppression of Israel by the surrounding nations had called into question Yahweh's honor as the God of Israel.

The events of Israel's national history, however, turned dark. As an act of divine judgment on Israel for her moral and spiritual failure, God allowed foreign overlords to dissolve the national kingship and carry the people into captivity. The later return from Babylon did not bring the expected national revival. Soon the struggling Jewish state once again became the helpless pawn in international power politics.

As their expectations for the establishment of justice within history were repeatedly dashed, prophetic voices grew increasingly pessimistic in their view of the present world. Articulaters of the hope of restoration lifted their gaze beyond history to the eternal, cosmic realm. Divine salvation would not come in the ongoing history of the nation. Instead, the seers began to look to a divine act breaking into history and establishing a new creation in accordance with the eternal pattern.

As this shift in outlook occurred, apocalypticism was born. In the words of Paul D. Hanson, "The security and repose of a timeless realm of the vision of myth established itself as the hope of a people made weary by an overly harsh world."[23]

It was into this situation that Jesus came and the earliest gospel message was proclaimed.

Apocalyptic and Millennium

The book of Revelation indicates that the question concerning the millennium arose quite early in Christian history. Actually, however, by introducing the concept of a thousand-year reign of Christ into Christian eschatology, the Jewish-Christian community was merely advancing a theme derived from the late apocalyptic writings.

The Old Testament prophets had explored the relationship between the eternal destinies of individual humans and the destiny of the corporate nation. The apocalyptic movement continued this exploration. The book of Daniel, for example, drew the two eschatological themes together through the doctrine of the resurrection. At the end of the age, righteous and unrighteous will rise from their graves to face judgment. The righteous will join the nation of Israel to share the blessings of the eternal messianic kingdom that will be located on this earth.[24]

Beginning in the second century B.C., however, apocalypticists began to alter this viewpoint.[25] They became conscious that the earth, although purified, could not be the fitting location of an eternal messianic kingdom. Two possible solutions to this problem came to the fore. One moved the focal point of the kingdom from earth to heaven, substituting the image of a heavenly Jerusalem for the earthly as the seat of the messianic rule.[26] The other alternative reduced the messianic kingdom to a temporal reality and transposed the goal of the resurrection of the righteous beyond that transitory kingdom to an eternal, heavenly realm beyond.[27]

The disagreement as to whether the messianic kingdom was eternal and heavenly or temporal and earthly brought a corresponding division within the ranks of the apocalypticists concerning the placement of the eschatological judgment. The first alternative—that of an eternal messianic kingdom in the eternal new heavens and new earth—demanded that the judgment precede and initiate the messianic rule. The other—that of a temporal, earthly kingdom—shifted the judgment to the end of that era.[28]

The vision of the millennium within the last canonical book brought the question debated by the ancient apocalypticists into Christian theology. And it remains a point of contention among Christians today. Do the

Second Coming of Christ and the resurrection of all humankind, together with the eschatological judgment and the inauguration of the eternal kingdom, occur as one grand event? Or are they separated by a temporal messianic rule lasting a thousand years? In other words, does the eternal kingdom of God come as the catastrophic end to human history in an unmediated fashion, or are we to expect an interregnum of a thousand years, a golden age on earth? And how does the millennial vision of Revelation 20 fit together with the transformation of the Jewish expectations for a temporal messianic kingdom into the New Testament emphasis on the present kingship of Jesus?[29]

In contemporary evangelical circles this question, and not that of the general validity of the apocalyptic world view that formed its original context, has emerged as the crucially divisive issue.

2

ANTICIPATING THE END

Millenarianism in the History of the Church

*I*n contrast to other ancient Near-Eastern cultures and even the Greek and Roman societies, the Hebrews developed a keen historical consciousness. This development came to a climax in what historians refer to as apocalypticism. The apocalypticists displayed an intense interest in setting forth the overarching pattern of history and seeing current events within the context of the whole. History, they believed, followed a preordained plot; it was a drama, and the great political events could be understood only in terms of their role in that drama. As a drama, history will have an end, they maintained, and this end will be inaugurated by God himself, who will break into history in judgment and glory. This divine act will be followed by a glorious messianic era.[1]

The drama of history likewise has a theme, the apocalypticists declared. They interpreted the theme of history in moral categories, for they viewed the world as the stage for a cosmic struggle between good and evil. To speak about the meaning and the lesson of the events of history the visionaries employed symbolic language. By this means they could disclose the deeper realities underlying past and present events. And they used this language to assure their audience of the certainty of a climax to history in the not-too-distant future. Apocalypticism, therefore, formed the context in which early Christian corporate eschatology developed.

Millenarian Thought in the Early Church

In keeping with the apocalyptic context in which the gospel was first proclaimed, the early Christians gained a sense that they were living in the final period of time before the consummation of God's program. Like the apocalypticists, the early Christians held to a rudimentary chronology of the end. The present era will climax with a time of trial during which the forces of evil will run rampant. This will be followed by God's intervention on behalf of the saints (see, for example, 2 Thess 2:1-12). This chronology was enhanced and expanded under the influence of the final book of the canon, the Revelation of John (also known as the Apocalypse, a name arising from the Greek term *apokalypsis,* rendered "revelation" in the English). In the twentieth chapter John the seer reintroduces into the Christian chronology the concept of a messianic era anticipated by the visionaries of the intertestamental period. He speaks of a thousand-year reign of Christ, commonly referred to as the millennium (from the Latin term *mille,* "thousand").

From this common canonical root arose varying expectations and interpretations concerning the messianic rule. In the vicinity of Ephesus, the location of the seven churches addressed by the book of Revelation (now western Turkey), a millenarian tradition developed that shares certain features with modern premillennialism. This tradition focused on the material blessings that will accompany the future rule of Christ over the renewed physical earth following the resurrection at the end of this age.

The church father Papias, for example, a contemporary of Polycarp of Smyrna who tradition claims was a disciple of John, set forth as a teaching derived from apostolic times "that there will be a certain period of a thousand years after the resurrection from the dead when the kingdom of Christ must be set up in a material order on this earth."[2] Papias poured into this thousand-year period mentioned in the book of Revelation certain features of the expectations for the messianic era articulated by Isaiah and other Old Testament prophets: "all the animals, feeding only on the produce of the earth, shall live in peaceful harmony together, and in perfect subjection to man."

Another approach to millenarianism filtered into Christian thought from Hellenistic Judaism and exercised a lasting impact on subsequent eschatology. This view was built on the "creation-day world-age" theory. Based on Peter's statement, "With the Lord a day is like a thousand years, and a thousand years are like a day" (2 Pet 3:8), it linked the seven days of creation set forth in Genesis 1 with seven millennia of world history. The theory allowed Christian chronographers, perhaps first in the vicinity of Antioch, Syria, to attempt to calculate the date of Christ's Second Coming to inaugurate the final millennium.[3] Common among these thinkers was the idea that Jesus had been born in the sixth millennium.[4]

The second-century church father and early apologist Justin Martyr linked the creation-day world-age theory with the premillennialism of Papias and the Ephesian tradition. He equated the seventh age with the millennial era. With conviction typical of many modern premillennialists, Justin reported, "I and others who are right-minded Christians at all points, are assured that there will be a resurrection of the dead, and a thousand years in Jerusalem, which will then be built, adorned, and enlarged as the prophets and Ezekiel and Isaiah and others declare." At the same time, he refused to make eschatology a test of orthodoxy, for he added, "Many who belong to the pure and pious faith and are Christians think otherwise."[5]

Perhaps the most complete expression of patristic premillennialism is found in the writings of the second-century bishop of Lyons, Irenaeus. His chronology of the end included a three-and-a-half-year rule of antichrist, who will desecrate the Jerusalem temple. His reign, however, will be interrupted by the return of Christ to consign him to the lake of fire and to bring the era of righteousness, "the seventh day," to the saints.[6] After the millennium occur the general resurrection, the judgment and the eternal state. Irenaeus envisioned that the millennium will be preceded by the resurrection of the righteous to fleshly bodies. Further, during this era creation will be restored to its primal state for the sake of the saints, as prophesied in Isaiah 65:20-25. Irenaeus offered a picturesque expansion of this expectation, which he perhaps derived from Papias:[7]

> The days will come, in which vines shall grow, each having ten thousand branches, and in each branch ten thousand twigs, and in each true twig ten thousand shoots, and in each one of the shoots ten thousand clusters, and in every one of the clusters ten thousand grapes, and every grape when pressed will give five and twenty metretes of wine. And when any one of the saints shall lay hold of a cluster, another shall cry out, "I am a better cluster, take me; bless the Lord through me."[8]

Irenaeus did not merely set forth the premillennial position, he also developed a theological rationale for the thousand years. The millennium is a necessary stage in the preparation of the righteous for eternity. Through their presence in this earthly kingdom they become accustomed to "incorruption," and thereby are prepared by a physical kingdom to inherit the completely spiritual realm. At the same time, the millennium functions as God's recompense for the earthly suffering of the saints. It is only just, he declared, that "in that very creation in which they toiled or were afflicted, being proved in every way by suffering, they should receive the reward of their suffering."[9]

The creation-day world-age theory that Justin and others employed did not necessarily lead to the materially oriented premillennialism of Irenaeus. This is exemplified by a work that probably predates the early apologist (being written sometime between A.D. 96 and 131), the *Epistle of Barnabas.* Although premillennialists often cite the author as an early proponent of their position, the situation is more complex. The Reformed premillennialist D. M. Kromminga argues that the epistle actually reflects certain features that mark modern amillennialism.[10]

Barnabas concluded from Genesis 1 that in six thousand years the Lord will bring the divine program to completion and inaugurate the sabbath rest,[11] a theme that apparently belonged to the Jewish tradition.[12] According to Kromminga's interpretation of *Barnabas,* however, although the seventh day prefigured in the creation narrative is an era of world history, it will not be superseded by another. Rather, it is identical with the eternal kingdom itself, symbolized in the eighth day, which will last forever.[13]

Although Kromminga's interpretation has not found universal agreement, it does point in the direction of the distinction between the outlook of the epistle and that of the patristic premillennialists such as Irenaeus. *Barnabas* brought together three themes: the Jewish concept of the repose of the seventh day, the Hellenistic concept of the seven eras of world history and the Christian emphasis on the importance of the eighth day.[14] Consequently, the work places its focus on the seven millennia giving rise to the eighth day, and not on millenarianism in the strict sense, as in later premillennialism.[15]

In addition to the connection between the seventh and eighth days, Kromminga found another characteristic in *Barnabas* that resembles modern amillennialism, namely, its exegetical method. The epistle is marked by a pervading anti-Judaism.[16] In keeping with this tone, *Barnabas* unhesitatingly applied to the church Old Testament promises originally given to Israel.[17]

On the basis of their preference for allegorical rather than literal exegesis, the Alexandrian church fathers had no place for any variety of millenarianism. Nor did a strong premillennial tradition develop in Rome. There were exceptions, however.

The most outstanding exception was Lactantius, tutor to Constantine's son, Crispus. His views concerning the physical pleasures to be enjoyed during the millennium paralleled those of Irenaeus: "The rocky mountains shall drip with honey; streams of wine shall run down, and rivers flow with milk."[18] But he moved beyond the tradition in linking the thousand years to anticipations of a golden age articulated by pagan thinkers who, he declared, had obtained some inklings of true doctrine:[19] "In short, those things shall then come to pass which the poets spoke of as being done in the reign of Saturnus."[20]

A second exception was Cyprian. Although he may not have advocated the premillennial position per se, like the apocalypticists he anticipated the coming of woes to accompany an early end of the world. Yet his rationale was different from theirs. Their expectations were based on the perception that the cosmic drama was drawing to a climax. Cyprian, in contrast, looked for a soon end of the world because he saw signs that nature was weakening through old age.[21] His thesis of the decline of nature exercised a powerful influence on subsequent eschatological thinking, even into the Reformation era, until it was replaced with the idea of progress indicative of the thinking that later became prominent in the modern epoch.[22]

For various reasons, the millennial expectation fell into disfavor in the post-Constantinian era. The anticipated chronology simply did not occur. No antichrist arose only to be vanquished by the gloriously returning Christ. Unexpectedly, the political situation was completely reversed. Rather than remain a small, persecuted sect at odds with the imperial government, Christianity became an institutionalized, privileged religion, whose adherents no longer stood in need of the comfort of future vindication that lay at the heart of premillennialism. Further, the Greek philosophical tradition, which dominated the theology of Alexandria, gained increasing influence on Christianity as a whole. Accordingly, salvation came to be viewed in terms of freeing oneself from matter, a conception at odds with the emphasis on the enjoyment of physical pleasures that typified the older expectation of a future millennium.[23]

The most significant factor in the demise of premillennialism, however, was the influence of the greatest theologian of the late patristic era, Augustine, bishop of Hippo from A.D. 395 to 431 Although once a premillennialist himself, Augustine came to reject this view because of its emphasis on the physical pleasures to be enjoyed during the thousand years— "that those who then rise again shall enjoy the leisure of immoderate carnal banquets, furnished with an amount of meat and drink such as not only to shock the feeling of the temperate, but even to surpass the measure of credulity itself." He rejected such ideas as believable "only by the carnal."[24]

The way toward Augustine's position had been paved by the work of another North African, the Donatist thinker Tyconius, from whose ideas the bishop drew.[25] In contrast to earlier exegetes but in keeping with the more allegorical exegetical method of Alexandria that he helped adapt to the emerging Latin theology, Tyconius understood the book of Revelation as a picture of the history of the church in the world, rather than as a prophecy of the end. Consequently, he interpreted the millennium as the present age, that is, the age of the church militant in the world. Augustine articulated a similar interpretation in his influential book *The City of God.*

In Book 20 of this work, Augustine set forth his interpretation of the central millennium text, Revelation 20. The linchpin of his exegesis is the claim that the second resurrection mentioned in the text, which sets the stage for the final judgment, refers to an event that accompanies the return of Christ, rather than coming a thousand years later. The "first resurrection," in turn, is an event of a totally different order. It is not a physical but a spiritual occurrence; it "regards not the body but the soul."[26] For Augustine, consequently, the first resurrection is a symbol referring to the personal spiritual experience of "passing from death to life," that is, of being raised from the death of sin into newness of life, which according to Catholic theology occurs in baptism. In keeping with this understanding he interpreted the casting of Satan into the bottomless pit as a reference to the divine restraining of the devil's full power of temptation so that the evil one is unable to seduce fully the elect. This was accomplished through the earthly ministry of Jesus.[27]

Augustine offered two possibilities for the meaning of the thousand years. Similar to the position articulated by the *Epistle of Barnabas,* this symbol could refer to the sixth millennium of God's program, through which the world was now passing and which would be followed by the eternal sabbath rest of the saints.[28] Or it could carry a more figurative sense, employing a number of perfection to represent the fullness of time, that is, "the whole duration of this world."[29]

By the time of Augustine's death, the nonmillenarian theology of Alexandria and Rome had engulfed the millennialism of Antioch and Ephesus. As a result, at the Council of Ephesus A.D. 431 the church condemned as superstition the belief in a literal, future thousand-year reign on the earth.

Augustine's various statements concerning the meaning of the millennium mentioned in Revelation 20 were not without some ambiguity. They could be (and were) readily understood to indicate that Christ's Second Coming should occur one thousand years after his first advent.[30] This implicit prediction, carrying as it did the authority of the bishop of Hippo, coupled both with the theme of the old age of the world and with a rise in political and natural disasters, resulted in a great sense of anticipation in parts of Christendom first as A.D. 1000 and then as A.D. 1033 approached.[31] When the years passed and the end did not come, this interpretation of the symbol in Revelation 20 required revision.

The necessary revision was forthcoming, based in part on a thesis readily at hand. For centuries theologians had been drawing a close link between the millennium of Revelation 20 and the church as the earthly kingdom of God. As the church became an established and integral part of society, it had lost much of its earlier apocalyptic fervor. In this new context many theologians had spiritualized the apocalyptic expectations and reinterpreted the kingdom of God in terms of the church on earth.[32]

The equating of church and kingdom could likewise claim the authority of Augustine. He had spoken of the church in the present as the kingdom of Christ and as sharing in Christ's rule.[33] This alternative reading of Augustine formed the center of the official teaching of the church on the matter through the Middle Ages.

Millenarian Thought in the Middle Ages

The outlook of the Middle Ages was dominated by static, as opposed to dynamic, concepts. The orthodox theologians viewed both the church and history in relationship to eternal, unchangeable realities. Their emphasis lay on the eternal teaching concerning the essentials of salvation that had been delivered to the apostles and entrusted to the church.

Medieval church theologians were not unconcerned with the interface between the process of time and the unchanging eternal pattern of reality at the foundation of the faith. But they described this relation in nonapocalyptic images. They no longer interpreted history by means of the image of a cosmic drama—as a drama complete with plot and climax—that lay behind millennialism. In its stead, most had substituted the image of the pilgrim people of God seeking a destination beyond history. Consequently, in the dominant medieval outlook the historical epoch since Christ's advent had no cosmic significance. It was simply the space between the two grand events of history, the Incarnation and the last judgment.

In keeping with this outlook, church theologians gave little attention to predictions concerning the end of the age and a future golden era on earth. The dominant eschatology was a modified Augustinianism that linked the institutional church to the kingdom of God. Participation in the rites of the church, it was believed, brought the believer into contact with the kingdom.

Typical of medieval thinking was the position outlined by "the angelic doctor" of the church, Thomas Aquinas. Aquinas anticipated no future, earthly millennial era. He did acknowledge that a new earth will follow the end of the age as predicted in Revelation, but its appearance will be quite different from the present world. No longer needed, plants and animals will cease to exist.[34] The blessed need no continuation of earthly life, for they will enjoy the vision of God. As for the events predicted in the book of Revelation, Aquinas acknowledged that they will occur. But they will happen suddenly, unpredictably and quickly. Consequently, prophecy provides no basis for anticipating the course of history, he asserted.

Nevertheless, the reference to a thousand years remained in sacred Scripture. Orthodox commentators offered various nonapocalyptic interpretations of the text. The figure referred to Christ's church on earth, to the human rest beyond time or to the repose of the saints between death and the resurrection. The latter position was set forth by the medieval thinker Aelfric and became the standard view among orthodox late medieval exegetes. According to Aelfric, the sixth age of human history is the era between the two advents of Christ; the seventh is not a literal stage of history but the state of death; and the eighth age is the eternal state that follows the resurrection.[35]

Not only did the nonmillenarian outlook become the standard for orthodoxy; beginning with the Council of Ephesus in the fifth century and throughout the Middle Ages, church leaders sought to suppress millenarianism. They promoted this campaign even to the point of altering the writings of premillennialists among the early church fathers, such as Irenaeus.[36] Despite these efforts and the nonmillenarian tone of official church teaching, however, millennial ideas persisted, and speculation concerning the date of the Lord's return continued both on the edges of church life and among certain orthodox theologians.[37]

Medieval millenarianism lay smoldering on the fringes of the church. It was present in popular religion, among the dispossessed of society and in many of the sects that cropped up along the edges of institutionalized Catholicism. A greater challenge to the official teaching, however, arose from the presence of millennial ideas within several of the acknowledged orders of the church.

Perhaps the central characteristic of medieval millennialism was its connection with ecclesiastical reform. Many millennialists pressed apocalyptic images into the service of their call for church renewal. They pointed to abuses present in the Roman Catholic church and maintained that church reform was the prerequisite for the dawning of the millennial golden era.

The reform-minded medieval millennialism, however, differed from the premillennialism present in the early church. In fact, it shares certain affinities with the postmillennialism of a later era. Millennialists in the Middle Ages looked forward to a golden era on earth occurring prior to the return of Jesus Christ, not subsequent to his second advent, as in premillennialism. And Christians were to be agents in ushering in the glorious age.[38]

Curiosity concerning the antichrist figure abounded during the Middle

Ages, even among orthodox thinkers. During this era a basic consensus concerning this figure developed. Emmerson summarizes the common medieval conception:

> Antichrist will be a single human, a man with devilish connections who will come near the end of the world to persecute Christians and to mislead them by claiming that he is Christ; he will be opposed by Enoch and Elias, whom he will kill, and will finally be destroyed by Christ or his agent.[39]

In its view of the time of antichrist's coming, the millennialism that developed in the Middle Ages resembles premillennialism. Like its modern counterpart it anticipated that the antichrist will appear prior to the thousand-year reign. Unlike its contemporary cousin, however, the association of the future millennium with church reform led many medieval reformers to equate this figure with whatever was perceived as hindering needed changes. They appropriated the expectation of the coming antichrist to denounce political or religious leaders who they perceived stood in the way of reform.[40] This, too, marks an important difference from the anticipation of a secular, political/military figure prevalent in premillennial circles today.

The fountainhead of much of the millenarian thinking of the Middle Ages lay in the late-twelfth-century Cistercian reformer Joachim of Fiore.[41] Although interested in the significance for prophecy of various combinations of numbers, including the seven ages of the world, his teaching focused on a threefold division of the historical drama. Central to Joachim's teaching was the conviction that the Trinity was built into the very fabric of the process of time, so that history expressed the divine inner relations. This principle was evident on the personal level in the experience of illumination of Scripture. From meditation on the letter of the Old and New Testaments proceeds spiritual intelligence. In the same way human history evidences the activity of the three trinitarian persons, culminating in the work of the Holy Spirit in what Joachim termed the third *status*.

In contrast to many interpretations of his thought, Joachim himself apparently did not see the three stages as chronologically sequential, with an *era* of the Spirit superseding those of the Father and the Son. The third state is not a temporal age, but a new quality of life that hovers over each of the other two. Hence, his position was not intended to incite ecclesiastical revolution. Nor did he envision the demise of the Roman Catholic church, but a transformation of its quality of life from activity to contemplation, from that of the *ecclesia activa* to that of the *ecclesia contempliva*.[42] To lead the church into this transformation—in apocalyptic terms, through the tribulation of the antichrist into the peace of the third *status*— Joachim anticipated the rise of two new spiritual orders. A hermit order would agonize for the church in tribulation, whereas a preaching order would labor in the world.[43] With this vision in view, he found in the Bible, especially in the seven seals in the book of Revelation, clues to the meaning of contemporary events. These in turn indicated that the world stood on the threshold of the grand events of prophecy.

Many of Joachim's enthusiastic disciples missed the distinction between "era" and *"status"* crucial to his thinking. They transformed the third *status* into an anticipated temporal age. Joachim's ideas were especially useful to those agitating for ecclesiastical reform. Reformists, such as the Spiritual Franciscans, believed that they, like he, had received new illumination. This illumination demanded that they both embody the true spiritual life of the future and lead the world toward it.[44] But as Joachim had indicated, the movement toward the renewal of the third *status* would lead through the tribulation of antichrist.

Some reformists cast the millennial vision in ecclesiastical terms. As a way of reconciling hope for renewal with loyalty to the church, many of them anticipated the rise of an "angelic pope" who would mark God's intervention and bring change to the center of the institution itself.[45] The angelic pope, however, would be opposed by antichrist, who, some insisted, would appear in the seat of the supreme pontiff himself.[46] Other Joachites recast the vision in political terms that juxtaposed a Savior-Emperor with the antichrist-tyrant.[47] In either case, visionaries saw in current events signs of the imminence of the dark night that would eventually give way to the millennial dawn.

Apocalyptic interpretations of history continued to be voiced here and there within Roman Catholic circles even after the Middle Ages gave way to the Renaissance. For some visionaries, Joachim's anticipation of a missionary order was fulfilled in the Jesuits. Others transported his main theme to the New World, using the categories of the new era of the Spirit to understand the significance of the discovery and evangelization of the native peoples found there by the Spanish explorers.[48]

Despite the repeated re-emergence of apocalyptic themes, however, the nonmillenarian outlook dominated the thinking of the church during the era of Augustine onward. As Ernest Lee Tuveson concludes, "the Apocalypse and the attitude toward history which it represented slumbered as a force in Western culture—except for some uneasy tossings—for more than a thousand years."[49] Yet it remained an explosive force that was most powerfully felt once the Protestant Reformation burst forth.

Millennial Thinking and the Reformation

Officially the churches of the Reformation continued the dominant nonmillennialism of the medieval Roman Catholic church. Wary of the chaos they perceived would arise from the revolutionary ideas of the more radical reformers, both Luther and Calvin spurned millenarianism in all forms. Yet despite the absence of official sanction, millennial expectations had played—and would continue to play—an important role in the Protestant conception of the significance of their movement.

The way for the Protestant employment of millennial themes in their struggle with the Roman church was already prepared by certain earlier radical voices calling for reform. One such reformer who subsequently enjoyed wide influence in English Reformation history was the fourteenth-century theologian and preacher John Wyclif, often hailed as "the morning star of the Reformation."[50] A harbinger of future uses of apocalyptic themes, he linked the papacy with the imagery associated with antichrist. Wyclif launched this dramatic innovation in response to the crisis that arose in the Roman Catholic church following the election of Clement VII as a rival pope to Urban VI in 1378, which dashed all his hopes for a papal-inspired reform of the church.[51] However, he apparently did not simply equate this eschatological figure with any one person or earthly institution.[52] Rather, under "antichrist" he lumped together the friars, the papacy and those bishops who opposed the reforming movement and its attempt to translate the Bible into English.[53]

As the Reformation progressed into a self-conscious movement, its thinkers revived apocalyptic themes, renewed interest in the book of Revelation and pressed those themes and that book into the service of church reform. In this way it marked somewhat of a continuation and development of the millennialism that had flourished on the fringes of the church throughout the Middle Ages. Nevertheless, certain important differences remained.

Perhaps the most radical change lay in the interpretation of the antichrist. Here Luther represents a subtle but monumental advance beyond his predecessors in the Middle Ages. Most of the medieval reformers did not attack the papacy as an institution, but only the worldliness and inertia of individual popes. Some even pinned their hopes on the rise of an "angelic pope" who would inaugurate reform. However, building from Wyclif a century and a half before him, Luther came to speak of the papal institution itself as antichrist. This view became standard fare in Protestant writings.[54] The adjustment in the identity of antichrist resulted in Protestants relegating to human action a significant role in defeating this foe. Because antichrist is an ecclesiastical institution, one may actively oppose and gradually undermine him.[55]

A second innovation developed through Luther's revised exegesis of the Apocalypse. In keeping with his antipapal polemic, Luther altered his interpretation of Revelation, as he came to see in it a prophecy of the history of the church. Consequently, he sought to match the various symbols in the book with events of church history. The tale of woes charted by the ancient seer climaxed in the reign of the pope, in Luther's viewpoint, who was singled out because the papacy was the chief stumbling block to the cause of church reform. This historicist reading of the book of Revelation remained the standard means of exegesis in Protestant circles well into the seventeenth century.[56]

Yet another difference may be detected in Luther's view of Revelation 20. While standing in the reformist tradition of the Middle Ages, Luther eschewed the millennial doctrine of the medieval apocalypticists. He did not anticipate a future era of peace and righteousness on the earth, but rather saw the biblical vision of the golden age as being fulfilled, beginning in the patristic era and concluding with the triumph of the papacy.[57]

The nonmillenarian apocalypticism of Luther also forms a stark contrast to the ideas perpetrated by certain of the radical reformers of the sixteenth century, from whose views both he and Calvin shrank back in horror. Perhaps the most well known of the radical millenarians was Thomas Müntzer. He anticipated a new age of enlightenment, which, he believed, he was directly inspired by the Holy Spirit to inaugurate.[58] Although beheaded in 1525 for his involvement in the Peasants' War, the ethos of his outlook lay behind the infamous Münster incident of 1534. Certain radical millenarians took over the town, proclaimed it the New Zion and anticipated the millennium. The next year Catholic and Protestant military forces put an end to the occupation.

As a reaction to the abuses in Münster, Catholics and Protestants alike rejected millenarianism as heretical.[59] Both likewise agreed that the military advances of the Turks were among the plagues predicted by the book of Revelation. The central point of contention between the two major antagonists in sixteenth-century Western Christendom lay, of course, in the interpretation of the two beasts of the thirteenth chapter of John's vision. Following Wyclif and Luther, Protestants quickly focused on a close linkage between the pope and the evil eschatological figure as one of the central features of their understanding of history. Catholics, in contrast, strongly denied this charge.

In this combative context Catholic theologians, including the Jesuit Francis Ribera, eager to exonerate the earthly head of the church, reintroduced the medieval futurist rendering of the prophecies of antichrist in order to counter the historicist reading typical of Protestants. The antichrist, they averred, was yet to come, and he would be a renegade Jew.[60]

Its link to Catholic apologetics was a factor that led English Puritans in the seventeenth century to reject the futurist hermeneutic *en masse*.[61]

Despite the centrality of the Continent for the development of Protestant ideas, it was in England and later in America that millennialism found its most important expressions.

Millenarianism in England

In reform-minded England millenarian ideas found exceptionally fertile soil. After the break with Rome, English Puritans cast their gaze not only on the distant Roman see but closer to home on the vestiges of papalism—that is, on all the papal practices remaining in the English church—as constituting antichrist, the archenemy of the true church. As they saw it, their task was to root out Romish practices in the English church, so that it might become truly reformed, opening the way for the glorious era of the church of Jesus Christ.

Like the Continental reformers from whom they drew inspiration, the early English Puritans followed the historical interpretation of the book of Revelation and viewed the millennium of Revelation 20 as having occurred in the past—roughly between the years A.D. 300 and 1300. Yet other ideas were also at work, and these brought a rebirth on English soil of a futuristic understanding of the millennial era.

The first important step in this direction was taken by Thomas Brightman. He revised the Reformed Augustinian concept of the millennium by introducing the idea of "the latter-day glory,"[62] which later played a significant role in American millenarian thinking as late as the beginning of the twentieth century. Brightman proposed two millennial eras, the first in keeping with the traditional Protestant dating of A.D. 300 to 1300 (Rev 20:2), but the second inaugurated by the rediscovery of the power of the gospel beginning with Wyclif (Rev 20:5). Brightman's characterization of this imminently dawning latter-day glory was optimistic: God would intervene to destroy the enemies of the church, the Jews would be converted and then Christ would return as Judge.

The expectation of a latter-day glory was advanced by the influential

English Congregationalist, John Owen. He anticipated a time of great spiritual prosperity for the church, both in purity of doctrine and worship and in success in mission to the nations. This era, however, would come not by the actions of humans, he cautioned, but by the manifestation of the power of Christ through the pouring out of the Spirit.[63]

Whereas Brightman and Owen represent a pristine postmillennialism, other thinkers set out on a course leading to premillennialism. Influential in this development was the move from Augustinian eschatology to millenarian thinking by the respected German Calvinist, Johann Heinrich Alsted. He predicted that the millennium would be inaugurated in 1694 as the third period of church history, when God would intervene to place Satan in the bottomless pit.[64]

In seventeenth-century England, however, the line between the two varieties of millenarian thinking was not strictly drawn.[65] More significant was the division concerning the time of the millennium. English theologians agreed that the promises of a new heaven and a new earth would be fulfilled. But they differed as to whether this fulfillment lay in time— in a glorious state of the church in the latter days prior to the final consummation—or in eternity—in a literal new creation that would include a renewed earth.[66] Consequently, an important theological line divided those thinkers who anticipated a future millennial era from other visionaries who believed that the thousand-year period lay in the past.

The millenarians, in turn, disagreed among themselves concerning the actual nature of the imminent millennial reign of Christ. Some believed that Christ would reign spiritually from heaven through his saints. For example, neither Joseph Mede, who labeled himself the first English Puritan millenarian,[67] nor Thomas Goodwin, who anticipated a recovery of the scriptural doctrine and church polity discovered by the Congregationalists, anticipated that the millennium would be inaugurated by the literal descent of Christ to the earth. Rather, in the golden age Christ would rule from heaven through the resurrected martyrs.[68] Yet others anticipated his literal presence on the earth.[69] Such differences, however, were marginal when compared to the broader millenarianism that united all such thinkers. As Bryan Ball concludes, "a millenarian was a millenarian regardless of how he explained the advent."[70]

In the same way, all thinkers were united in their belief in the literal return of Christ, despite differing expectations concerning the details. Ball summarizes the situation: "It could therefore be said of the coming rule of Christ, that while a majority expected Him to come and inaugurate a Kingdom *for* the saints, the millenarians held that He would either reign *through* the saints or *with* them."[71]

From the time of the reign of Mary in the sixteenth century to the Commonwealth era in the seventeenth, Puritans agreed that papal influence, which most writers declared was symbolized by the two beasts of the book of Revelation,[72] would soon be destroyed by the intervention of God.[73] But as the Puritan movement moved toward its climax and hopes of reform, which had reached a feverish pitch in the Commonwealth era, were dashed by the Restoration, certain millenarians offered more radical innovations. Increasingly important grew the idea that the human agents were to be involved in the work of overcoming antichrist and completing the Reformation. At first the Puritans had placed their hope in the magistrate or Parliament. Now, however, the time had come for the saints, the heirs of the kingdom, to take matters into their own hands, for the imminent kingdom was to be established *by* the saints.[74]

The most widely known group of radicals were the Fifth Monarchy Men, who called for a "Reformation without tarrying for one." They advocated taking up arms to wrest the government from the opponents of Christ and thereby to establish the millennial kingdom. In this way "the fifth monarchy," the rule of Christ, would replace the four monarchies delineated in the visions of the book of Daniel (chaps. 2, 7). Fifth Monarchists transferred the scene of the final confrontation to England, and political leaders and current political developments formed the context for their interpretation of the antichrist figure, which they preferred to speak of in terms of the "little horn" (Dan 7:8). From biblical prophecy they sought to divine the date of the final conflict and the inauguration of the millennium. Their millennial vision formed the basis for a program of reform in the present. All profane persons were to be expelled from government and the laws of God would be established, including not only the moral law but all the judicial laws and penalties scattered throughout the Torah.[75] The Fifth Monarchists' call for political reform was paralleled by advocacy of ecclesiastical changes. The national church was to be replaced by a type of voluntary Congregationalism.[76]

The closing decades of the seventeenth century saw the demise of the Fifth Monarchy movement. Many members shed their more activist leanings for the quietism of other Congregational bodies. This new quietism came to be epitomized in another group of radicals that arose at mid-century. The Quakers turned away from the theologically based political struggle of the Monarchists and placed in the center another dimension of the Puritan struggle, the struggle within the soul. They exchanged the millenarian hope of a future temporal kingdom on earth for the presence of a spiritual kingdom within the individual.[77]

With the Quakers, English Puritan apocalypticism had culminated in an internalized eschatology. In the meantime, however, millenarianism had been transferred to the shores of the New World. There it would blossom and color the ethos of the new nation for three centuries.

American Millenarianism
The English colonies on the North American continent and the nation that was born from them has never been "Christian" in the sense that the majority of its inhabitants have been professing believers. At the same time, one significant, if not dominant, theme that accounts for the ethos of the nation has been the Protestant outlook toward history. Under various phrases many students of American history have called the United States "the nation with the soul of a church," to use the well-known description coined by Sidney Mead.

The genesis of the Protestant ethos in America lies in the original founding of the New England colonies. The Puritans who sailed from the Old World transplanted on the American shore the Protestant burden of overcoming antichrist in anticipation of the latter-day glory.

Typical of the New England outlook was the postmillennial orientation of John Cotton. He offered a spiritual interpretation of the first resurrection, viewing the symbol as referring to the reformation of the church, the resurrection of persons dead in sin and a renewal of churches dead in apostasy.[78] Cotton's exegesis of the first resurrection as the anticipated reformation of the church offered an explanation for the relocation to the New World, for theirs was "an errand into the wilderness" undertaken for the sake of Christ's church, and this in terms of concern for obedience to the sovereignty of God.[79]

Although millenarian ideas were integral to the early colonial world view, it was the Great Awakening of the 1740s that etched a type of postmillennialism on the colonial soul. The experience of the revivals made this type of millenarianism, in the words of H. Richard Niebuhr, "the common and vital possession of American Christians,"[80] for they brought the remote possibility of the coming of the kingdom very near.

Although many perceived the millennial significance of the awakenings, the systematization of millennialism in the New World context fell to Jonathan Edwards, who has been termed "the father of American postmillennialism." Edwards fostered a revival of the Puritan emphasis on history as the scene of God's continuing activity through the struggle of the true church against the forces of evil. He applied this framework to church history in *A History of the Work of Redemption* (published posthumously in 1774 from a series of sermons delivered in 1739). Edwards's *History* traced the entire flow of salvation history from the fall to the consummation. In this work, the author built from the English Protestant historiography, including the rise of the papal antichrist over whom the people of God would soon be victorious. But Edwards envisioned that the scene of battle had been transferred to New England. The revivals that were just dawning in 1739 marked the beginning of the final phase of God's work. As a result, although no specific date for the event could be set, the victory of God's people could not be far in the future.

The expectant postmillennialism espoused by Edwards and others anticipated a golden age prior to the physical return of Christ. The reign of

Christ comes in the hearts of his people, proponents argued. But it affects the whole world as well. The millennium will be a time of great learning, universal peace and both spiritual and material enjoyment.[81]

Church bodies that hitherto had contented themselves to stand on the fringe of colonial society came to share the postmillennialism of the Puritan establishment. Typical of this development was the transformation experienced by the eighteenth-century New England Baptists under the leadership of the Massachusetts pastor Isaac Backus, who was a key shaper of the Baptist outlook of the era.[82] Like his denominational forebears and the entire Puritan movement, Backus was interested in church reform. For the context in which to articulate his call to reform, Backus borrowed the postmillennialism of Jonathan Edwards. An era of peace and righteousness would soon dawn, possibly beginning in the New World, and would then spread throughout the world. After this era, Christ would return to earth. The inauguration of the millennium would come about as the church gained the victory over antichrist.

While following the basic ethos of the establishment Puritans who viewed their movement in terms of the struggle to rid the church of antichrist, Backus differed from the dominant religionists concerning the identity of the vestiges from which the church needed to be purified. He determined that the mark of the beast spoken of in the book of Revelation is found in infant baptism and religious taxation.

Central to Backus's position was a significant alteration of the Protestant interpretation of antichrist. For him, this figure did not refer to a specific ecclesiastical institution (the papacy), but to the illegitimate mingling of church and state. Whereas Protestants typically linked both beasts of the Apocalypse with Rome, Backus turned the apocalyptic imagery back on the New England establishment. He agreed that the first beast was Rome; but the second beast arose within the Protestant church itself, as Protestants, following the very error of the church against which they protested, united church and state and persecuted dissenters. Consequently, he asserted, when the church as a whole would come to reject infant baptism and religious taxation, the union of church and state erroneously set up in New England would be broken. This would signal the defeat of antichrist, and the golden era of the rule of Christ through Christ's obedient church would dawn.

As the nineteenth century loomed on the horizon Backus and others sensed that the millennial era was arriving. This mood dominated the thinking of the American churches for the next hundred years. Edwards's *A History of Redemption* was widely read,[83] and the millennialism it espoused provided the theological basis for Christian involvement in a host of causes, each of which was seen in turn as the last great evil to be vanquished before the golden age could be inaugurated. Consequently, in the words of Ernest Sandeen, "America in the nineteenth century was drunk on the millennium."[84]

As the century unfolded, the cause of Christ and the aspirations of the new nation came to be linked in the minds of many people. Under this influence the dominant postmillennialism underwent a transformation. No longer was the field of conflict the church, from which antichrist must be expelled in order that Christ might reign supremely. Rather, the nation, or its social systems, came to be seen as the focal point of God's activity in challenging evil and establishing his rule through his people.

Perhaps nowhere was this American Christian utopianism speaking the language of the Apocalypse more pronounced than in the antislavery movement. Christian abolitionists rallied their forces by harnessing the spirit reflected in the "Battle Hymn of the Republic" with its apocalyptic-based lyrics. When victory came, postmillennial optimism anticipated a new day for the nation. In the words uttered by Edward Beecher in 1865, "Now that God has smitten slavery unto death, he has opened the way for the redemption and sanctification of our whole social system."[85]

But the victory over slavery did not result in the millennial era. Other evils remained in the land. As a result, the postmillennial spirit with its vision of a Christianized society fostered other reformist movements—women's suffrage, temperance and even the social gospel.[86]

Conservative theologians continued to articulate the biblically oriented postmillennialism of the Puritans, as is evidenced by the systematic theologies of Charles Hodge and Augustus Hopkins Strong. Yet a new attitude was clearly in the wind that affected even the conservatives. The American spirit became saturated with a secularized postmillennialism. Americans became convinced that the new nation had a mission to extend its influence across the continent and throughout the world. As American nationalism cast its spell over the heritage of postmillennialism, American Christians accepted the idea of a national "manifest destiny." The kingdom of God would most assuredly move out from the United States as this nation served as a beacon of Christianity and democracy to the rest of the world.[87] The ecclesiastical reformist expectation of a divine intervention into church life that would bring about a victory over antichrist in the church had been completely transformed into the social reformist expectation of human progress in history that would rid the world of ignorance and transform the structures and institutions that stifle the human spirit.

Just as the nineteenth century witnessed the ascendancy of postmillennialism, the twentieth solidified its demise.[88] Two world wars, the threat of a nuclear Armageddon and the tenacity of evil despite the best of human efforts convinced many Christians that the world was indeed not standing on the verge of the golden age, at least not one that would come except by some catastrophic infusion of divine grace. Where interest in eschatology remained in mainline churches, it took largely the form of amillennialism. Among evangelicals, however, a rebirth of premillennialism lay on the horizon.

Although postmillennialism had dominated the American churches during the nineteenth century, premillennialism had not disappeared. To those who continued the historicist exegesis of the Apocalypse set forth in the Reformation, the exile of the pope at the hands of the French in 1798 appeared to be the fulfillment of Daniel 7 and Revelation 13. On both sides of the Atlantic some thinkers took the matter a step further and employed biblical prophecy to calculate the date for the Lord's return, but with catastrophic results. One such prediction, William Miller's claim that the event would occur on October 22, 1844, served to discredit premillennialism among evangelicals for a generation.[89]

During the closing decades of the nineteenth century, however, a new variation on the premillennial theme, dispensationalism, was imported into America. This system had the potency to replace the waning postmillennialism, at least in conservative circles. The new outlook substituted a thoroughgoing futurist exegesis of the key prophetic texts for the historicist interpretation of its older sibling.

Dispensationalism is noted for its division of salvation history into a series of distinct time periods, called "dispensations." The division of time into periods, of course, was not new. Beginning in the patristic era, the creation week formed a paradigm for the ages of history. However, some historians find a more immediate precursor to dispensationalism in the seventeenth-century Dutch Calvinist and covenant theologian Johannes Cocceius. Although he was not a premillennialist, Cocceius divided the one covenant of grace, which spans all of history from the fall to the eschaton, into several dispensations, and thereby described the history of redemption as a series of covenants.[90]

The innovation in early dispensationalism, therefore, was not the division of history into periods of time. What was new was the strict literalism in interpreting Bible prophecy,[91] which set the predictions of Daniel and Revelation into the future and demanded a reintroduction of Israel, rather than the church, as the major subject of biblical prophecy.

Contemporary dispensationalism usually traces its origins to the Plymouth Brethren movement in England and the influence of John Nelson Darby. The Brethren were a separatist group who left the Anglican church because they believed it was apostate.[92] Sometime after 1830 John Darby, who had developed a system of dispensations somewhat similar to the earlier work of Cocceius, added an extraordinary innovation, the pretribulation rapture. The true saints of God, he declared, would be taken out of the world prior to the future tribulation period. The apostate church, however, would remain behind to experience the horrors of the rule of antichrist.

Much speculation has surrounded the source of Darby's theory of the pretribulation rapture. Opponents claim that it originated about 1832 in an outburst of tongues speaking in the breakaway church of Edward Irving. Indeed among the Irvingites there was keen interest in the restoration of "the apostolic gifts" such as healing and speaking in tongues. In fact, many nineteenth-century premillennialists anticipated a restitution of Pentecostal charisma in the last days.[93] Yet there is little historical support for the supposed connection between this phenomenon and Darby's teaching.[94]

In the closing decades of the nineteenth century a type of dispensational premillennialism that drew its foundation from Darby spread rapidly within conservative circles in the American church. The religious establishment had been thrown into chaos by the social and intellectual ferment of the post-Civil War era. In an attempt to maintain traditional orthodoxy in the face of these changes, conservatives banded together in a loose coalition. Dispensationalism was able not only to win a place within the conservative coalition but eventually to become the dominant partner.

In part, the initial success of this theological orientation was due to dispensationalist involvement in the Bible conference movement that flourished during the last quarter of the century. The most widely known of these was the annual Niagara Bible Conference, which composed a statement of faith in 1878 that included an affirmation of premillennialism. A series of prophecy conferences were subsequently held in various parts of the nation. These came to be dominated by dispensationalists as well.

Dispensationalism also profited from the modernist-fundamentalist controversy.[95] Because of its claim to employ a literal hermeneutic in the attempt to set forth a system of thought that reflects the theology of the Bible itself, the movement aligned itself with nondispensational fundamentalists in opposing the modernist approach to the Bible and to biblical theology. Adherents of the new premillennialism played important roles in the founding of interdenominational fundamentalist organizations as well as in the disputes that led to the splits within the ranks of the northern Baptists and the Presbyterians.[96] In these situations, dispensationalists presented themselves as the defenders of the faith of the Bible. In time, many evangelicals became convinced that this system was the only theological outlook that took the entire Bible seriously.

The Bible institute movement, in which several dispensationalists played key roles, also served to advance the cause of the movement.[97] Beginning with Moody Bible Institute (1886) conservatives founded several schools as a means of preserving orthodoxy, as the major church seminaries were taken over by modernists. These schools focused on mission rather than academic pursuits, and they fostered the training of lay Christian leaders. Nearly all of the new schools were doctrinally committed to dispensationalism. Consequently, they produced a large group of eager Christians committed to both traditional orthodox doctrine and the newer premillennialism.

Crucial events and changes during the twentieth century likewise favored dispensationalism. They served to turn attention toward the new premillennialism and gave its interpretation of prophecy the air of empirical verification. The tenacity of the social problems of the world led many Christians to abandon the orientation toward human efforts in building the kingdom, characteristic of postmillennialism, for the premillennial emphasis on the necessity of God's intervention for the establishment of the golden age. Liberalism appeared to have completely engulfed the mainline denominations, indicating the presence of the great apostasy anticipated by dispensationalism. The significant political occurrences of the century—two world wars, the rise of the European common market—and a host of other less spectacular new items appeared to confirm the dispensational interpretation of prophecy.

But above all, the return of Jews to Palestine, climaxing with the founding of a Jewish state in 1948 and its subsequent success in establishing itself in the midst of hostile neighbors, gave dispensationalism a wide hearing and confirmed for many the correctness of its interpretation of biblical prophecy. The sense of intrigue was heightened by the dispensationalist claim that Russia was the evil kingdom of the north, which many proponents asserted within the context of the global competition between the United States and the Soviet Union that characterized the "cold war" era.[98] As a result, in the eyes of many conservatives this specific viewpoint came to be seen as *the* biblical eschatology.

Factors such as these converged to make dispensationalism the dominant eschatology of fundamentalism and evangelicalism in America by the middle of the twentieth century.[99] Large numbers of conservative Christians came to equate any denial of the tenets of this system with the denial of the faith of the Bible itself. Writing concerning the dispensational variety of premillennialism, church historian Timothy Weber concludes,

> For many fundamentalists and evangelicals today, the premillennial second coming, the divinity of Jesus, the virgin birth, the resurrection, the substitutionary atonement, justification through faith, and the infallibility of the Bible come as a self-contained doctrinal package, allowing no additions or subtractions.[100]

In recent years, however, the success of dispensationalism has been paralleled by a growing questioning of the received dispensational orthodoxy. Adherents themselves have been tinkering with the system, modifying some of its more objectionable features. Others have abandoned it completely. There are signs that the dominance of this viewpoint—at least in its classical expression—may be on the wane,[101] just as was the fate of other eschatological systems in previous eras. Whether this is indeed the case, and if so, what eschatological viewpoint will eventually replace dispensationalism, remain open questions.

3
BRINGING IN
THE KINGDOM

The Heritage of
Postmillennialism

*N*o self-respecting scholar who looks at the world conditions and the accelerating decline of Christian influence today is a 'postmillennialist,' " concluded Hal Lindsey in his best seller *The Late Great Planet Earth* (1970).[1] With this comment, the well-known popularizer of dispensationalism merely restated, albeit perhaps in less gentle words, what his colleagues had been asserting for several decades. Already in the 1930s, Alexander Reese, for instance, wrote, "Here one can make the arbitrary statement that the postmillennial interpretation of Origen, Jerome, Augustine, and the majority of the Church theologians ever since, is now as dead as Queen Ann, and just as honorably buried."[2] J. Dwight Pentecost, on the other hand, placed its downfall somewhat later in history: "Postmillennialism is no longer an issue in theology. World War II brought about the demise of this system."[3]

Such statements betray an unfortunate failure on the part of some critics to give adequate due to the importance of the postmillennialist position. Lindsey, whose viewpoint is no longer shared by most contemporary dispensationalist scholars, erroneously depicted postmillennialists as believing "that the Christians would root out the evil in the world, abolish godless rulers, and convert the world through ever-increasing evangelism until they brought about the Kingdom of God on earth through their own efforts." He also chided them for rejecting the literalness of much of the Scripture and for believing in "the inherent goodness" of humankind.[4]

Contrary to Lindsey's caricature, postmillennialism was not the construct of starry-eyed utopian liberals.[5] On the contrary, it was the dominant position among American evangelicals in the late eighteenth century and throughout most of the nineteenth century. Evangelical thinkers from Jonathan Edwards to Archibald Alexander Hodge and Augustus Hopkins Strong, who held uncompromisingly to the doctrine of the glorious return of the risen and exalted Lord, were convinced that postmillennialism best reflected the eschatology of the Bible itself. Their outlook differed fundamentally from both secular and liberal Christian utopianism. They were optimistic concerning the future, to be sure. But their optimism was born out of a belief in the triumph of the gospel in the world and of the work of the Holy Spirit in bringing in the kingdom, not out of any misconceptions concerning the innate goodness of humankind or of the ability of the church to convert the world by its own power.

The popularity of postmillennialism was evidenced in 1859 as the *American Theological Review* characterized the situation by stating that this viewpoint was the "commonly received doctrine" among American Protestants.[6] Postmillennial themes were likewise incorporated into some of the grand hymns of the century. Our evangelical forebears set forth to conquer their spiritual foes singing, "Lead On, O King Eternal." The conflict they engaged in and its resolution were couched in postmillennial terms: "For not with swords loud clashing, Nor roll of stirring drums;

With deeds of love and mercy, The heav'nly kingdom comes." This postmillennial vision culminated in the great worldwide missionary thrust, as
the church took seriously the admonition of the hymnwriter, "O Zion
haste, thy mission high fulfilling."

Not only have critics misinterpreted the position they reject, their pronouncements of the death sentence on postmillennialism came premature-
ly. It is true that by the middle of the twentieth century this view had been
supplanted by premillennialism as the most influential eschatology among
evangelicals. But in the years since Lindsey wrote its obituary, postmillennialism has experienced a revival in interest. Recently the classical
postmillennialism of the nineteenth-century theological giants and of
twentieth-century adherents such as Loraine Boettner has been given a
new lease on life by at least one mainline evangelical theologian, John
Jefferson Davis.[7]

In addition to the reformulation of the classical version, several varieties
of postmillennialism have appeared under the broader evangelical umbrel-
la. Perhaps the most prominent of these is the "reconstructionism," or
"dominion theology," set forth by thinkers including Rousas Rushdoony,
Greg L. Bahnsen and David Chilton. Beyond the classical postmillennial
emphasis on personal conversion, this newer variation espouses a political
agenda for the establishment of a Christian republic not too dissimilar
from that of the Fifth Monarchists during the Puritan era in England.

Furthermore, certain postmillennial themes have been influential
beyond the boundaries of evangelicalism, for they have found an echo,
whether consciously or unintentionally, in certain contemporary theological movements such as liberation theology in South America.

Postmillennialism might command the loyalties of only a minority of
theologians today.[8] Nevertheless, it is not the discredited remnant of a
misguided past its opponents sometimes suggest.

The Main Features of Postmillennialism
As Hal Lindsey's characterization indicates, of the major eschatological
positions, postmillennialism is probably the most maligned and misunder-

stood. Among evangelicals, the viewpoint is often suspect because it is erroneously linked to the older liberalism, which focused primarily on societal transformation rather than personal conversion.

Of course, a secularized version of postmillennialism did lie behind certain currents of nineteenth- and early twentieth-century progressivism. And American Protestant liberalism did incorporate certain themes from postmillennialism. Hence, its articulators replaced expectations of catastrophe and divine intervention with an emphasis on evolutionary development and human achievement. They looked to education, legislation and the "gradual process of remedial treatment" as the solutions to the ills of human life. In all of this, they envisioned the world as constantly growing better.[9]

Conservative postmillennialists, however, have always adamantly distanced themselves from any naturalistic "pseudo-postmillennialism."[10] According to Loraine Boettner, the latter "regards the Kingdom of God as the product of natural laws in an evolutionary process." Orthodox postmillennialism, in contrast, "regards the Kingdom of God as the product of the supernatural working of the Holy Spirit in connection with the preaching of the Gospel."[11] The central aspect of postmillennialism, therefore, lies not in societal transformation per se, but in the spread of the gospel and the conversion of a great number of persons.

Like many amillennialists, postmillennialists often appeal to Augustine for the foundation of their position.[12] In a manner similar to the postmillennial view, his interpretation of Revelation 20 did indeed anticipate the thousand years as occurring prior to the Second Coming of Christ. Yet in an important way Augustine's position differed from modern postmillennialism. Contemporary postmillennialists anticipate the golden age still in the future, rather than commencing with some point in the New Testament era as Augustine suggested.[13]

What became the theologically conservative postmillennialism of recent centuries finds its actual genesis in developments within English Puritanism.[14] Many scholars suggest that the founder of modern postmillennialism was the English divine Daniel Whitby (1638-1725).[15] Whitby set forth postmillennial ideas in an essay carrying the descriptive title "A Treatise of the Millennium: Shewing That It Is Not a Reign of Persons Raised from the Dead, but of the Church Flourishing Gloriously for a Thousand Years After the Conversion of the Jews, and the Flowing-In of All Nations to Them Thus Converted to the Christian Faith." This essay was published in 1703 in Whitby's widely read book *Paraphrase and Commentary on the New Testament.* Yet several themes of this eschatology were articulated by certain seventeenth-century Puritan divines and were incorporated into some of the important Puritan ecclesiastical documents in both Old and New England.[16]

Whitby's scheme was paralleled in New England by Jonathan Edwards's *A History of Redemption.* In good Protestant fashion Edwards linked the church of Rome with the figure of antichrist and recounted the struggle of the true church against this enemy of the Lord throughout the Reformation era. But then, building on those biblical prophecies that he believed remained yet unfulfilled, the New England Puritan anticipated the not-too-distant victory over the forces of antichrist, Islam and heathenism, which will mark the destruction of Satan's earthly kingdom. This "glorious work" will be accomplished in the midst of a time of darkness as the Spirit of God is poured out "for the wonderful revival and propagation of religion."[17] Although Satan will then launch a fierce counterattack, the gospel will prevail, the Jews will be converted, and the kingdom of Christ will encompass the globe in fulfillment of Old Testament promises and the visions of Revelation. The long period of the church's prosperity[18] that then follows will, however, end with a great apostasy, as the nations are again deceived by Satan and threaten the church. In response, Christ will appear in judgment, bringing the work of redemption to completion.[19]

The basic postmillennial orientation as delineated by thinkers such as Whitby and Edwards formed the foundation for the eschatology that flowered in the great systematic theologies of nineteenth-century American evangelical Protestantism.

The central tenets of this modern postmillennialism were succinctly set forth at the turn of the century by the eminent Baptist theologian Augustus Hopkins Strong:

> Through the preaching of the gospel in all the world, the kingdom of Christ is steadily to enlarge its boundaries, until Jews and Gentiles alike become possessed of its blessings, and a millennial period is introduced in which Christianity generally prevails throughout the earth.[20]

The same basic position has been echoed more recently by the conservative Presbyterian thinker J. Marcellus Kik:

> The post-mill looks for a fulfillment of the Old Testament prophecies of a glorious age of the church upon earth through the preaching of the gospel under the power of the Holy Spirit. He looks forward to all nations becoming Christian and living in peace one with another. He relates all prophecies to history and time. After the triumph of Christianity throughout the earth he looks for the second coming of the Lord.[21]

As these statements indicate, postmillennialists view the millennium as a long era of universal peace and righteousness that comes as the result of the preaching of the gospel, the saving work of the Holy Spirit in the hearts of individuals and the Christianization of the world.[22] They anticipate a golden age of spiritual prosperity for the entire world that comes at the end of, but is a part of, the church age.[23] It is, in the words of Strong, "the culmination of the work of the Holy Spirit, a universal revival of religion, a nation born in a day, the kings of the earth bringing their glory and honor into the city of God."[24] The golden age, in turn, will climax in the Second Coming of Jesus.

Both premillennialism and postmillennialism, therefore, anticipate a future kingdom era on this earth. Hence, both share a basic millenarian outlook. Nevertheless, modern postmillennialists differ from premillennialists concerning the relationship between the present and the anticipated kingdom age.

One point of difference focuses on the transition between the two eras. In contrast to the catastrophic beginning of the millennium anticipated by premillennialists, according to postmillennialism the transition to the kingdom era is smooth.[25] Like the coming of summer or the beginning of the modern era, the advent of the millennium cannot be pinpointed, for it comes as the result of a slow process,[26] although the long preparation may be followed by a sudden consummation.[27] The future arrives as the outworking of forces that already are active in the world.[28] As a result, the millennium may dawn without its inauguration being perceived. And given the symbolic nature of the time span in Revelation 20, its duration may exceed a literal one thousand years.[29]

Likewise the two eschatologies differ concerning the nature of the kingdom era. In contrast to the discontinuity that premillennialists tend to emphasize, the postmillennial vision of the thousand years focuses on the continuity of the future age with the present era. In many ways, life in the golden age is quite similar to life in the present.[30] Marriage and the natural process of birth, for example, will continue. Most important, the church will keep its place in the program of God as the outward, visible expression of the inward presence of God's Spirit.

The changes that will emerge in the future age will be differences of *extent,* not *content.*[31] The gospel will continue to be preached as it is now. However, a heightened acceptance and influence of Christian principles in human affairs will arise. The millennium will include the experience of the positive blessings that flow from the worldwide penetration of the gospel and the diminishing of evil influence in human affairs. As the Holy Spirit regenerates human beings, their changed character will lead to reforms in the social, economic, political and cultural spheres. A high moral and spiritual life will characterize that time, for Christianity will become the transforming influence not only over the lives of individuals but also over the nations. This heightened spirituality will result in the great material prosperity promised in both the Old and the New Testaments.[32] And as humans engage in the task of proper management of the earth assigned to them before the fall, a marvelous transformation will occur in nature.[33] In short, in the words of Loraine Boettner, "Life during the millennium will compare with life in the world today in much the same way that life in a Christian community compares with that in a pagan or irreligious community."[34]

Postmillennialism incorporates expectations such as these into a specific eschatological chronology. Most adherents of this viewpoint would subscribe to an order of events similar to the following: As the gospel spreads throughout the earth and brings its divinely intended and Spirit-energized results, evil (and perhaps its personal representation in the form of antichrist)[35] is eventually routed and the millennium arrives. During this era the nations live in peace, for Satan is "bound" and thereby evil is temporarily restrained. After the thousand years have ended Satan is loosed to lead a short-lived rebellion, the final conflict of evil with righteousness,[36] whether this be understood as a spiritual battle of truth against error[37] or in terms of political persecution.[38] Satan's rebellion is ended by the triumphal return of Jesus. The Second Coming is followed by the general resurrection, the judgment and the eternal state—heaven and hell.

The Biblical Basis of Evangelical Postmillennialism

Evangelical postmillennialists believe that their eschatology reflects the teaching of the Bible. As a millenarian viewpoint, of course, it builds its primary case from a futurist interpretation of John's vision. A thousand-year reign of Christ will occur on the earth prior to the end of human history.

As in premillennialist apologetics, the foundation for the postmillennialist expectation of a future thousand-year golden age lies in the interpretation of the rider on the white horse found in Revelation 19:11-21. This text is, in the words of Loraine Boettner, "a vision setting forth in figurative language the age-long struggle between the forces of good and the forces of evil in the world, with its promise of complete victory."[39]

Postmillennialists generally agree with premillennialists, and against many amillennialists, that the events symbolized in Revelation 20 follow chronologically after those of chapter 19. In contrast to premillennialists, however, postmillennialists argue that the rider on the white horse of chapter 19 is not to be interpreted as the Lord in his eschatological Second Coming. Rather, the image is of the Lord victorious over his enemies through the preaching of the gospel within the church age.[40]

That the rider intends to represent the victory of Christ in the proclamation of the good news is evident from a specific detail of the image: a sword comes out of the mouth of the rider. The interpretive key to this detail lies in Hebrews 4:12, "For the word of God is living and active." It is "sharper than any double-edged sword."

That the vision refers to the church age and not the Second Coming is evident by John's declaration that the scene is heaven, not the earth: "I saw heaven standing open, and there before me was a white horse, whose rider is called Faithful and True" (Rev 19:11). Hence, the risen Christ is in heaven from where he engages in spiritual warfare against his foes.[41] In other words, in typical apocalyptic fashion the vision draws aside the veil so that the seer is able to perceive otherwise hidden spiritual realities (compare Acts 7:56).

According to postmillennialists, therefore, the triumph of the rider on the white horse refers to the advancing victory of the Son of God over the world accomplished by the proclamation of the gospel throughout the church age,[42] which in turn inaugurates the thousand-year era of Revelation 20. Despite their vain attempts, neither the beast nor the kings of the earth are able to thwart the reign of Christ that comes about through the victory of the gospel. Postmillennialists argue that the vision of chapter 19 is quite different from the depiction of Christ's Second Coming found in the middle of chapter 20. The latter text speaks of the doom of Satan and the great white throne judgment, which imply the return of the Lord to judge the world (compare Mt 25:31). Because Revelation 19 depicts a process that occurs in history and not the Second Coming, the golden age precedes, rather than follows, the Lord's return.

The conclusion postmillennialists draw from the vision of the rider on the white horse, namely, that it refers to the spread of the gospel in history and not the Second Coming of Christ, is confirmed by the nature of the two resurrections that bracket the millennium in John's vision (Rev 20:4-5). Postmillennialists find it impossible that both could be physical resurrections, the first being a resurrection of the righteous and the second of the unrighteous. Such an interpretation (which is central to the premillennial apologetic) contradicts the clear teaching of Scripture that the Second Coming will mark the rising of all from their graves for the general judgment (for example, Mt 16:27; 25:31-33; Jn 5:28-29; 2 Cor 5:10; 2 Thess 1:6-10; Rev 20:11-15).[43]

As to the exact nature of the first resurrection anticipated in John's vision, although there is some variation among postmillennial interpreters, nearly all link the symbol to the Christian martyrs. John Jefferson Davis, for example, views it in terms of a rebirth of the martyrs' cause: "The 'first resurrection,' then, refers to the future restoration and vindication of the cause for which the martyrs died."[44] Others interpret the symbol in terms of a rebirth of the martyrs' spirit. This position dates to Whitby, is found in briefer form in A. A. Hodge,[45] and was repeated by James Snowden.[46] But no one has improved on Strong's articulation:

> We may therefore best interpret Rev. 20:4-10 as teaching in highly figurative language . . . a period in the latter days of the church militant when, under special influence of the Holy Ghost, the spirit of the martyrs shall appear again, true religion be greatly quickened and revived, and the members of Christ's churches become so conscious of their strength in Christ that they shall, to an extent unknown before, triumph over the powers of evil both within and without.
>
> Thus, the text does not refer to the second advent, but to great spiritual changes in the later history of the church, which are typical of, and preliminary to, the second advent and resurrection, and therefore, after the prophetic method, are foretold in language literally applicable only to those final events themselves.[47]

The balance between the spiritual resurrection prior to the millennium and the physical resurrection following the era, which Strong and other postmillennialists find in Revelation 20:4-5, parallels the balance between a spiritual coming of Christ prior to the thousand years and his physical coming after that time. As a result of Christ's spiritual coming at that point, the saints reign with him spiritually, "in the wonderful advances of his kingdom."[48]

For postmillennialists, the vision of the rider on the white horse offers a symbolic picture of an idea that is central to the entire New Testament, namely, the progress of the gospel throughout the church age. Jesus himself presented this theme in the parables of the kingdom in Matthew 13.

Especially important to postmillennialists are the four parables that compare the kingdom of heaven to processes of growth.[49] According to postmillennialist exegesis, the parables of the mustard seed and the yeast (Mt 13:31-33) teach that the gospel influence begins small, but spreads progressively until it is found throughout the world. The presence of the gospel in human hearts results in the influence of Christian principles in society, which in turn brings about the long-expected era of peace and righteousness. The parables of the weeds and the net (13:24-30, 47-50) indicate the mixed nature of the growth of the kingdom. In this age the kingdom will never be without the presence of evil; yet as the kingdom advances the weeds and the bad fish constitute a comparatively small part of the whole.

The parables of the weeds and the mustard seed, on the one hand, and the yeast, on the other, indicate that kingdom growth occurs both within a specific believer or location (intensively) and from individual to individual or throughout society and its institutions and activities (extensively). In these ways both individuals and the mass of humankind come to be governed by Christian principles. The kingdom, in other words, eventually covers the earth (extensive growth) and transforms the individual life and the world (intensive growth).[50]

This crucial theme of the progress of the gospel, which postmillennialists find in Matthew 13 and Revelation 19, is paralleled by a related emphasis, the New Testament declaration of the absolute power of Christ. According to Matthew's account of the Great Commission, the risen Lord based the sending of the disciples—and by extension, his commissioning of the church throughout the age—on his own reception of authority: "All authority in heaven and on earth has been given to me. Therefore go . . ." (Mt 28:18). Because of Christ's authority, the church now has the mandate to spread the gospel throughout the world. Not only do postmillennialists desire to take this command seriously, they believe that the church possesses all the resources necessary to fulfill its mandate.

Further, postmillennialists emphasize the implications of Christ's reception of authority. In the words of James Snowden, "All authority includes all power of every kind that is applicable to this task. Jesus Christ can never have any more power than He has now, for He now has all there is."[51] Consequently, postmillennialists argue, we do not need to wait for a future kingdom age beyond his catastrophic return as the era of his rule over the earth. Instead that rule will begin in this age as the church is successful in fulfilling its mandate. As the church is obedient to this command, the lordship of Jesus is advanced in the world. The spread of Christ's rule in this manner will eventually inaugurate the era of peace and righteousness.

Millard Erickson, himself a premillennialist, succinctly summarizes the contrast between the two millenarian views based on Matthew's Great Commission text: "Premillennialists assert that Christ the King is absent and will do great things when He returns; postmillennialists assert, however, that according to this passage Christ *is* present and will be to the end of the age. Thus that power to conquer and reign is available to us in the present."[52]

The postmillennialist viewpoint, with its emphasis on available power, lays the lack of its use, and therefore the lack of success in the worldwide gospel proclamation, to the charge of the church. In commenting on the figure of the chain employed in Revelation 20:1, J. Marcellus Kik turns for a moment from exegete to preacher:

> Unfortunately the Church of today does not realize the power that Christ has given her. Christ has placed in her hands the chain by which she can bind Satan. She can restrain his influence over the nations. But today the Church bemoans the fact that evil is becoming stronger and stronger. She bemoans the fact that the world is coming more and more under the control of the Devil. Whose fault is that? It is the Church. She has the chain and does not have the faith to bind Satan even more firmly.[53]

Similarly John Jefferson Davis asserts: "The most serious obstacle to the success of the church's mission is not the power of its spiritual opponents, but the church's own weakness of faith and partial grasp of the invincible resources which are hers in Christ Jesus."[54]

The progress of the gospel as it is proclaimed under the authority of Christ is linked to another theme as well, the far-reaching effects of Christ's work of redemption. Just as humankind fell in Adam, so also humankind is the object of redemption.[55] This emphasis does not lead postmillennialists to universalism, that is, to the belief that every individual human will eventually be saved. But at the same time, they hold out hope for the salvation of a vast number of humans, anticipating that the saved will far outnumber the lost.

Postmillennialists find warrant for the contrast between the large company of the redeemed and the small number of the lost in scriptural imagery.[56] The realm of the redeemed is a great kingdom, whereas the abode of the damned is confined to being a prison, a lake or a pit. The saints and angels are an innumerable company, in comparison with which the number of the lost pales in insignificance.

The nineteenth-century Calvinist theologian William G. T. Shedd offers a vividly articulated summary of this contrast. Hell, he said,

> is only a spot in the universe of God. Compared with heaven, hell is narrow and limited. The kingdom of Satan is insignificant in contrast with the kingdom of Christ. In the immense range of God's dominion, good is the rule, and evil is the exception. Sin is a speck upon the infinite azure of eternity; a spot on the sun.[57]

More recently Loraine Boettner finds in the description of the great white throne judgment (Rev 20:15) an indication that those whose names are not written in the Lamb's book of life "are the exceptional—we may even say, rare—cases."[58]

Postmillennialists draw the theme of the progress of the gospel and its attendant corollaries from the New Testament. This does not mean, however, that they ignore the Old Testament. On the contrary, they hold that one of the most pervasive themes of the Old Testament is that the glory of the Lord will fill the earth and the nations will worship Yahweh (for example, Num 14:21; Ps 86:9; 97:5; Is 2:2-3; Zech 9:10; and messianic texts such as Ps 47; 72; and 110).[59] Charles Hodge, for example, argues from Isaiah 45:22-23 that "the true religion shall prevail over the whole earth. Jehovah shall everywhere be recognized and worshipped as the only true God." Texts such as this, Hodge notes, were applied by the New Testament to the church age.[60] As a result, the conversion of the Gentile world is assured. The mandate of proclamation, however, has been assigned to the church in this age, and under the authority of Christ and by the power of the Holy Spirit it can be successful in this task.

Likewise important for the postmillennialism is the prophetic anticipation of a future golden age.[61] As do the Christian millenarians after them, the prophets awaited a time of peace and righteousness for the world within history. One crucial Old Testament text is Isaiah's vision of a new heaven and a new earth (Is 65:17-25), which the Apocalypse later expanded in the Christian context. In contrast to premillennialists, who interpret the scene as a new material order inaugurated by Jesus' return, postmillennialists see it as referring to a moral and spiritual revolution in human affairs fostered by the gospel.[62]

Postmillennialists, like many nondispensationalist interpreters, find the fulfillment of the general expectations of the Old Testament prophecies in the church, rather than in a future, restored Israel. On this basis, they pour the prophetic expectations of a future golden age into the mold provided by the millennial vision of the Apocalypse. But because the goal of God's work in the Old Testament is attained in the church, the anticipated blessed era comes as the culmination of the church age and forms the era of the victory of the church in the world.

The postmillennial approach means, of course, that its adherents do not interpret literally the prophetic texts predicting a future glory for Israel. The object of these visions, they argue, is the church. However, they adamantly deny the charge of their critics that this hermeneutical approach constitutes an incipient liberalism. On the contrary, they "spiritualize" such statements, in the words of Loraine Boettner, "because we regard this as the only way on which their true meaning can be brought out."[63]

In defense of a spiritualizing hermeneutic of Old Testament texts, post-millennialists offer a biblically based apologetic. They point out that many prophecies concerning Christ's first coming were not fulfilled literally, but in some spiritualized manner (such as Gen 3:15; Mal 4:5; Is 40:3-5).[64] In fact, it was their expectations of a literal earthly kingdom and political ruler that caused many Jews to fail to recognize Jesus as their Messiah at his first coming.[65] Further, the New Testament itself finds in events surrounding the infant church the fulfillment to certain Old Testament anticipations concerning Israel's future glory (such as Acts 2:16-21; 15:14-18).[66] Finally, a literal fulfillment of many prophecies would mean a restoration of Jewish national life in a way that would necessitate a return to the old covenant, which, according to the New Testament, has been replaced by the new covenant within the fellowship of the church.

The Old Testament prophets, postmillennialists assert, rightly envisioned a glorious era. But because it was yet future, it could only be intelligently described by employing the thought-forms and the religious and political structures with which people of the day were familiar. They readily utilized the vocabulary of the old economy, which focused on the land of Palestine, the temple and the sacrificial system, and the kingship, to speak of the future messianic era they awaited. The prophets, therefore, could only imagine the future age, in which the whole world would worship Yahweh, in terms of the elevation of Jerusalem as the center of worldwide worship and the establishment of the ideal theocracy in Israel as the political center of the earth. In the light of the New Testament, however, we now know that these prophecies are fulfilled in the glorious victory of the church (for example, Heb 12:18-23).

Such a heightened, nonliteral fulfillment is in keeping with the nature of prophecy as understood by postmillennialists. Prophecy is not "history written beforehand." Rather, its primary purpose is, in the words of Boettner, "to inspire faith in those who see its fulfillment, and only secondarily to inform us of what is going to happen in the future."[67] Although

it is different from how many people view prophecy, Boettner's understanding can claim New Testament precedence. Peter's epistle declares
that the prophets were not cognizant of the object of their vision of the
sufferings and glory of Christ, for they were not serving themselves, but
the church (1 Pet 1:10-12).

In accordance with postmillennial hermeneutics, Boettner interprets
Isaiah 2:2-3, for example, as fulfilled

> in that the Gospel took its course out from Jerusalem as the disciples
> went under orders to evangelize all the world, with the Church over the
> centuries gradually coming into a position of world-wide prominence,
> gradually increasing in power and becoming more influential in the
> lives of men throughout the world until it stands out like a mountain
> on a plane.[68]

The same hermeneutical approach, however, leads John Jefferson Davis
to give the text a yet future referent. To him it speaks of "the latter day
spiritual exaltation of the Christian church," at which time the "pervasive
impact of the gospel in the life of the nations produces a state of affairs
where warfare and the production of its implements cease."[69]

In either case, postmillennialist exegesis moves from the principle that
the church is in some sense the new Israel, "the true Zion and the heavenly
Jerusalem."[70] Consequently, the expectations of a glorious future for the
nation of Israel envisioned by seers under the old covenant find their
fulfillment in the yet future golden age of the church that will culminate
the present age of the new covenant (although some postmillennialists also
hold out hope for a conversion of Jews in the future).[71] For this reason,
setting forth on a spiritual plane an interpretation of prophecies that by
the necessities of the day were limited to a material horizon, postmillennialists conclude, is the only way to understand correctly the intent of the
Bible as a whole, of which these texts are a part. Like Augustine in the
fifth century, modern postmillennialists argue that to read out of the visions of the Old Testament a literal, physical and political rule of Christ
on the earth after the close of the church age, as premillennialists do, is
to fall victim to the old tendency to "Judaize" Christianity.[72] At the same

time, these prophecies, together with the vision of the millennium in Revelation, must be taken seriously, contra amillennialism. They refer to a golden age of the church yet in the future.

Although focused on the Bible, the postmillennialist apologetic often moves beyond the biblical texts to human history to garner support. Its adherents note the great advances that have been made since the coming of Christ that spark hope for a Christianization of the world prior to the Lord's return.[73] Postmillennialists do not deny that there have been times of apparent setback, nor do they hide from the continuing presence of problems in the world. At the same time, they claim that in general conditions have improved since the first century, when the world at large was "groping helplessly in pagan darkness."[74] They also point to the availability of Bibles and of the gospel itself throughout the world in a manner unparalleled prior to the present. In short, although the world may not be improving daily, the general direction of history since the coming of Christ has been upward, thereby offering a tangible indication that the golden age will indeed one day arrive in its fullness.

Reconstructionism

The previous section focused on the tradition of postmillennialism that runs from the nineteenth-century evangelical theologians to Loraine Boettner and, more recently, to John Jefferson Davis. But other varieties of postmillennialism have emerged in recent decades as well and have offered important reformulations of the major classical themes.

One of the most important of these newer expressions of postmillennialism bears the name "reconstructionism," or "dominion theology." Despite whatever shifts in emphasis they set forth, reconstructionists remain part of the larger stream of postmillennialism. They incorporate into their system the main features of the evangelical postmillennial tradition described above, and even incorporate many of the classical postmillennial arguments within their basic apologetic. At the same time, in at least one place, namely, in their program for society, reconstructionists move beyond the postmillennialism of mainline evangelical adherents.

Although an interest in society is integral to postmillennial thinking in general, reconstructionists take this theme a step farther than mainline evangelical postmillennialists. They boldly assert that our Christian duty moves beyond the sphere of individual moral holiness to include a public and social responsibility.[75] Reconstructionists articulate this thesis in terms of the idea of "dominion." "God," writes Rousas Rushdoony, "called Adam to exercise dominion in terms of God's revelation, God's law," and through redemption and regeneration humankind is recalled to this task and privilege.[76]

The concept of dominion is not unique to reconstructionism, of course. But dominion theology marks a radical point of departure from contemporary Christian thinking in its claim that our God-ordained obligation includes enforcing obedience in society to the divine law revealed in the Bible.[77] In fact, the goal of reconstructionists is nothing less than the establishment of "a Christian Republic, where God's law rules."[78] In a sense, this thesis constitutes a twentieth-century radicalization of the older Calvinist ideal of the Christian commonwealth.[79]

Reconstructionists boldly declare in the midst of an increasingly pluralistic society that the civil magistrate is accountable to God to enforce those aspects of the divine law outlined in the Bible that are applicable to society,[80] including the "just recompense" for every crime as set forth by God himself through the Scriptures.[81] This means even instituting the death penalty for the offenses so punishable under the Mosaic law.[82] By following God's laws a nation can be well pleasing in the sight of God, and God will abundantly bless it for honoring the divine law and the divine Lawgiver.[83]

Despite the apparent victory of secularism in Western society, reconstructionists, evidencing a truly postmillennial spirit, remain optimistic concerning the fulfillment of what they perceive as the Christian social responsibility. The Bible declares that all authority has been given to Christ, and consequently it promises that his rulership will increase until it becomes worldwide in scope. More specifically, the Great Commission promises not only that the nations will be evangelized, but that they will also be discipled, that is, taught to observe God's laws.[84] The Lord's anointed will bring forth justice among the nations; a "Christocracy" will be established throughout the world;[85] and the church, as it fulfills its mandate, will be instrumental in bringing about the rule of Christ.[86]

Dominion theologians point to the pessimism of the prevailing premillennialism and its corollary emphasis on the rapture of the church out of the world—which they bemoan as merely a doctrine of escape from the world[87]—as contributing to the current retreat of the church. Because they do not believe society can be altered, proponents of "defeatist" eschatology, which assumes that the gospel will fail, do not work for the transformation of the world.[88] Therefore defeatist Christians actually abet the enemy,[89] dominion thinkers theorize.

In place of pessimistic premillennialism, reconstructionists preach "dominion eschatology," an optimistic world view that focuses on the victory of the gospel in the here and now, not merely in the far-off future. They call on the church to be busy at its mandate and thereby establish "a Christendom that will someday embrace the entire world."[90] For in salvation, God "gives us the world, and turns it into the Garden of Eden."[91]

The Critique of Postmillennialism

Despite its dominance in the nineteenth century and its defense by able adherents today, postmillennialism is not currently a widely held viewpoint. Consequently, it remains under attack from adherents of other eschatological positions. To date, critics have tended to focus mainly, although not exclusively, on mainstream evangelical postmillennialism. The reconstructionist variety, in contrast, until recently[92] has not received the attention its advocates believe it deserves,[93] with the possible exception of the interest shown by those critics who focus on its relationship to the New Religious Right.[94] Of course, criticisms of the wider postmillennial tradition do indeed target its newer expressions, insofar as they critique the foundation underlying all variations on the basic postmillennial theme.

An obvious point of difference between proponents and opponents lies in the classical postmillennialist exegesis of the central text at issue in the millennium debate, Revelation 19:11—20:10. This will come to light more clearly in subsequent chapters as the alternative interpretations are set forth. Beyond this central issue, critics find postmillennialism deficient at several points.

One often-repeated criticism, which was crucial in the decline of the popularity of the view,[95] argues against postmillennialism on the basis of current events. Many critics see the present world situation as the Achilles' heel of this eschatological viewpoint. They wonder how anyone can continue to cling to the idea of progress given the events of recent history, such as the wars and crises that have plagued humankind especially since the beginning of the twentieth century. For many Christians the observation "the world is simply not getting better and better" immediately eliminates the postmillennial viewpoint from further consideration.[96]

Defenders of postmillennialism, however, find this objection unwarranted. They argue that critics are guilty of setting up a straw man when they think that they have destroyed postmillennialism by arguing against an oversimplified idea of progress. This eschatological viewpoint does not in fact envision the unabated linear process of human progress seen in it by its critics.[97] Neither each successive year nor each successive decade will by necessity show marked improvement in society. Postmillennialists anticipate ebb and flow in history, rather than simple linear development. Until the revival and widespread conversions predicated on the work of the Holy Spirit through the worldwide proclamation of the gospel, they argue, sin will continue to dominate. Beyond the oscillations of history, however, many postmillennialists discover a pattern of progress.[98] The general direction of history, they suggest, is upward. Taken as a whole, the era since Christ's first advent reflects the progress the gospel has brought to human affairs.

Further, this criticism of postmillennialism is incorrect. Critics claim to decimate postmillennialism by noting that the world is growing worse, not better. Such critics err, however, by invoking a truncated horizon. When a longer view of history is substituted for the short view taken by critics, postmillennialists maintain, the progressive flow of history emerges. Contemporary adherents of this eschatology readily admit that we have witnessed certain reversals. Nevertheless, when the horizon of comparison is shifted beyond the short term to encompass the great sweep of history, the pessimistic conclusion of critics evaporates. Thus, postmillennialists ask, Who would argue that the great advances of recent time have not brought marked improvement to the world? Who would trade life in the present century for life in the ancient Roman Empire? For the postmillennialist apologist rhetorical questions such as these lay to rest the erroneous criticism that the world is not improving.

The critics' objection is also improper. It builds from the wrong source. Theology is to be determined from the Bible as confirmed by the general sweep of history, and not from the daily newspaper, postmillennialists declare. In response to the criticism leveled against this system, reconstructionist David Chilton speaks on behalf of postmillennialism in general: "We are not to derive our theology from the newspapers or the evening news. Our faith and hope must be drawn from the unfailing Word of the sovereign God, who brings all things to pass according to His unalterable will." Consequently, "the question is not whether current conditions seem favorable for the worldwide triumph of the gospel; the question is only this: *What does the Bible say?*"[99] This principle is echoed by the mainline evangelical postmillennialist John Jefferson Davis, who succinctly states, "The decisive factor in any determination should be biblical exegesis, not some attempt to read the 'signs of the times.' "[100]

Perhaps the arguments for and against postmillennialism based on current conditions are in the end by their very nature inconclusive. Today's pessimistic portrait of a world on the verge of self-annihilation could become dated by an unanticipated breakthrough tomorrow. On the other hand, however, as amillennialist critic Anthony Hoekema notes, "Even if one should agree . . . that the world is indeed getting better, how would this prove that the world is moving on toward a millennial golden age?"[101]

A second objection argues that the postmillennial understanding concerning the ultimate number of the redeemed does not square with the

Scriptures. Critics accuse postmillennialists of teaching that nearly all humankind will come to Christ, or at least nearly all who are alive during the time immediately before and during the millennium. In contrast to such optimism, critics point out, Jesus indicated that the number of the saved would be relatively small (Mt 7:14).

This objection demands a clarification of the postmillennial position. Conservative postmillennialists are not universalists; they do not teach that every human being will be converted. Instead, their emphasis rests on the theme of the powerful influence of Christianity in society. Even though Christians might at no time actually constitute the majority of the world's inhabitants, during the period that will climax in the millennium the influence of the gospel will grow until it pervades the world.

At the same time, while avoiding universalism, postmillennialists do remain optimistic concerning the converting power of the gospel. The Bible declares, they point out, that the number of those who will be saved is vast. The Scriptures portray heaven as a great city and a kingdom, in contrast to hell, which is described as a prison, a lake or even a pit.

Many premillennialists, however, actually agree with postmillennialists concerning this point. They, too, anticipate that in a future millennial era the gospel will hold sway not only in human society as a whole, but also in the hearts of the vast number of people. Writing from a dispensationalist perspective, Herman Hoyt, for example, expresses amazing agreement with postmillennialism "in holding to the conviction that through the provision of redemption a greater part of the human race will be saved."[102] And as in postmillennialism, the great advance will come about by the proclamation of the gospel: "In the period of the tribulation and millennium, the greatest period of evangelization in the history of the world will take place."[103] However, premillennialists relegate the period of the advance of the gospel to the era commencing with Christ's return and not prior to it as in postmillennialism.

The millenarian viewpoints coalesce, therefore, in the expectation of a great future era of gospel prominence in the world. Both pre-and postmillennialists anticipate a great evangelistic thrust and spiritual harvest dur-

ing the future millennium. The point at issue between the two positions
is how that era is inaugurated.

A third criticism of postmillennialism comes closer to the central issue
at stake among the competing eschatological viewpoints. At issue in the
discussion among the major millennial positions is the proper understanding of the biblical expectation of the nature of the end of the age. Each
of the viewpoints emphasizes a different dimension of that expectation.

Critics of postmillennialism charge that this eschatology in all its varieties fails to reflect the more complex description of the end time found
in the New Testament. The various texts paint two quite different pictures
of the events that set the stage for the final events of history. The optimistic theme emphasized by postmillennialism is undeniably present. But
the New Testament also sounds a pessimistic note. Although certain texts
give warrant for eschatological optimism, the Bible also indicates that
spiritual and moral conditions will worsen as the end approaches (for
example, Mt 24:4-7; 2 Tim 3:1-5).[104]

If a widely held interpretation of Luke 18:8 is correct, then the eschatological pessimism that exists side by side with the optimistic theme in
the New Testament was present already in the expectations of Jesus
himself. In speaking of the future intervention of God to bring about
justice in response to the prayers of the saints, the Master asks, "When
the Son of Man comes, will he find faith on the earth?" This query is best
understood as a rhetorical question reflecting Jesus' concern that the faith
of many will grow cold through the lengthy delay of the parousia.[105]

Failure to give adequate account of the pessimistic strand of New Testament teaching concerning the end time led certain earlier postmillennialists to err in the direction of unbridled optimism about the nearness of the
millennium. James H. Snowden, for example, writing at the height of
World War 1, asserts that the successful conclusion of the conflict will
forever put an end to militarism.[106] Fortunately, many of Snowden's heirs
have been chastened by such premature "date-setting" into a more cautious
stance. Mainline evangelical postmillennialists are less likely today to make
pronouncements concerning the nearness of the golden age, while contin-

uing to hold uncompromisingly to the power of the gospel eventually to achieve its goal.

Nevertheless, even the chastened postmillennialism articulated by contemporary evangelical proponents does not move far enough in accounting for the eschatological realism of the New Testament. The presence in the texts of both optimism and pessimism suggests that the Lord will come at a season that is both "the best of times and the worst of times," to utilize the well-known phrase from Charles Dickens. By emphasizing the progress of the gospel in history climaxing in the millennial era, however, postmillennialists often fail to present adequately the complete, two-edged New Testament picture of the end.

Yet it appears that some postmillennialists are not oblivious to this problem. In fact, classical postmillennialism offers tacit agreement with this criticism of the general position. On the basis of Revelation 20:7-10, the classical view anticipates that the golden age will conclude with a Satanic rebellion that Christ himself will squelch. Consequently, the unbridled historical optimism critics see in postmillennialism becomes in the final analysis a more down-to-earth realism.

Conclusion

Despite its weaknesses, postmillennialism has at least two interrelated contributions to make to contemporary Christianity. First, it offers a needed reminder that the reign of God is in one sense a present reality.[107] Both pre- and postmillennialists agree that the fullness of the kingdom era lies yet in the future. In a manner not paralleled by their premillennialist cousins, however, postmillennialists emphasize the availability in the present of the resources of the glorious future reality.

Second, its unquestioning optimism concerning the work of God through the proclamation of the gospel and the activity of the church in the world stands as a major contribution of postmillennialism. This optimism is the natural result of the emphasis on the present availability of kingdom resources. Christ is exercising authority now, postmillennialism declares, and through the Holy Spirit shares his authority with his people;

no wonder postmillennialists enjoin the church to be optimistic as it takes up the challenge of its mandate in the world. Postmillennialism serves to encourage the saints of God in their struggle with the active yet soon to be bound and ultimately defeated forces of evil.

The encouraging optimism of postmillennialism is especially needed in a day when pessimism is widespread in the church. Many Christians are convinced that the world situation is progressively worsening. As a result of this opinion, they easily fall victim to fatalism and discouragement. All attempts to alter the inevitable downward course of events is totally futile, many believe. In this situation, postmillennialism would rally the people of God with Jesus' words "Occupy until I come" (Lk 19:13 KJV). Postmillennialism stands as a clear admonition to us to be busy at the Lord's work, knowing that our labor is not in vain in the Lord (1 Cor 15:58).

4

A FUTURE
KINGDOM
FOR ISRAEL

The Ascendancy of Dispensationalism

*I*f postmillennialism was the great loser in the twentieth century, the great winner was a variety of premillennialism commonly called "dispensationalism." By the midpoint of the century this eschatological orientation had become the most widely held viewpoint among fundamentalist and evangelical Christians in America. Not only did it replace what had been the dominant eschatology of the nineteenth century, it also so overwhelmed other varieties of premillennialism that in the minds of many it came to be seen as the only legitimate representative of that viewpoint.[1]

So pervasive was its success that by mid-century in many circles the classical dispensational scheme of biblical interpretation and its chronology of the end times had become standards of right belief. For some conservative Christians any move away from this eschatology constituted an attack on the doctrine of Christ's Second Coming itself.[2] Clarence Bass's experience was repeated by others who came to reject the tenets of the system during the 1950s, that era of ferment within evangelicalism. Bass reported in 1960:

> Even today some of my dearest friends are convinced that I have departed from the evangelical faith. No affirmation of my belief in the cardinal doctrines of the faith—the virgin birth, the efficaciousness of Christ's death, the historicity of the resurrection, the necessity of the new birth, even the fervent expectancy of the personal, literal, actual, bodily return of the Lord to the earth—will convince them, because I have ceased to "rightly *divide* the word of truth."[3]

In certain sectors of the church, such attitudes persist into the present. Fortunately, however, they have largely vanished from contemporary dispensational scholars, who are making a conscious effort to seek more common argument with adherents of other eschatological viewpoints.

Many factors account for the success of dispensationalism in the twentieth century. Not to be overlooked is its espousal of a literal hermeneutic, or system of Bible interpretation, in the midst of the extended fundamentalist-liberal controversy.[4] But perhaps the single most significant event that solidified in the minds of many the correctness of the dispensational scheme of the end times was the "rebirth of the state of Israel," the establishment in 1948 of an independent Jewish political entity in Palestine. This event, coming as it did as the climax to events set in motion by the British victory over the Turks during World War 1, gave credence to the dispensationalist integration of Old Testament predictions concerning a return of the Jews to possess their ancestral homeland.

Equally important, the presence of Israel in Palestine, occurring within the context of the rise of the Soviet Union—seen by many proponents as the end-times king of the north[5]—added immense plausibility to dispensationalist predictions of worldwide military conflicts focusing on the Middle East immediately prior to the return of Christ. As historian Dwight Wilson noted, "The juxtaposition of events in 1948 brought in the succeeding months a sense of expectation that would not be equalled again."[6] Since 1948, the prophetic significance of the rebirth of Israel as a divine act preparing for the final conflict of the age has been a central assertion of dispensationalism.[7]

The success and widespread credibility enjoyed by dispensationalists today forms a stark contrast to the meager beginnings of this eschatology in the nineteenth century. Although its exact historical genesis seems to be shrouded in mystery, most historians agree that dispensationalism as it is now known was given its first systematic articulation by the Irish Anglican clergyman John Nelson Darby, an influential leader in the Plymouth Brethren movement.[8] During the nineteenth century Darby's followers imported his theology to the United States.

More influential than Darby's writings in the shaping and spread of dispensationalist ideas in America was the publication in 1909 of the Scofield Reference Bible, an edition of the King James Version that contained the annotations of C. I. Scofield. For the next decades Scofield's understanding stood as the standard interpretation of dispensationalism, and his comments were viewed by many readers as reflecting the only valid interpretation of the biblical texts.

Since the early heyday of dispensationalism, adherents have tinkered with the thinking of Darby and Scofield. In the 1960s mid-century revisions were solidified in a new edition of the revered study document, the New Scofield Reference Bible. Despite changes introduced by its editors, the work retains many of the central features of the earlier dispensationalism. The viewpoint delineated in the two editions of the Scofield Reference Bible and articulated by luminaries such as John F. Walvoord and Charles Ryrie may be termed "classic dispensationalism."

Beginning in the 1980s, certain dispensational scholars launched an even more radical rethinking of the system. As a result, there now exists alongside of classical dispensationalism a growing circle of "moderate," "modified" or "progressive" dispensationalists who no longer accept many of the features of the older view. It would be a mistake, therefore, to view dispensationalism as a static, monolithic viewpoint. The modified variety prevalent in educational institutions has yet to filter through the church, however. Consequently, the older, "classic" dispensationalism remains a potent force in evangelicalism.[9]

The Main Features of Dispensationalism

Dispensationalists share with all premillennialists the central belief that Christ's Second Coming will be premillennial; it will occur *before* the future golden age on earth. But beyond this fundamental tenet that unites it with its eschatological cousins, dispensationalism constitutes a vision quite different from any of its rivals.

The name "dispensationalism" is derived from "dispensation," a word found in the King James Version of the Bible (see 1 Cor 9:17; Eph 1:10; 3:2; Col 1:25), which refers to the administration of God's earthly household.[10] As their name suggests, dispensationalists divide salvation history into epochs, or eras, of the economy of God in order thereby to distinguish the different administrations of God in directing the affairs of the world.[11]

Scofield defined a dispensation as "a period of time during which man is tested in respect of obedience to some *specific* revelation of the will of God."[12] On this basis, he found seven such epochs in the Bible: innocency, conscience, human government, promise, law, grace and kingdom.[13] Contemporary progressive dispensationalists have grown uncomfortable with both the Scofield definition and the tendency among their forebears to multiply dispensations. Some now focus on as few as two—the old and the new covenant eras.[14]

According to older dispensationalist thinking, each successive epoch entails a specific and progressive[15] revelation of what God requires of human beings, as well as the human stewardship of that revelation.[16] During each dispensation, humankind fails to live in obedience to the test,[17] and consequently each epoch climaxes with the judgment of God. Charles Ryrie, former professor of theology at the staunchly dispensationalist Dallas Theological Seminary and important shaper of the classical expression of the system, offers this summarization:

Dispensationalism views the world as a household run by God. In this household-world God is dispensing or administering its affairs according to His own will and in various stages of revelation in the process of time. These various stages mark off the distinguishably different economies in the outworking of His total purpose, and these economies are the dispensations.[18]

Dispensationalists were not the first to divide salvation history into epochs of God's administration.[19] Already in the patristic era, for example, theologians found in the six days of creation a schema of human history. Augustine concluded his influential *The City of God* by outlining the six ages of history that will climax in the seventh, the eternal sabbath rest for the people of God.[20] Many theologians throughout the Middle Ages followed a similar pattern.[21] Nevertheless, the actual way in which the early dispensationalists approached this activity did constitute an innovation.[22] In a manner unparalleled by previous thinkers, Darby and Scofield emphasized the differences among the successive divisions of history. The sharp distinctions introduced by Darby, however, have been moderated by contemporary progressive dispensationalists, who place whatever dispensations of time they find in the Bible under the one program of God in establishing his rulership over the earth.

Dispensationalism is characterized by a division of salvation history into distinct epochs, whether seven[23] or two in number. But its *sine qua non* principles as a specific eschatological viewpoint lie elsewhere.[24] Dispensationalism, especially in its classical expression but also to a lesser extent in its current progressive form,[25] may be best described as a unique combination of two central tenets[26] that arise out of a specific hermeneutic or system of biblical interpretation.

The first basic tenet of dispensationalism concerns the relation between God's Old Testament and New Testament people. Classical dispensationalism maintains a thoroughgoing separation of, even a metaphysical distinction[27] between, Israel and the church.[28] At its heart is the principle that there are two peoples of God. Traditionally dispensationalists have asserted that Israel is God's national people, whereas the church of Jesus Christ constitutes God's spiritual or heavenly people.[29] Progressive dispensation-

alists have softened the older radical distinction between the two, preferring to speak of "a united people of God" within which lie certain distinctions.[30]

It would be an unfortunate misunderstanding to assume that the dispensationalist differentiation between Israel and the church suggests that
there were no saints in the Old Testament era. What the distinction intends is a denial of the inclusion of the redeemed of both the Old and New
Testaments as together comprising the one church, characteristic of other
eschatological systems.[31] Dispensationalists of all varieties adamantly reject the contention that the church is the New Israel.[32] In the words of
Charles Ryrie, "dispensationalism insists that the people of God who have
been baptized into the Body of Christ and who thus form the Church are
distinct from saints of other days or even of a future time."[33]

In the older dispensationalism the distinction between Israel and the
church corresponds to a distinction between two phases of God's program
for salvation history. One program is connected with the specific, earthly
nation of Israel. The other concerns the heavenly, international body called
the church. The first program—the nation of Israel—focuses on the land
of Palestine and includes God's promise to bestow material blessings on
the physical descendants of Abraham. The second program—the church
of Jesus Christ—centers on heaven and the spiritual blessings God has
for those from every nation who acknowledge Jesus as Savior and thereby
become Abraham's spiritual children.[34]

While continuing the older expectation of a restoration of Israel to the
land of Palestine, progressive dispensationalists no longer employ spacial
categories (heavenly and earthly) to speak of the distinction between Israel
and the church. Instead they prefer temporal, kingdom-oriented terms,
arising from their emphasis on the difference between the present, inaugurated dimension of the kingdom of God and its future consummation.
The church is the focal point of God's activity during the present era of
the inaugurated kingdom. It is, in the words of Darrell Bock, "the show-
case of God's present reign through Messiah Jesus, who inaugurates the
fulfillment of God's promises."[35] Israel, in contrast, will again come into

focus when Jesus returns. At that time, the Lord "will restore Israel's role," which includes "certain political, earthly expectations tied to Israel."[36] In this way, progressive dispensationalists seek to carve out a middle position between the classical variety and nondispensationalism.[37]

Dispensationalists assert that the distinction between Israel and the church, however it is to be envisioned, carries an important implication. Foundational to the proper understanding of the message of the Bible, they argue, is a clear understanding of the distinctive roles of the two. Even though both together may comprise the one people of God, there remain significant differences. The Bible student ought not to confuse Israel and the church. This advice is most pronounced in the exhortations of classical dispensationalists. Only by understanding the intended focus of a text, they declare—whether it is concerned with Israel or with the church—can the interpreter obey Paul's exhortation to Timothy (2 Tim 2:15) to be found faithful in "rightly dividing the Word of Truth."[38]

According to the dispensationalist reading of the Bible, in contrast to the nondispensational understanding of the church as the fulfillment of the Old Testament, the New Israel, neither phase or aspect of God's program is yet complete. The classical view expresses this understanding in terms of suspension and parenthesis. The Israel phase, which began with Abraham, was suspended when the Jews rejected Jesus as their Messiah. Consequently, the church phase, which is a parenthesis in God's Israel program, was inaugurated at Pentecost. The advent of the church, however, did not spell the end of God's program for Israel. God neither abrogated the divine promises to his Old Testament people nor enmeshed them into the church.[39] Consequently, someday God's program for the church will be completed. When this happens focus will be placed once again on the divine intentions for the national people of Israel. At that time the nation will accept its true Messiah, an event that will signal the fullness of the kingdom age, the glorious era of peace and righteousness known as the millennium.

Progressive dispensationalists no longer employ the older terminology to describe this expectation. Some do retain the idea of the church as in some sense a parenthesis, but they understand this idea in a salvation-historical, rather than a metaphysical, sense. What was unknown to the Old Testament writers, they declare, was the fact that Jesus would accomplish God's program in two stages, not one, corresponding to his two advents. In this sense, the church, which is the focus of Jesus' work inaugurated at his first advent, is a type of parenthesis in the fuller program of God.[40]

Whereas the first tenet of dispensationalism concerns the relation between Israel and the church, the second focuses on the close of the present age and the final epoch of history that lies beyond it. Dispensationalism sets forth a specific understanding of the nature and purpose of the tribulation—the seven-year period of worldwide distress lying in the not-to-distant future—and the significance of the millennium, the golden age predicted by the prophets and by the twentieth chapter of the Apocalypse. Both of these periods of time are best understood in terms of their function within God's program for Israel.

Dispensationalists declare that neither the tribulation nor the millennium properly concern God's purposes for the church. Rather, both focus on the divine dealings with Israel. Of course, in the tribulation God's wrath will be poured out on the earth. But more important for an adequate understanding of the purpose of the events of those days is the premise that Israel is once again in the center of God's action at that stage of history. God will use the tribulation in order to prepare the Jews to receive their Messiah, Jesus, at his return. This focus is even more prominent in the glorious thousand-year era. Although the church may also play a role in it, the primary purpose of the millennium is to serve as the time during which God will finally complete the Old Testament promises to Israel.

In keeping with these two foundational tenets, classical dispensationalists are interested in offering a detailed eschatological chronology. Although there are dissenting voices, most anticipate that the current church age will one day be brought to a close by the secret, pretribulational rapture of the (true) church. At this event the Christians who have died, together with the believers who are alive, will meet the Lord in the air. The returning Jesus takes his church to heaven to stand before "the judgment seat of Christ" and to celebrate "the marriage supper of the Lamb" (Rev 19).[41] This rapture is pretribulational; it occurs prior to the tribulation period. (Some dispensationalists, however, argue that the rapture is midtribulational, that is, that the first three and one-half years of the tribulation precede the rapture.[42] And within the ranks of dispensationalism there are several scholars who defend the posttribulational view.[43])

Meanwhile on earth the appearance of the antichrist marks the beginning of the seven-year tribulation. During this time the antichrist rules over the world, and God's wrath is poured out on the earth. But by suffering under the political treachery of antichrist, Israel is prepared to be converted back to God. The tribulation period climaxes with a military conflagration in Palestine.[44] In the midst of this Battle of Armageddon, Jesus Christ returns with the armies of heaven and routs the enemies of Israel. In addition to the deliverance his victory means for the Jewish people, "the Lord destroys every hostile force that would challenge His right to rule as Messiah over the earth."[45] Israel acknowledges Jesus as Messiah, and the thousand-year kingdom is established on the earth.

As in many other premillennial eschatologies, the millennium anticipated by dispensationalism is the time of Christ's earthly reign. He will be physically present on earth, and from Jerusalem he will rule over all the nations of the world. All humankind will live together in peace and safety, because Satan will have been bound and cast into the bottomless pit. But unlike their eschatological cousins, nearly all dispensationalists anticipate that Israel, not the church, will be prominent in this age. The millennium is the occasion for God to fulfill the Old Testament prophecies to bless the nation. Therefore, during the thousand years Israel will enjoy presence in the land of Palestine and prominence among the nations.[46]

The dispensationalist chronology concerning the events that follow the thousand years parallels premillennialism in general. At the close of the millennial era, Satan is freed from his prison. He gathers the unbelieving nations in a rebellion against Christ's government. However, his rebellion is short-lived, for it is squelched by fire from heaven. Then come the general resurrection (including the resurrection of the unrighteous), the judgment and the eternal state.[47]

The Biblical Basis of Dispensationalism

Like adherents of the other conservative viewpoints, dispensationalists believe that their system of eschatology accurately reflects the teaching of the Bible itself. But to an extent greater than is claimed by defenders of other systems, its proponents argue that their view arises out of the consistent employment of a literal hermeneutic, especially as applied to the Old Testament and the book of Revelation.

Classical dispensationalists set forth as the central hermeneutical maxim for all valid biblical interpretation the literal approach to the Bible.[48] Consequently, in Charles Ryrie's opinion, the primary goal of dispensationalist expositors is to accept the text of Scripture "at its face value,"[49] that is, to give to every word "the same meaning it would have in normal usage, whether employed in writing, speaking or thinking."[50] Dispensationalists readily admit that the Bible employs symbols, of course, but argue that unless there is good contextual indication that a figure is indeed a symbol, it must be interpreted literally. However, dispensationalist writers rarely take their commitment to literalism to the extreme of the nineteenth-century premillennialist Isaac P. Labagh. He theorized that the bottomless prison for Satan envisioned by Revelation 20:3 was located in the center of the earth, which, because it is constantly revolving, has neither top nor bottom.[51]

Apologists such as Charles Ryrie[52] argue that the literal, normal or plain interpretation of the Bible is in keeping with the divine intent in giving language to humankind as a means of communication. Further, the prophecies concerning Christ's first coming were fulfilled literally, indicating that the literal method of interpretation must be correct. And if this method is not followed, Ryrie claims, all objectivity in exegesis is lost.

Progressive dispensationalists have demonstrated a greater willingness than their forebears to acknowledge the presence of symbols in the Bible. And they seek to avoid interpreting biblical symbols in the "wooden" manner that readily arises when imagery is taken at its face value.[53] While more conscientious in employing interpretive resources and the findings of modern biblical scholarship, progressive dispensationalists nevertheless remain committed to the literal approach to biblical texts.

Dispensationalists find a primary application of their hermeneutic in the promises of Old Testament prophecy. In fact, they accuse conservative exegetes who readily employ the literal approach to other biblical texts of suddenly resorting to allegorizing or spiritualizing when confronted with prophecy.[54] Against adherents of other eschatological viewpoints, therefore, dispensationalists adamantly argue that we must employ the literal hermeneutic consistently. Hence, we are to interpret divine promises given through the prophets, like other texts, as they were given,[55] at least insofar as they provide the promise of an eschatological renewal for Israel.

The literalist hermeneutic leads dispensationalists to anticipate that prophecies concerning Israel (and perhaps the surrounding nations) will be fulfilled sometime in the future basically as they were originally given. Use of the literal method means as well that promises originally directed to Israel must someday become the experience of the nation. Such promises focus on Israel's future possession of the land of Palestine and their enjoyment of physical blessings.[56]

Classical dispensationalists take this principle to an extreme not generally found among their progressive heirs. On the basis of an application of the hermeneutic to the vision of Ezekiel, for example, some expect that the Jerusalem temple will be rebuilt in exact accordance with the plan and proportions given in the prophecy.[57] A few even declare that the Old Testament sacrificial system will once again be instituted, not to provide cleansing for sin, however, but as a reminder of Christ's sacrifice and as an object lesson for children born during the millennium concerning the need for the new birth.[58]

Because of their desire to employ consistently a literalist approach to Scripture, dispensationalists are reticent to exhaust the intent of Old Testament promises in any "spiritualized" fulfillment. Classical dispensationalists argue that these texts cannot refer to the spiritual blessings received by the church. Their progressive heirs are more willing to connect the church with Old Testament expectations, but they too anticipate a yet future fulfillment to promises given to national Israel, invoking the principle of multiple fulfillment in support of their approach.[59]

Dispensationalists reject the older thesis that the church is the culmination of God's activity in the Old Testament era. The church is simply not the New Israel.[60] The New Testament itself denies that thesis, they argue. On several occasions Paul contrasts natural Israel and the church, indicating that "Israel" continues to mean the physical descendants of Abraham (for example, 1 Cor 10:32; Rom 9:3-4, 6).[61] Rather than the fulfillment of what God began with Israel, according to classical dispensationalists, the church is an interruption, or "parenthesis," in the divine program for Israel. Progressive dispensational thought has softened this stance, seeing the church as the first in a two-stage program of kingdom inauguration.[62]

Classical dispensationalist thinkers derive the far-reaching thesis concerning the discontinuity between Israel and the church as a logical, albeit indirect, conclusion from the strict employment of the literalist approach to the Bible. The church is not mentioned in the Old Testament, they argue, and therefore it constitutes a "mystery," a plan of God not revealed to the Old Testament prophets.[63] In the same way, the absence of references to the church in the description of the tribulation era found in Revelation (specifically chapters 4—18) suggests that the church is not present during this period of time. Because the church is present neither in the Old Testament nor in the tribulation—that is, during those periods when God is working specifically with Israel—it must be a parenthesis in God's program.

Again at this juncture, the classical argument has been softened by progressive dispensationalists. Robert Saucy, for example, explains that the mystery nature of the church in relation to the Old Testament does not mean that the union of Jew and Gentile in the church was unknown to the prophets. Rather, "the revelation of this previously hidden mystery relates primarily to the actualization or realization through Christ of that which the prophets foretold and longingly anticipated."[64] Nevertheless, even for progressives, the central maxim remains intact: Israel and the church are to be kept separate, insofar as they are the focus of two different stages of prophetic fulfillment.[65]

Classical dispensationalists argue that the conclusion concerning the parenthetical nature of the church, derived from the Bible as a whole, is also evident in several biblical texts. But above all, one specific Old Testament passage, which for many interpreters stands as the crucial prophecy, is important in establishing this thesis—Daniel's vision of the "seventy sevens" (9:20-27).[66]

Christian exegetical tradition has generally interpreted the sevens of Daniel's vision as prophetic years. As a result, the prophecy anticipates that God's program for Israel would be completed after 490 years, which began with some historical point related to the return of the Jews to Palestine after the Babylonian exile. Although some evangelicals have recently argued for other alternatives,[67] especially a Maccabean context for the fulfillment of this prophecy,[68] conservative commentators have traditionally agreed that the first sixty-nine weeks of prophetic years came to an end at the advent or sometime during the ministry of Jesus. The point at issue among them is the time of the seventieth week.

The nondispensationalist conservative interpretation, which some label "the traditional view,"[69] asserts that the final week followed immediately after the sixty-ninth week, terminating in the crucifixion of Christ and leading eventually to the destruction of the nation of Israel in A.D. 70. The entire prophecy, therefore, focuses on the first advent of Christ and his accomplishment of the messianic vocation.[70]

In its classical expression, dispensationalism sets forth a significant alteration to the traditional exegesis. Generally, adherents place the close of the sixty-nine weeks at the point when Jesus offered the kingdom to Israel and himself as Messiah (that is, Palm Sunday). But this offer was rejected by the nation. As a result, the kingdom was postponed, at least in its earthly fullness, and Jesus went to the cross.[71]

The older dispensationalism saw in this thesis concerning Israel's rejection of their Messiah at his first coming an even more crucial and far-reaching conclusion: The seventieth prophetic week has been placed in abeyance. When Israel rejected Jesus, "God's prophetic clock" was stopped—to employ the metaphorical language popularized by the older view—and consequently the church program, which was unknown in the Old Testament, was inaugurated. One future day the church phase of God's program will be completed, and the church will be raptured. That event will commence the restarting of God's prophetic clock to tick off the seventieth week of Daniel's prophecy, which is the seven-year tribulation period. During these years, the kingdom will once again be heralded to Israel; this time, however, it will meet with success, and the theocratic kingdom—the millennium—will be inaugurated.[72]

Here again, progressive dispensationalists have moved beyond the classical view. They no longer speak in terms of the church as a substitute for a failed kingdom program.[73] Nevertheless, similar to their forebears, they employ a literal hermeneutic, which readily leads to the basic dispensationalist understanding. If Old Testament promises to Israel do not find their complete fulfillment in the New Testament church, some important distinction must remain between Israel and the church. The church cannot be the completion of what God began with the ancient Hebrews, but must be either a separate phase (classical dispensationalism) or an inauguration phase (progressive dispensationalism) in the divine program for the ages. In the same way, if Old Testament prophecies concerning the possession of the land of Palestine must one day come to pass, a future golden age is required as the era during which God pours out material blessings on the nation of Israel.[74] Dispensationalists, whether classical or progressive, argue that a future millennium in which Israel is prominent constitutes the only logical interpretation of Old Testament messianic prophecy.[75]

Less immediately obvious is the biblical case for what in the minds of most people is the chief characteristic of dispensationalism, the pretribulation rapture (or the two-stage return of Christ, as it is sometimes called). This doctrine is central to classical dispensationalism. Although generally voicing no objections to the older view, progressive thinkers tend to devote less attention to it. Dispensationalist writings—especially those of classical articulators—offer at least five major arguments supporting this doctrine.

First, the pretribulation rapture is demanded by the nature or purposes of the tribulation.[76] This seven-year period is the time of "Jacob's trouble" (Jer 30:7), that is, a latter-day trial during which Israel will turn to the Lord (Deut 4:27-30).[77] Hence, the purpose of the tribulation concerns God's dealings with Israel, not the church. Further, during the tribulation God's wrath is poured out on the world (1 Thess 5:9; Rev 6:17; 11:18). Because the church is not the object of God's wrath (1 Thess 5:9),[78] it simply cannot experience the horrors of those years.[79] On the contrary, God has promised to exempt the church both from the future eschatological divine wrath 1 Thess 1:10; 5:9) and from the time of wrath (Rev 3:10).[80] God's purposes for the tribulation, then, suggest that only Israel—and not the church—can be present on earth during this time.

The imminence of the blessed hope of the believer is a second argument supporting the pretribulation rapture.[81] Paul encourages Christian living during this age on the basis of a "blessed hope" that can be realized at any moment (Tit 2:11-13; 1 Thess 1:9-10). Dispensationalists interpret this hope to be the rapture of the church. The imminence of the rapture (the blessed hope) implies that no other event in "God's prophetic timetable" can stand between it and the present.

Dispensationalists argue likewise for the imminence of the rapture on the basis of the difference they find between texts dealing with this occurrence and those focusing on the Second Coming.[82] Rapture texts contain no mention of any signs or events that precede it, whereas second advent texts generally also speak of what leads up to and signals the return of Jesus.

The Mount Olivet Discourse (Mt 24) offers a prime case of a Second Coming text. Paul Feinberg summarizes the argument: "Matthew 24 is by far the most exhaustive and in my judgment relates events that will occur throughout the Tribulation. In Matthew 24:32-51 our Lord makes it clear that these signs are to alert the believer that His coming is near."[83] Clearly the believers being alerted in this text are not members of the church as it now is present on the earth. They will have been translated through the rapture. Rather, in view here are the "tribulation saints," those converted during that future period. Many dispensationalists emphasize that the primary focus of Jesus' discourse are believing Jews, those who will come to acknowledge Jesus as their Messiah through the kingdom proclamation during the time of Jacob's trouble.

On the basis of considerations such as these, no affirmation is dearer to a great number of dispensationalists than the claim that the "translation of the Church is the next event in predictive prophecy."[84] In fact, some adherents find abhorrent any suggestion that the rapture could occur after the tribulation. Anything other than the pretribulation rapture would entail a denial of the imminence of the blessed hope, for the believer would know at the beginning of the tribulation that the rapture is now seven years in the future.

Third, the pretribulation rapture is demanded by the book of Revelation. As suggested earlier, dispensationalists note that the church, after having been dominant in the first three chapters, is totally absent in Revelation 4—18, which describes the tribulation period. (Actually, the word does not occur after chap. 3 until chap. 22.)[85] Instead of the church, the people of God mentioned in these chapters are the 144,000 chosen and sealed from among the tribes of Israel. From its absence in the text, dispensationalists conclude that the church is absent from the earth during the tribulation.[86]

Some dispensationalists interpret Revelation 4:1 as a veiled reference to the rapture. The call of the angel to the seer and John's subsequent transporting into heaven are symbolic of the rapture of the church.[87] In the same way, the twenty-four elders represent the "Church rewarded," that is, the church as raptured and present in heaven while the tribulation rages on earth.[88]

This interpretation of Revelation 4 is confirmed by the significance many adherents find in the promise given to the godly Philadelphian church (Rev 3:10), that it will be "kept from the hour" of trial that is soon to transpire on the earth.[89] In fact, the early systematic theologian of dispensationalism, Lewis Sperry Chafer, labels this text "the determining passage"[90] concerning this doctrine. The Philadelphia church symbolizes the godly, pure, separated church of the end time. This church will be rewarded for its faithfulness by experiencing the rapture prior to the tribulation. By means of the rapture these true believers are "kept from the hour," in fulfillment of the promise to the Philadelphia church.

The fourth argument for the pretribulation rapture arises from Paul's declaration that the restrainer must be removed before the revelation of the man of sin (2 Thess 2:6-8). Although the apostle does not reveal the identity of the restrainer, many dispensationalists suggest that it can be nothing other than the church or the Holy Spirit[91] working through the church to curb iniquity.[92] This interpretation arises in part from Jesus' declaration to his disciples that they are salt and light in the world. As salt and light, the church exerts a preservative force in human affairs, preventing evil from becoming as widespread and intense as it potentially could be. Once the church is removed from the world, however, the way is open for the full development of evil, which occurs during the tribulation. The church (that is, the Holy Spirit operative through the church), therefore, must be removed before the man of sin, the antichrist, can be revealed. For this reason the rapture must be pretribulational.

Finally and most important, the pretribulation rapture is demanded by the dispensationalist system itself.[93] This is readily evident in the classical expression of the system. If there are two peoples of God and two phases of God's program in the world, and if the Israel phase has been placed in abeyance during the church age, then the pretribulation rapture follows logically. The church phase must come to an end before the Israel phase can once again re-emerge. God's program for the church must be brought to completion—which will occur by means of the rapture—before God's program for Israel can continue.

Less evident is the theological importance of the pretribulational rapture for progressive dispensationalism. It remains plausible, albeit not necessary, that the church will be raptured before God acts to bring the promised territorial and political restoration to Israel.

The Critique of Dispensationalism

Although dispensationalism gained the following of many evangelicals as the events of the twentieth century unfolded, it by no means won the uncritical support of the entire movement. Beginning around mid-century, several prominent voices within evangelicalism began to raise questions concerning the correctness of this theological system in its classical expression. The questions posed to classical dispensationalism by its critics have not fallen on deaf ears. On the contrary, the critical engagement with the system has been one factor instrumental in fostering some of the changes introduced recently by progressive dispensational thinkers.

The discussion of the classical viewpoint focused on the literal hermeneutic that stands at its basis, as well as on the doctrine of the pretribulation rapture and on the dichotomy between Israel and the church. To the extent that contemporary dispensationalism has moved beyond the older formulations of these hallmarks the comments of critics of the system may no longer be germane. Nevertheless, since dispensationalist scholars retain certain features—albeit in modified form—of the tradition with which they consciously identify themselves, the older discussion retains certain points of ongoing relevancy.

The dispensationalist hermeneutic has generated a keen debate between proponents and critics. Nondispensationalists accuse dispensationalists of employing an oversimplified approach to the Bible. More specifically, they reject the claim that the Old Testament promises to Israel demand a literal fulfillment.

This criticism is especially targeted at classical dispensationalism. In rejecting the literalism of its proponents, critics appeal to the New Testament, which as "the only divinely inspired commentary on the Old Testament" forms the pattern for Christian exegesis of the divine promises to Israel. They offer several specific examples of the New Testament use of the Old.

According to Luke's account of Pentecost (Acts 2:15-21), for example, Peter found in the events of that day the fulfillment of Joel's prophecy concerning the day of the Lord (Joel 2:28ff.), including the predictions of cosmic disturbances. He applied Joel's vision not to national Israel, but to the church. Luke's rendering of James' speech at the Jerusalem Council (Acts 15:14-18) offers a similar nonliteral interpretation of Amos' prophecy of a future divine re-establishment of the Davidic kingship (Amos 9:11-12). The prophet anticipated an eschatological re-emergence of Israel as a dominant nation under the reign of David's greater son, the Messiah. But the leader of the Jerusalem church claimed that the fulfillment of this text was the coming of the Gentiles to faith in Jesus.[94] Likewise, Jeremiah's vision of a day of a new covenant between God and Israel (Jer 31:31ff.) appears to be a prophecy of an eschatological re-establishment of Israel. But the book of Hebrews declares that this day has already arrived, for it was fulfilled in the first coming of Christ (Heb 8:6-12).

As these and other examples indicate, nondispensationalists claim that the inspired authors of the New Testament found fulfillment in the church for certain Old Testament promises originally given to Israel. In addition, some interpreters note that other promises, such as dominance over Israel's neighbors and even possession of the land of promise, were declared fulfilled already in the Old Testament era. Hence, in reporting the conquest of the land, the book of Joshua claims that all God had promised to do for Israel had been accomplished (Josh 23:14; 11:23; 21:43; see also 1 Kings 4:20-21).[95] And later prophecies of a regathering of Israel pointed to the return from exile that began following the edict of Cyrus.

Considerations such as these lead critics to conclude that the hermeneutic of classical dispensationalism is faulty. Consequently, they reject as well the theological system that arises from the literalist hermeneutic. It is erroneous to demand the strict separation between Israel and the church asserted by classical dispensationalism, they argue; it is likewise unwarranted to understand the tribulation and the millennium in terms of a program of God for Israel apart from the church.

Progressive dispensationalists voice amazing agreement with critics of the older system on these matters. Based on texts such as Acts 2 and 15, they readily acknowledge that Old Testament promises find fulfillment in the church. And they have long ago rejected the older suggestion that

Israel and the church are parties to two separate new covenants,[96] acknowledging on the contrary that Israel and the church participate in the one new covenant of Jeremiah 31.[97] At the same time, progressive dispensationalists assert, against their critics, the validity of a progressive or two-stage fulfillment of certain Old Testament prophecies. Consequently, Joel 2, for example, finds only its initial fulfillment in the church. Yet the final and complete fulfillment, the outpouring of God's Spirit on all—including Israel—is in the future.[98] For critics, the newer dispensationalism offers a welcome step in the right direction. Nevertheless, the modified view has yet to present a conclusive apologetic for the validity of the principle of progressive fulfillment. If Old Testament promises to Israel are fulfilled in the church, as progressive dispensational thinkers admit, then why must there be yet a more complete, literal fulfillment to the nation lying in the future?

Although it is not the focal doctrine of classical dispensationalism, no other tenet of the system has raised as much controversy as the pretribulation rapture. This controversy is warranted since the teaching is closely related to both of the central theological assertions of the dispensational eschatology. The pretribulation rapture facilitates the removal of the church from the earth prior to the tribulation, so that God can fulfill the Old Testament promises to Israel. Objections to this teaching generally move in two directions.

First, critics question the exegesis of certain New Testament texts that dispensationalists cite in support of the pretribulation rapture. One such passage is the Mount Olivet Discourse (especially Mt 24:1-41). As noted earlier, many dispensationalists claim that Jesus directed this prophecy largely to believing Jews who will live during the end-time tribulation period and who will carry the kingdom message throughout the earth. Consequently, while perhaps differing with each other on the exact details, dispensational exegetes agree in inserting the rapture of the church somewhere prior to verse 14 ("And this gospel of the kingdom will be preached in the whole world as a testimony to all nations, and then the end will come").[99]

Yet critics find no warrant for this conclusion. The text, they assert, is addressed to the church as a whole, and indicates only one coming of the Lord, a coming that occurs after the tribulation.[100]

Some nondispensationalists fear that relegating Matthew 24:14 to the tribulation will actually undercut the evangelistic program of the church. George E. Ladd, for example, maintains that the doctrine of the pretribulation rapture as applied to this text "sacrifices one of the main motives for world-wide missions, viz., hastening the attainment of the Blessed Hope."[101] In Ladd's opinion "it is impossible to conceive of a stronger motive for world evangelization and for the salvation of the lost than the realization that Christ is waiting to return until the Church has completed this mission."[102] Of course, if the proclamation in Matthew 24:14 is not the spread of the gospel by the church in this age but the propagation of the good news about the kingdom by believing Jews during the tribulation period, as many dispensationalists understand the verse, then Ladd's argument may lose some of its punch.

Another debated text is 2 Thessalonians 2:1-13. Here Paul suggests that both the coming of the Lord for the saints and the day of the Lord occur after the apostasy and the revealing of the man of sin. Dispensationalists readily identify the church or the Holy Spirit as the restrainer who blocks the way for the lawless one, and thereby they find in this text a reference to the rapture. Critics disagree.[103] They call dispensationalists to task for going beyond what the author actually states. Because Paul does not identify the restrainer, the claim that the rapture is in view here is pure speculation, critics argue.

Not only does this text not support the pretribulational rapture, critics declare, it actually anticipates the presence of the church during the tribulation. Appealing to a principle of interpretation known as the Granville Sharp rule,[104] nondispensationalists claim that Paul viewed the Lord's coming and the day of the Lord as the same event, and he anticipated that they will happen simultaneously and in conjunction with each other.[105] They note further that the message of the text builds from the knowledge that its recipients already possess knowledge that will keep them from falling prey to the lawless one during the day of deception. Paul writes as though Christians need to be warned against the danger of deception by the antichrist. Thus, the thrust of the passage presupposes the presence of believers in the tribulation.

A final text is Titus 2:13, which speaks about "the blessed hope" for which believers wait. Critics note that the event discussed here is not the imminent secret rapture, so central to dispensational teaching; rather, it is nothing less than the glorious appearing of Christ himself. The occasion toward which the text directs our gaze is the epiphany of Christ's glory, which even dispensationalists admit occurs at the end of the tribulation. The implications of this observation are significant. Nondispensationalists argue that the New Testament explicitly says that Christians are to *look for* an event that is preceeded by the tribulation years.[106]

On the basis of this text, critics accuse dispensationalists of misplacing the "blessed hope" of the believer. Ladd passionately summarizes this contention:

> To insist that the Blessed Hope must be escape from the Great Tribulation is to place the emphasis where the Scripture does not place it. ... The Word of God everywhere assures us that in this age we are to expect tribulation and persecution. The last great persecution of Antichrist will indeed be worse and more fearful than anything the world has ever seen; but when we contemplate the history of martyrdom, why should we ask deliverance from what millions have already suffered?[107]

In addition to the exegesis of specific texts, critics often follow a second major line of criticism. They claim that the doctrine of the pretribulation rapture actually necessitates a violation of the literalist hermeneutic of dispensationalism, especially in the Apocalypse.

A vivid example of purported dispensationalist spiritualizing is the suggestion by some interpreters that Revelation 4:1 is a veiled reference to the rapture. As plausible as the interpretation might seem, critics charge, a literal hermeneutic would obviously necessitate the rejection of such a view.[108]

Some dispensationalist commentators, following a line of exegesis that predates the movement itself, interpret the seven churches of the opening chapters of the book in a symbolic, nonhistorical fashion. They see these churches as a prophecy of the seven successive epochs of Christian history. At the climax of the series stands the lukewarm Laodicean congregation, which represents the apostate church of the end times, symbolized subsequently in the book by the great whore. Critics wonder how dispensationalists can violate their literalist hermeneutic in this manner. However, commentators such as Norman Harrison find warrant for the symbolic interpretation in the text itself, namely, in the arrangement of the epistles relative to the geographic location of the original churches: "It is significant that they are located, geographically, and in the order named, in a circle, suggestive of the entire cycle of Church history."[109]

A more lively debate focuses on the dispensationalist treatment of the promise to the Philadelphia church, "I will also keep you from the hour of trial that is going to come upon the whole world to test those who live on the earth" (Rev 3:10). Many dispensationalists move beyond the "natural" reading of the text, which understands this church as a historical, first-century congregation in Asia Minor, and claim that the recipient of the promise of the text is the faithful church of the last days.

In addition to the question of the validity of the symbolic interpretation of the Philadelphia church, protagonists and antagonists debate the dispensationalist assertion that Revelation 3:10 speaks of a pretribulation rapture. Critics point out that the text itself does not explicitly mention such an event. On the contrary, it may actually presuppose the presence of believers during the tribulation.[110]

The focus of the debate lies with the interpretation of the promise that the Philadelphians would be "kept from" the hour of trial. This phrase ("kept from"), dispensationalists declare, must be read in the light of the descriptions in the promise that seem to refer to a coming worldwide time of testing. The promise, therefore, is that believers will be spared from this testing, which could only be realized if they were not on the earth when the testing happens.

Critics build their rebuttal from what they see as the parallel to this promise given in one petition of Jesus' prayer: "My prayer is not that you take them out of the world but that you protect them from the evil one" (Jn 17:15). Because both texts employ the same Greek construction, non-dispensationalists argue that just as Jesus prays for God's gracious protection of the disciples in the face of Satanic onslaught, so also he promises the Philadelphia church not an escape through a secret rapture but his gracious protection in the presence of the coming trial.

Dispensationalist interpreters reply that John 17:15 actually supports their position. From his study of the parallel Greek construction, Paul Feinberg adds an interesting twist to the debate:

> Just as the disciples were not in the Evil One, so the Philadelphians would not be in the hour of testing. The promise of our Lord is to keep them outside the hour of trial. If this be so, it does not describe the Rapture per se. Instead it looks at the results or consequence of the Rapture.[111]

An additional problem with the dispensationalist use of Revelation lies in the placement of the vision of the marriage supper of the Lamb (Rev 19:6-9), which dispensationalists often cite in support of the pretribulation rapture. According to the dispensationalist hermeneutic, the book of Revelation follows a chronological order; that is, the order of events presented there is the order in which these events will occur. However, one cannot maintain the strict chronological approach within the block of material that comprises Revelation 17—19 without contradicting the dispensational order of future events. In this section the declaration of the marriage supper of the Lamb (19:7-8) comes after the proclamation of the destruction of the great prostitute (vv. 1-3), which is likewise the fall of Babylon (chap. 18). Both of these events preceed the victory of the rider on the white horse, who premillennialists see as the returning Christ (19:11-21). According to the dispensationalist chronology, the marriage supper transpires in heaven during the tribulation prior to the fall of Babylon, which in turn occurs at the time of Christ's triumphal return. But this is not the chronology of Revelation 17—19.

The nondispensationalist premillennial advocate George Eldon Ladd, following D. M. Kromminga,[112] offers an alternative understanding of the vision of the marriage feast. He claims that Revelation 19:6-9 is best seen as a "prophetic hymn" or a "hymn of anticipation" of the reunion of the church with Christ, and not an actual portrayal of the event. Rather than occurring before the tribulation, the wedding transpires in Revelation 20, "at the Revelation of Christ in glory." [113]

Considerations such as these lead nondispensationalists to conclude that in the final analysis the pretribulation rapture is necessitated more by the dispensationalist system, especially in its classical expression, than by actual exegesis. If a distinction between Israel and the church is presupposed by the Bible student, the doctrine of the secret rapture readily emerges from the New Testament. But the texts that adherents cite in support of their position do not so much explicitly teach the pretribulation rapture as may merely be shown to be consistent with it.

The lack of clear statements in the New Testament that set forth the doctrine of the pretribulation rapture leads critics to call for a more exegetically based proof of the dispensationalist doctrine. This call is based on the hermeneutical principle that, to employ Ladd's words, "in disputed questions of interpretation, the simpler view is to be preferred," so that "the burden of proof rests upon the more elaborate explanation."[114] In this case, the more elaborate explanation is the pretribulation view, for it divides the coming of Christ into two aspects, his coming for the saints before the tribulation and his coming with the saints after that period. Unless a tight case can be derived from the Scriptures, critics argue, it is best to anticipate the simpler, nondispensational chronology.

At the heart of dispensationalism is the distinction between Israel and the church. The strict dichotomy between two peoples of God characteristic of classic dispensationalism has likewise come under the scrutiny of critics. Nondispensationalists reject the older dispensationalist claim that the church was fully unknown in the Old Testament and therefore constitutes a second, "mysterious" phase of God's program in the world. Critics point out that the prophets envisioned a time when Gentiles would be included in the worship of Yahweh (such as Is 66:17-24; Zech 14:16-21) and consequently ask how this prophetic vision differs from what came to fruition in the establishment of Christ's church.

In fact, nondispensationalists argue, the inclusion of the Gentiles with Israel in the worship of God stands as the climax to the major vision of the entire prophetic movement. They point to Paul's word to the Galatians, "the Scripture foresaw that God would justify the Gentiles by faith, and announced the gospel in advance to Abraham: 'All nations will be blessed through you ' " (3:8). Hence, Paul claims that the vision of the union of all peoples as Abraham's offspring was made known even prior to the existence of the Israelite nation. In fact, the eventual inclusion of the nations in the reign of God was the hope of Abraham and the patriarchs,[115] as well as the content of the Abrahamic covenant.[116]

On the basis of considerations such as these, some critics offer an interesting twist. They invert the classical dispensationalist thesis of parenthesis. Rather than the church age being a parenthesis in the program of God with national Israel, opponents claim the reverse, namely, that the era of national Israel "was but a parenthesis in the midst of human history since the fall."[117] The central goal of salvation history, they argue, has always been the establishment of the new covenant, which lay at the foundation of God's dealings with Adam, Abraham, David and the Israelite nation.[118]

Critics likewise question the classical dispensationalist interpretation of the seventy weeks of Daniel. Traditionally the church has seen this prophecy as being messianic and as ending in the era of the Roman Empire. Nondispensationalists argue that the traditional interpretation, which assumes that the seventy weeks occur in strict succession, is more in keeping with a literalist hermeneutic than is the gap theory employed by dispensationalists. There is insufficient internal data to warrant an interruption of over nineteen centuries between the sixty-ninth and seventieth weeks of the prophecy.

Finally, nondispensationalists suggest that the strict dichotomy between Israel and the church, so characteristic of classical dispensationalism, is a violation of New Testament teaching, which emphasizes the continuity between the New Testament and the Old Testament. For example, we cannot fully understand Jesus' ministry apart from its Old Testament setting. Old Testament concepts, such as the remnant, are implicit in Jesus' actions, including the choosing of twelve disciples. Likewise, Jesus' reference to "my church" (Mt 16) is reminiscent of the Deuteronomic "congregation of Yahweh" (Deut 23:1; 1 Chron 28:8).

Paul explicitly teaches the unity of the work of God in both testaments. For him there is but one people of God, "one tree" to which the gentile branches have been added (Rom 11) and "one commonwealth" of which Gentiles have now become a part (Eph 2:11, 22). The book of Hebrews echoes this theme. The new covenant is the fulfillment of the old, which has passed away.

Above all, nondispensationalists assert, the New Testament presents the coming of Jesus to die for the sins of the world as the central, eternal plan of God. Christ's death—and consequently the founding of the church to proclaim the gospel of forgiveness through Christ—is not some second-order program subservient to God's working with Israel. Thus, classical dispensationalists have found themselves continually protesting the charge of their opponents that their teaching downplays the cross.[119]

Concerning the crucial issue of Israel and the church, progressive dispensationalists seek to offer a middle ground between the classical view and its critics. They readily acknowledge that the prophets foresaw the union of Jews and Gentiles in the salvation accomplished by Christ.[120] They set forth as well the unity of the work of God in history. However, while moving far in the direction of the critics of classical dispensationalism, progressive thinkers nevertheless maintain enough of the older distinction between Israel and the church to dissatisfy critics. Although no longer asserting a strict separation between a heavenly people and an earthly people, the newer dispensationalism reserves certain apects of the one new covenant (specifically its territorial and political dimensions) to the future restored nation of Israel. Consequently, even progressive thinkers are willing to speak of Israel and the church as "distinguishable covenant participants" who "comprise differing peoples."[121] From the perspective of nondispensationalists, this distinction only serves to continue the dispensationalist denial that the church is the climax of the divine program inaugurated in the Old Testament. And this is the basic objection critics lodge against dispensationalism in any form.

In addition to the more academic questions discussed above—hermeneutics, the pretribulation rapture and the relationship between Israel and the church—classical dispensationalists have been keenly interested in "understanding the times" for the sake of setting forth the chain of events predicted by the biblical writers. The older intent continues into the present in the form of the "popular" variety of dispensationalism that focuses on end-times scenarios. Beyond the problems already mentioned, classical dispensationalism, especially as it gives impetus to the quest for the chronology of the end, runs the risk of falling prey to other dangers. Fortunately, progressive dispensationalists have themselves acknowledged many of these problems and join in challenging others to avoid them.

One danger is the heightened pessimism that characterizes classical dispensationalism. Not unlike the prognosis of many secular doomsayers, the scenario its proponents anticipate offers little hope for improvement in world conditions this side of the catastrophic action of God that will spell the end of the age.[122] In this way, the classical dispensationalist vision of the end times serves to augment and heighten the pessimism inherent in premillennialism in general.

Older dispensationalists, however, have repeatedly rejected the suggestion that theirs is a pessimistic eschatology. They rebut the claim by asserting that "pessimism" is not the proper word to describe a view that sees God at work in the major events and trends in the world today. In its stead they sometimes offer the term "realism," for they neither ignore nor are discouraged by the somber aspects of the present age.

It is certainly true, for example, that dispensationalists have stood at the forefront of efforts aimed toward world evangelization. Such efforts would appear to dispel the charge of pessimism. However, at least in the past, the dispensationalist missionary challenge has tended to be that of dispersing information, in contrast to the challenge to Christianize the entire world that has marked the efforts of others.[123]

Not only is this underlying pessimism evident in the dispensationalist approach to missions, it has led many proponents to take a cautious stance toward social and political involvement. Engagement, when it has occurred, has generally been highly selective, focused on individualistic, moralistic and short-term goals.[124] Classical dispensationalists tend to be, in the words of Assemblies of God minister Dwight Wilson, "pessimistic, fatalistic, nonpolitical, and nonactivist."[125]

This heightened political pessimism was present already at the genesis of the dispensationalist movement in Britain. Darby's nineteenth-century colleagues, in contrast to millenarians of the seventeenth century, were political reactionaries. In the words of historian Ernest Sandeen:

> Since the course of history led straight to judgment, change could only produce a crescendo of corruption. Catholic emancipation, the Reform Bill, democracy, industrialization—the millenarian opposed them all, but with a sense of resignation born of the knowledge that the world must grow more evil day after day.[126]

Another danger arises out of classical dispensationalism's greatest point of appeal, which traditionally has been its ability to mediate the assurance in the midst of turbulent times that God is in control. As a "pessimistic eschatology," classical dispensationalism has continued to offer believers what historian Timothy Weber terms an "ironic comfort." Proponents are able to find a place within the divine plan for the bewildering world events of our day. He concludes, "As long as the world remains a terrifying place, seemingly bent on its own destruction, the premillennialist [that is, classical dispensationalist] world view will have the ring of truth for many."[127] Yet the assurance that provides the system's appeal is also a source of temptation. End-times forecasters often give the appearance of overconfidence concerning their ability to know the future. Weber chides this eschatology for being "inherently guilty of historical and theological 'overassurance.' "[128] Not only do its adherents know where history is going, they know how it will get there.

The classical dispensationalists' overconfidence concerning the end-time scenario and their pessimism concerning the effect of the church in the world coalesce in the doctrine of the pretribulation rapture, which highlights yet another grave danger. Pretribulation rapturism runs the risk of actually capitulating to the secular mindset it seeks to avoid, for its chronology of the future fits well with the spirit of the age.

The doctrine of the pretribulational rapture and the classical dispensational concept of the church are intertwined. The view that sees the purpose of the church as calling the "heavenly body" out from the world, a body that will then be raptured away from the world and its troubles, risks forgetting that the church was placed in the world for the sake of Christ's message coming to the world.[129] All too often the practical outworking of the expectation of a pretribulation rapture degenerates into a flight from the world, rather than engagement with the task of finding solutions to the deep problems that confront humankind.[130]

Equally dangerous is the promise of escape from persecution that often forms a corollary to the doctrine of the pretribulation rapture. Although dispensationalism rightly emphasizes that Christians are commanded to be diligent at all times and to expect the Lord's coming, no student of eschatology dare promise believers that they will be spared trial. Paul's words to Timothy are clear: "All who live godly lives will be persecuted" (2 Tim 3:12). The teaching that Christians will be spared the tribulation by means of the rapture runs the risk of holding out a false hope.

Suspicion of involvement with the task of seeking solutions to the world's problems and the expectation of being caught away from the time of trial—these two attitudes so readily connected with dispensationalism—fit well with the escapist mentality of contemporary Western society. The similarity is evident in the proliferation of Hollywood superhero fantasy productions, which reveal an uncanny resemblance to the popular end-times scenario: A violent redeemer figure from the realm beyond the earth in the nick of time rescues the innocent humans from wicked, demonic adversaries.

It is interesting to note that the type of dispensationalism that divines a specific end-times scenario focusing on military confrontation in the world and escape for believers is most popular in lands such as the United States where the church faces no persecution but where social problems appear to be spinning out of control. Could it be that this eschatological system is actually a form of modernism, caught in the escapism so prevalent in contemporary thinking?

Modifications to Dispensationalism

The type of dispensationalism that continues to be widespread among evangelicals is influenced largely by the older classical variety. Emerging from dispensationalist educational institutions, however, is another approach that takes seriously scholarly discussions with critics of the system. These discussions have been enriching for all participants. One positive outcome has been a growing awareness that broad areas of agreement exist between proponents and opponents.

Already in 1963, Roy Aldrich offered four points of universal evangelical agreement.[131] All agree that God's program includes several divisions of time, of which two—the age from Moses through Christ and the church age—comprise perhaps 93 per cent of the Bible. All agree that the Bible presents only one way of salvation, justification by faith. All agree that God's moral law has application in every area. And all acknowledge that the saints of every age have much in common. Aldrich called for a greater emphasis on the points of agreement as a means of overcoming the divisions caused by differing eschatological viewpoints, a call that has been subsequently echoed by several thinkers.

As noted above, debates with its critics have led as well to dramatic developments within dispensationalism itself. Consequently, the system has changed drastically over the course of the twentieth century. Such alterations have made a coming together of evangelicals of varying eschatological viewpoints more plausible in recent years than in the earlier stages of the history of the movement.

Several changes have already occurred. An earlier, more radical variety dubbed "ultradispensationalism," which separated not only Israel and the church but also the Petrine and Pauline churches,[132] has virtually disappeared. Beginning at about mid-century, more moderate dispensationalists became sensitive to criticisms leveled against certain tenets of the system. Even the Scofield Reference Bible, the chief standard for dispensationalist teaching, has come under revision.[133] Mid-course modifications to the system moved the dispensational movement back from the brink of heresy toward which earlier, more radical proponents tended. As a result, it has been able to join the mainstream of evangelicalism and serve as a welcomed and potent force for the renewal of biblical authority in certain areas of the church.

Beginning in the 1980s "progressive dispensationalists" further blunted the rough edges of the system. Joining critics of the older view in rejecting as inadequate the strict literalist hermeneutic of earlier thinkers, they no longer adhere to the sharp distinction between Israel and the church, but place both under the one program of God for the world—the inauguration and consummation of the divine rulership. Acknowledging that the new covenant promised to Israel (Jer 31) is inaugurated in the church, progressive dispensationalists prefer to speak only of a functional or historical, rather than a metaphysical, distinction between Israel and the church. Above all, progressive dispensationalists repudiate the tendency toward end-times speculation so characteristic of adherents of the older view.

Changes such as these have allowed dispensationalists and nondispensationalists to draw closer together.[134] In fact, there is talk of a "growing rapprochement" within evangelicalism between covenant and dispensational theologians.[135]

Dispensationalism today is in a state of fluidity. No longer are the rigid distinctives of the past held to with unswerving certainty. Many progressive dispensationalists are no longer certain as to exactly what are the defining tenets of the system that commands their allegiance.

Participants in the newer discussion, however, retain—albeit in modified form—certain major emphases of the system.[136] Above all, even those theologians who have given up the older terminology of a "heavenly people" versus an "earthly people" and who do not speak of a metaphysical distinction remain loyal to the assertion of some type of distinction between Israel and the church. Ethnic Israel, they argue, continues to have a special place both in the present but especially in the future aspects of the New Testament teaching concerning God's program in history.[137] On this basis, these thinkers continue to expect some type of future for Israel in fulfillment of Old Testament prophecy, apparently apart from the inclusion of believing Jews in the church. Old Testament promises concerning the land of Palestine, they add, suggest that this future focuses on a Jewish millennium.[138]

These viewpoints, even in their less radical expressions, run the risk of a crucial theological danger, namely, the reduction of the centrality of the church. Although important distinctions do exist between Israel and the church, the New Testament clearly teaches that the church is neither a secondary nor a preliminary program, but the crowning product of all God's activity in history. Older dispensationalists such as Charles Ryrie indicate that the goal of history is not the church, but the millennium. During that era God will fulfill the divine promises to national Israel.[139] Ryrie's view begs critics to ask how the church fits into the anticipated Jewish millennium.[140] To the extent that dispensationalism in any form subordinates the church to Israel (albeit perhaps not overtly or consciously) it risks becoming a Judaizing tendency in the church.[141]

With the moderating of its position dispensationalism came to lose its best apologetic. Critics accused the older proponents of teaching that each dispensation contained a unique way of salvation. The former view set forth a genuine soteriological difference between Israel and the church. Israel—both past and future—could be saved through the sacrificial system, whereas the church was united to Christ.

During the twentieth century most dispensationalists came to reject that view, acknowledging that in every era salvation comes only by faith in Christ's work (Gal 3:8).[142] But this acknowledgment, although correct, introduces problems of internal consistency.[143] More important, it raises the question of the theological importance of any separation within the one people of God. If the means of salvation are the same in every age—faith in God's salvific work—then in what sense can we speak of any ultimate theological significance for Israel in distinction from the church?

Progressive dispensational theologians have attempted to come to grips with the theological significance of Israel apart from the older indication of the nation comprising a soteriologically distinct people. Robert Saucy, for example, asserts that Israel plays an ongoing role as a channel of divine revelation and as a participant in the completion of the salvation of the world.[144] Saucy focuses on Israel's role as an object lesson of God's dealing with all humankind and as a model of societal salvation. Others, building from Romans 11:11-14, locate Israel's importance within the context of the role of the eschatologically reingrafted nation in the midst of the gentile nations. Peter Beyerhaus reflects this approach when he concludes, "Israel forms the decisive eschatological linkage between world-evangelism and the establishment of the messianic Kingdom."[145]

Despite attempts such as these, one wonders if in the end the newer suggestions can avoid the problems of the older dispensationalist dichotomy between Israel and the church. It simply may not be possible to construct a separate theological understanding for Israel that does not detract from the primacy of the church in the program of God for the salvation of the world.[146] Does not the suggestion that Israel has yet a role to play in that program apart from the inclusion of the Jews within the worldwide fellowship of people who acknowledge Jesus as Savior, Messiah and Lord necessarily encroach on the finality of what Christ accomplished in the establishment of his church as the one people of God in which all racial barriers have been eradicated? And how can Israel serve both as a type of the kingdom inaugurated at Christ's first advent but consummated only at his second and as a distinct ethnic group possessing theological importance alongside of the spiritual kingdom of Christ—the church?[147]

Opponents of dispensationalism rightly assert that the crisis of theological significance for Israel apart from the church follows naturally from the viewpoint of the New Testament itself, which emphasizes the one body of the faithful of all ages. The book of Hebrews, for example, presents the Old Testament saints not as belonging to national Israel but rather as a cloud of witnesses, an unbroken chain of faithful people who provide New

Testament believers with a legacy of faith (chap. 11). This theme is present even in the Old Testament. Already for the prophets it is the remnant of God, the faithful Israel, who are important as the heirs of God's promises. In the New Testament, this remnant becomes associated with Jesus as those who acknowledge his messiahship. Therefore, rather than a distinction between Israel and the church, the Bible places the crucial division within Israel itself—a division between the remnant, who are the faithful of God, and the apostate, who according to Jesus are the children of Satan (Jn 8:44).

Consequently, nondispensationalists conclude that the future of national Israel can lie only with spiritual Israel,[148] that is, with those physical descendants of the patriarchs who respond in faith to the one gospel of the saving action of God in Jesus the Messiah. This fact does not change, even though there may be a great future day in which the world will witness a mass turning of Jews to their Messiah.

Issues such as these remain a source of disagreement between, and consequently an ongoing agenda for, contemporary dispensational theologians and their nondispensational discussion partners. As progressive dispensationalists continue to grapple with the central problem of the relationship of Israel to the church, they constitute perhaps the most significant development in the larger dispensationalist movement. This more scholarly dispensationalism presents an eschatological orientation far different from that produced for popular consumption by less creative minds. Fortunately, with this more cautious dispensationalism lies the future of the movement and its ongoing contribution to evangelical theology.

5
MILLENNIAL BLESSINGS FOR THE CHURCH

Historic Premillennialism

Although dispensationalism has remained the dominant eschatological viewpoint among the movement as a whole, its unchallenged monopoly on the allegiance of evangelicalism began to wane during the second half of the twentieth century. This development was especially evident within evangelical academic circles. Beginning in the 1950s several influential scholars came to reject the central tenets of the reigning eschatology, claiming they were contrary to sound biblical teaching and out of step with the historic position of the church.[1] But offering an alternative outlook proved more difficult than criticizing dispensationalism.

Many of the evangelical thinkers who rejected classical dispensationalism remained staunchly premillennial. Consequently, for guidance in the constructive theological task they took another look at the history of doctrine. To their delight, they discovered that a tradition of nondispensational premillennialism had been present in the church since at least the patristic era. The efforts of nondispensationalists to set forth an alternative system to replace the one they rejected coalesced in the articulation of an eschatology now commonly known as "historic premillennialism." The term is intended to convey the idea that the position of its proponents forms the contemporary continuation of the premillennialism that characterized Christian thinkers throughout church history.

The Main Features of Historic Premillennialism

Historic premillennialism embodies the same basic outlook and follows the basic chronology that typifies all current expressions of premillennialism. The present age will climax with a period of tribulation and the return of Jesus Christ. The Second Coming will mark the judgment on the antichrist and the resurrection of the righteous. At the parousia Satan will be bound, and the era of peace and righteousness will commence on the earth. After the millennium, Satan will be loosed to lead a brief rebellion. This will be followed by the general resurrection, the judgment and the eternal state.

The teaching essential to all varieties of premillennialism, therefore, is that the Second Coming is, as the name itself indicates, premillennial; it occurs prior to the thousand-year golden age. At his return the Lord will establish his reign, which contemporary premillennialists anticipate will be earthly and during which Christ will be physically present.[2] Rather than come as the result of a gradual process of progressive growth, the millennium will be inaugurated cataclysmically, dramatically and visibly. It will not come as an extension of positive processes already present within history, but in the context of, and as a contradiction to, the deterioration of earthly conditions that will precede Christ's return.

As Millard Erickson correctly notes, the linchpin of premillennialism is the doctrine of two bodily resurrections.[3] The first will occur at the Lord's return. The righteous of all ages will rise in order to share in the millennial reign of Christ. Only after the golden age will the rest of the dead come forth from their graves, an event that, however, will place the wicked in the presence of the judge who will consign them to their eternal destiny.

All premillennialists share certain expectations concerning the thousand years.[4] During the golden age, Christ will exercise political authority and righteous rulership over the entire world.[5] As a result, for the first time in human history, universal peace will encircle the globe. The harmony within the human family will spill over to all of creation, for the effects of the Fall experienced by nature will be lifted. This age will be characterized by the cessation of hostilities among the animals and between humans and animals (Is 11:8-9; 65:25).

Despite such similarities, the two major contemporary varieties—dispensationalism and historic premillennialism—give evidence to important differences. In the eyes of most evangelicals, the distinctive feature of historic premillennialism is its doctrine of the posttribulational rapture, as opposed to the pretribulational rapture taught by most dispensationalists. The church will be present in the tribulation period, the duration of which may or may not be seven years. We should not minimize this difference in the anticipated eschatological chronology, and in a sense the point has formed the focus of discussion between exponents of the two varieties of the one system. Nevertheless, it would be an oversimplification to suggest that the rapture is the main point of contention between these two premillennial viewpoints.

Because many adherents moved to this position from the classical dispensationalism of the 1950s, the emerging historic premillennialists were quick to mark off the distinctions that separated their view from its next of kin. In 1960, Clarence Bass offered a summary of the tenets central to his adopted eschatology. Historical premillennialism, he states, holds

> that the church is indeed the spiritual Israel; that the covenantal relations of God to Israel have indeed passed over to the church; that the promises to Abraham may be fulfilled in some measure in the church; that the kingdom offered by Christ was a spiritual kingdom which was instituted in the hearts of those who believe; that the church is neither

a parenthesis nor an intercalation, but the culminative display of God's total redemptive plan; that the millennium is to be a personal reign of Christ over a spiritually oriented kingdom rather than a theocratic, Jewish oriented one; that the blessed hope is the return of Christ, rather than the rapture of the church, and that the grace of God is indeed the principle by which *all* men of *all* periods are brought to God.[6] As Bass's summary indicates, at the genesis of the movement during the middle decades of the twentieth century historic premillennialists rejected the two central tenets of dispensationalism as formulated at that time, as well as the literalist hermeneutic on which they were based. These thinkers denied that the Scriptures teach a radical dichotomy between Israel and the church. Instead, in keeping with what they saw as the historic position of the Christian tradition, they viewed the church as the fulfillment of God's work in the Old Testament.

Since the work of Bass and other historic premillennialists, progressive dispensationalist scholars have also come to reject the older dispensationalist hallmark of a radical dichotomy between Israel and the church. The newer dispensationalism, however, continues to insist on a future work of God with ethnic Israel, a work that fulfills God's distinctive covenantal commitment to the nation. The future fulfillment of God's promises to Israel remains, therefore, at the foundation of the ongoing differences between historic premillennialism and contemporary dispensationalism.

Historic premillennialists continue likewise to reject the dispensationalist understanding of the tribulation and the millennium, which views them in terms of God's program for his Old Testament people. These eras do not belong to some purported Israel phase of salvation history, historic premillennialists argue. Rather, both—but especially the millennium—must be understood in terms of the broader purposes of the divine program for history, purposes that focus ultimately on the church.

Historic premillennialists view the thousand-year reign in terms of its function as a further stage in God's redemptive purpose in Jesus.[7] Specifically, it is a higher outworking of Christ's prerogatives as Lord of history, which began at the ascension when Jesus was enthroned at the right hand of the Father. His triumph over his foes, however, is not yet complete (1 Cor 15:25), and in this age his reign is not apparent to all, being visible only to the eyes of faith. At the parousia, however, Christ's lordship will become public, complete and universal; then everyone will pay homage to the name of Jesus (Phil 2:10-11).

In historic premillennial thought, the nature and purpose of the thousand years are linked as well to the doctrine of creation. As the era of perfection occurring within history, the millennium is God's opportunity to demonstrate his faithfulness to his creative purposes by completing his plan of salvation. For a thousand years all creation will enjoy the idyllic, peaceful conditions God intended at the completion of the six days of Genesis 1.

But most important, historic premillennialists argue that the millennium is the time in which the church reigns with Christ. During the golden age, the Lord exercises his rightful rulership over the earth. But there is more to the thousand years than his own political sovereignty. Beginning with Irenaeus in the second century, premillennialists have argued that it is only proper that those who have been faithful to Christ should participate in his rule.[8] Consequently, the millennium offers the opportunity for their Lord to reward believers for their steadfast service.

The Biblical Basis of Historic Premillennialism

Historic premillennialists have generally argued that the church will be present in the eschatological tribulation period, although this is not the distinctive feature of their eschatological system. This position is based on what they perceive to be the general sweep of the biblical teaching concerning tribulation, their understanding of the New Testament presentation of the return of Christ and their exegesis of certain specific texts.

The posttribulation rapture position arises out of the biblical expectation—found in both Old and New Testaments—that the typical experience of the saints of God will be tribulation (see, for example, Jn 16:33; Acts 14:22; Rom 5:3; 1 Thess 3:3; 1 Jn 2:18, 22; 4:3; Rev. 1:9).[9] The trials believers undergo, however, must be differentiated from the experience of God's

wrath, from which the faithful are spared.[10] The trials endured by the
people of God reach their climax in the eschatological tribulation, which,
posttribulationists argue, the Bible presents as a period of great persecution of the saints on the earth and a time of God's wrathful judgment on
the unbelieving world.[11] But in the midst of the trial, believers are shielded
by the guarding hand of God (Rev 3:10; 7:14).[12]

The belief that the rapture will come after the tribulation arises likewise
out of the New Testament descriptions of the return of Christ. Posttribulationists note that several Greek terms are employed to describe that
event. Of these, one word—*parousia*—is especially vivid. It is best translated "presence," referring to the final coming of Christ to be present with
his people. They note as well that this event, which is the object of the
believer's hope and expectation (1 Thess 2:19; 3:13; Jas 5:7-8; 1 Jn 2:28),
is consistently presented in the New Testament as occurring after the
tribulation (for example, Mt 24:3, 27, 37, 39; 2 Thess 2:8).[13] Posttribulation
apologist Douglas Moo concludes,

> a study of the vocabulary employed in describing the return of Christ
> paints a uniform picture: believers are exhorted to look for and to live
> in the light of this glorious event. And, while some texts obviously place
> this coming *after* the Tribulation, there are *none* which equally obvious-
> ly place it before the Tribulation.[14]

Because of the context in which it will occur, the rapture anticipated by
posttribulationists differs from that awaited by pretribulationists. The latter teach that Christ will meet his saints in the air and then whisk them
off to heaven for the marriage supper of the Lamb that occurs simultaneously with the tribulation period on the earth. Posttribulationists, in contrast, view the rapture in terms of the imagery of the subjects of a king
going out to meet their sovereign as he returns to his domain. Believers
form, as it were, a great welcoming party for the returning Lord.[15]

The chief argument for the correctness of this imagery is linguistic. It
lies in the use in two other places of the term *apantēsis,* which Paul uses
in the central rapture text, 1 Thessalonians 4:17, to refer to the believers
meeting their Lord in the air. One of these texts (Mt 25:6) is likewise

eschatological, and it employs an image borrowed from oriental wedding practices. At the announcement that the bridegroom is coming, the wise virgins comprise part of the welcoming party that goes out to meet him and then accompanies him to the wedding feast. The other text uses this term to designate the action of the believers in Rome who went out to the town of Three Taverns to meet Paul and accompany him into their city (Acts 28:15-16).

The posttribulationist appeal to specific texts as teaching their view moves in two directions. On the one hand, they claim that the three principal passages that describe the rapture—John 14:3; 1 Corinthians 15:51-52; 1 Thessalonians 4:13-18—give no indication that this event can be separated from the final manifestation of Christ. Rather, these texts favor locating the rapture after the tribulation and at the same time as the Second Coming.[16] On the other hand, they assert that certain other texts, including 1 Thessalonians 5:1-11; 2 Thessalonians 1—2; the Mount Olivet Discourse and the book of Revelation positively teach the posttribulational position.[17]

More important than the specific question of the place of the rapture in relation to the tribulation for the dialog among proponents of the major eschatological viewpoints is the question of the basic premillennial chronology. Contemporary voices who adhere to the "historic premillennial" view have been untiring apologists for the general premillennial chronology. Their case is built on both a biblical and a theological foundation.

The biblical support for the doctrine of a thousand-year reign of Christ following his Second Coming arises from the combination of the many prophecies of a future era of peace and righteousness with the one text in which a thousand-year reign is explicitly mentioned. This text, Revelation 20:1-10, provides the chronological structure for the doctrine of the millennium. The prophecies add the content.

Revelation 19—22 forms the explicit biblical foundation for the position articulated by contemporary premillennialists.[18] These scholars see in the closing chapters of the Apocalypse a vision of the events of the eschaton arranged in chronological order. Revelation 19:11-16 pictures the return of

Christ as the conqueror coming to destroy his enemies. After dealing first with his human political opponent, the triumphant Lord turns his attention to the evil power that lay behind this wicked leader. According to what George Eldon Ladd calls "the most natural reading" of Revelation 20:1-10, the destruction of Satan occurs in two stages separated by the millennial era. Christ's cosmic opponent is incarcerated for a thousand years, and then following the final eschatological battle that this archenemy inspires, Satan is banished to the lake of fire.

Central to the premillennial position is the interpretation of the two resurrections noted in Revelation 20, which sees both as physical, bodily events. All premillennialists are in agreement that a literalist hermeneutic must be employed in this case, and its use leads to a premillennial eschatology. Ladd offers a concise statement of the underlying principle: "Unless there is some reason intrinsic within the text itself which requires a symbolical interpretation, or unless there are other Scriptures which interpret a parallel prophecy in a symbolic sense, we are required to employ a natural, literal interpretation."[19]

On the basis of this principle, premillennial exegetes conclude that the author of Revelation 20 had two bodily resurrections in view. The linchpin of the argument rests on the use of the same Greek word, *ezēsan* ("they came to life"), to refer to both resurrections. Does the "living" of the righteous souls mentioned in verse 4 refer to a physical resurrection, as is the case with the "living" of the "rest of the dead" mentioned in verse 5?

In contrast to other New Testament texts (such as Jn 5:25-29; 11:25-26; Lk 9:60), which contain such internal indications, premillennialists find in Revelation 20:4-6 no contextual clue that requires the literal interpretation for the second reference but a spiritual understanding of the first. The passage describes both the first and second resurrections in identical terminology, and no other features of the text indicate that the two events are different in kind.[20]

Consequently, the point of the text is simple. In the words of Ladd, "At the beginning of the millennial period, part of the dead come to life; at its conclusion, the rest of the dead come to life."[21] Any other interpretation, adherents of this view claim, is an arbitrary, theologically motivated, biased[22] violation of hermeneutical principles, one that only attributes chaotic thinking into the mind of the biblical author.[23] Apologists often refer to Henry Alford's strong rejection of other options voiced in the middle of the nineteenth century:

> If, in a passage where *two resurrections* are mentioned, where certain *souls lived* at the first, and the rest of the *dead lived* only at the end of a specified period after that first,—if in such a passage the first resurrection may be understood to mean *spiritual* rising with Christ, while the second means *literal* rising from the grave,—then there is an end of all significance in language, and Scripture is wiped out as a definite testimony to anything.[24]

Premillennialists find support for their exegesis of Revelation 20 in several New Testament texts, which although they do not explicitly teach the doctrine nevertheless implicitly suggest two resurrections.[25] For example, literally translated, Philippians 3:11 speaks of an "out-resurrection out from among dead ones," an indication that Paul anticipated he would participate in a resurrection that would separate him from other dead persons (see also Lk 20:35). Several passages imply either a partial resurrection (1 Thess 4:16), a distinction between a resurrection of the righteous and a resurrection of the wicked (Lk 14:14) or a two-stage resurrection (Dan 12:2; Jn 5:29).

But the most significant confirmatory text is 1 Corinthians 15:23-26. Premillennialists see in Paul's words an indication that Christ's triumph over death comes in three stages. The first, Jesus' own resurrection as "the firstfruits," has already occurred (v. 23); two remain future. The resurrection of "those who belong to him" occurs "when he comes" (v. 23). A millennium later occurs the grand event of the end, "when he hands over the kingdom to God the Father" (v. 24). Premillennial apologists claim that the interjection of "then" between verses 23 and 24, which separates the apostle's reference to the resurrection of the righteous from his mention of "the end," indicates that Paul anticipated an interregnum of undefined duration between the parousia and the final consummation of history.[26]

Some premillennialists argue that such an interval between the resurrection of the righteous and the resurrection of the unjust is necessitated by the biblical doctrine of judgment.[27] The Scriptures indicate that believers are involved in the eschatological judgment in a double capacity; they will be judged and will act as judges. But this double role demands that their status be determined before they engage in the judging function. For this to occur, the judgment must come in two stages—a judgment of the righteous, followed sometime later by that of the wicked. The millennium constitutes the era that separates the two stages of the eschatological judgment.

Into the framework of the premillennial scenario deduced from Revelation 20:1-10 and confirmed by other biblical texts, adherents pour the various Old Testament prophecies of a future golden age. However, as noted earlier, the content of the millennial reign that contemporary historic premillennialists find in such promises leads to a parting of ways with their dispensationalist cousins. While they agree concerning the fact of a future millennium, the two varieties of premillennialism disagree concerning its exact nature.

According to historic premillennialists the object of the prophesies of a golden age is not a future regathered nation of Israel, as in dispensational thought, but "spiritual Israel"—the church. The group that will enjoy the millennial blessings, therefore, is not composed of an end-times restored nation of Israel, the natural offspring of Abraham, but the true Israel of God composed of Abraham's spiritual children in all generations. The difference concerning the identity of the group that will be prominent in the reign of Christ arises as a result of the hermeneutic offered by historic premillennialists. While arguing for a strict literal exegesis of Revelation 20:4-5, they conclude that other considerations demand a less than literal approach to Old Testament prophecy.

The overriding considerations that move historic premillennialists away from prophetic literalism are largely connected to the New Testament interpretation of the Old. Rather than echo the claim of classical dispensationalists that the prophecies about the first coming of Christ were literally fulfilled, historic premillennialists find that the New Testament reinterprets the Old in the light of the Christ event.[28] This is evident, for example, when the Evangelists apply to Jesus' life and ministry Old Testament texts such as Hosea 11:1 and Isaiah 53:5-6, which in their contexts are not prophecies of the coming of the Messiah.

Even more significant, however, the New Testament applies Old Testament prophecies concerning the future of Israel to the church and thereby identifies the church as "spiritual Israel" (such as Paul's use of Hosea in Rom 9:24-26). Historic premillennialists adamantly assert that the New Testament knows but one undivided people of God—not two, as in classical dispensationalist teaching,[29] not even one people internally divided, as in progressive dispensationalism. They readily admit, of course, that the New Testament church as a distinct social organization began at Pentecost. Nevertheless, they do not find that this precludes the biblical teaching that there is but one "church of the firstborn" (compare Heb 12:23) that unites without separation Old Testament saints and New Testament believers (Heb 11:40). The "bride" of Christ embraces the entire company of the redeemed—both Israel and the church.[30] This company, therefore, and not national Israel, will participate in the rule of the bridegroom during the thousand years.

We ought not to minimize the importance of this hermeneutical issue. Historic premillennialists perceive that the crucial difference between their view and that of dispensationalism, at least in its classical expression, hinges exactly on the question as to which testament is to have hermeneutical priority. Ladd, in fact, sets this forth as "the basic watershed" between the two. "Dispensationalism," he writes, "forms its eschatology by a literal interpretation of the Old Testament and then fits the New Testament into it. A nondispensational eschatology forms its theology from the explicit teaching of the New Testament."[31]

In addition to the priority of the New Testament in interpreting prophecies delivered in the Old, the case for historic premillennialism over against the classical dispensationalist variant arises from the Christology of the foundational documents of the church concerning the present reality of the kingdom.[32] Beginning with his ascension, Christ assumed an exalted position in heaven (Heb 1:3; 2:7-8; 10:12-13), historic premillennialists assert. Therefore, he now reigns as the vice regent of God with the goal of subjecting every hostile power (1 Cor 15:24-26) so that his lordship may be universally confessed (Phil 2:9-10).

The ascension Christology historic premillennialists find in the New Testament means that the kingdom proclaimed by Jesus, although future, is also a present, albeit a largely invisible, reality. Ladd has eloquently argued this thesis, declaring

> that the Kingdom of God is the redemptive reign of God dynamically active to establish his rule among men, and that this Kingdom, which will appear as an apocalyptic act at the end of the age, has already come into human history in the person and mission of Jesus to overcome evil, to deliver men from its power, and to bring them into the blessings of God's reign.[33]

Quite obviously, premillennialists who have such a pronounced conception of the present reality of the kingdom find little place for the total relegation of the kingdom to a future dispensation that they perceive among some of their eschatological cousins. However, refinements to the classical dispensationalist outlook by contemporary progressive proponents, who agree with historic premillennialists on this point, have served to close the gap between the two positions.

Given their conception of the one people of God, their application of Old Testament prophecies to the church and their concept of the present nature of the kingdom of God, what, apart from the literal exegesis of Revelation 20:1-10, keeps historic premillennialists premillennial? What prohibits them from moving all the way to amillennialism, with its rejection of the anticipation of a distinctive golden age within history?

In the final analysis, their bulwark against amillennialism is based on two considerations. First, historic premillennialists do not completely merge Israel and the church. In contrast to the tendency among classic amillennialists to discount any future role for the nation in God's program, they note that Paul clearly expected a future for racial Israel (Rom 9—11).

The exegete must, in the words of Douglas J. Moo, "distinguish carefully between prophecies directed to Israel *as a nation* (and which must be fulfilled in a national Israel) and prophecies directed to Israel as *the people of God* (which can be fulfilled in the people of God—*a people that includes the church!*)."[34]

In addition to their greater openness to a future for Israel within God's purposes, historic premillennialists are prevented from moving to amillennialism by the radical difference they find between the present order and the eternal state. The difference is so great, premillennialists argue, that we can speak of the age to come only as lying *beyond history,* rather than either within or as a continuation of the historical process. But the demonstration of Christ's glory, they add, cannot be relegated to the new heaven and the new earth beyond history. Rather, Christ's lordship must be demonstrated to *this* world, if Christ is indeed ruler of history.[35] In this way, then, historic premillennialists conclude that a messianic reign within human history is necessitated by New Testament Christology. And this messianic reign will occur during the thousand years.

The Critique of Historic Premillennialism

Historic premillennialists have attempted to carve out a distinctive position between dispensationalism on the one side, and amillennialism on the other. Over against the distinction between Israel and the church posited by the dispensationalism from which many of them came, these thinkers agree with the amillennial emphasis on the church as the spiritual Israel. They employ a "spiritualizing" hermeneutic that transfers to the experience of the church the prophetic expectations of a future glorious age for Israel.

At the same time, historic premillennialists are unwilling to employ universally the spiritualizing hermeneutic. They do not resign Israel to oblivion, but agree with their dispensationalist cousins that there remains yet some future role for Israel in the divine economy, albeit only as the nation turns to Christ and thereby becomes a vehicle of blessing to the world.[36] And they stubbornly cling to the literalist hermeneutic when the meaning of the thousand years of Revelation 20 is in question. Not all prophecy can be spiritualized, they argue, and not every dimension of the future hope for the people of God may be relegated to the eternal state beyond the culmination of history.

Because they are caught in the middle, as it were, contemporary adherents of historic premillennialism find themselves fighting on two fronts. When engaging in discussions with dispensationalists, especially adherents of its classical expression, they direct their polemic against the literalist hermeneutic and the emphasis on Israel that arises out of it.[37] But they defend a literal approach to the Bible and the physical, earthly dimensions of God's future purposes when confronting amillennialists.[38]

As a result of the double direction characteristic of their apologetic, critics from both the dispensationalist and the amillennialist persuasions charge historical premillennialists with inconsistency. Both assert, for example, that the historic premillennialist hermeneutic is inconsistent. Dispensationalists complain that they are not consistently literal in approaching Scripture. Amillennialists, in contrast, see them as too literalistic. They wonder why historic premillennialists demand a fulfillment within history of the glorious blessings promised to God's people.

Critics from both persuasions claim that historic premillennialists are likewise inconsistent in their understanding of Israel. Many amillennialists challenge them to consistency in seeing the church as the spiritual Israel. Historic premillennialists readily apply to the church various Old Testament promises originally given to Israel. Such promises find their fulfillment in the blessings the church will enjoy in the millennial era. But amillennialist critics wonder why these "spiritualized" promises require a future age for their "literal" fulfillment. Dispensationalists, in contrast, wonder why historic premillennialists cannot see that their acknowledgment of some distinction between Israel and the church naturally leads to a greater emphasis on the future fulfillment of God's promises to the nation.

In short, dispensationalists complain that historic premillennialists have set out on the road to amillennialism. Amillennialists, in turn, encourage them to make the complete break with premillennialism demanded by their rejection of dispensationalism.

Apart from the purported inconsistency of the historic premillennial position, amillennialists voice two additional reservations concerning historic premillennialism—the question of harmonization and the validity of their claim to continuity of tradition.

Amillennialists assert that no variety of premillennialism can be harmonized successfully with biblical teaching. Certain features of the standard premillennial chronology simply do not square with other biblical texts and emphases.

For example, critics are not convinced that the premillennial conception of the kingdom fully reflects the teachings of the New Testament. This is evident in its understanding of the time of the kingdom. By its very nature, premillennialism is oriented toward emphasizing that aspect of the kingdom that views it as a future, physical domain. In the end it is the earthly rule of Christ during the millennium. But the New Testament gives great emphasis to the kingdom as a present, spiritual rulership (see Lk 12:27; 22:29; 17:20-21; Jn 18:36). The mediatory rule of Christ is now, critics argue.[39]

Historic premillennialists, notably George Eldon Ladd, and more recently progressive dispensationalists have sought to develop a comprehensive understanding of the concept of the kingdom that encompasses both its present and future dimensions. Yet because of the emphasis they must place on a literal thousand-year reign, premillennial proposals, however comprehensive, cannot avoid giving prominence to the future, physical dimension of the kingdom. Even Ladd, despite his strong acknowledgment of the present reality of the kingdom, in the end concludes that "the kingdom is ultimately future."[40]

The discrepancy critics find between the premillennial understanding of the kingdom and that of the New Testament extends to the length of the kingdom age as well. Premillennialists view the future kingdom as a temporal reign. It will last only a given length of time (whether one thousand years or an indefinite length of time),[41] after which it is replaced by eternity. But the Bible declares that the kingdom is eternal.[42] The angel promised Mary at the annunciation that the reign of the Messiah would be unending: "The Lord God will give him the throne of his father David, and he will reign over the house of Jacob forever; his kingdom will never end" (Lk 1:32-33).

Critics also find that the millennium anticipated by premillennialists contradicts the teaching of the New Testament concerning the future era. According to the premillennial vision, this era will include the ongoing propagation of the species, and it will close with a Satanic-inspired insurrection of unbelievers. At the same time, premillennialists declare that the golden age will occur after the resurrection of the righteous, indicating thereby that this era is "the age of the resurrection" predicted by the Bible. Amillennialists question these two assertions. Because physical marital relations are no longer present in the resurrection (Mt 22:30), how can propagation of the species occur in that age, as premillennialists anticipate?[43] And if the resurrected righteous do not have children, how does a group of rebellious unregenerate persons arise at the end of that age?

One solution presupposes the presence in the millennium of unresurrected unbelievers, who then marry and produce offspring. But the assertion that such persons will populate the millennium is problematic in light of New Testament teaching. Paul declares that the kingdom era is only attained by means of the resurrection (1 Cor 15:50). And Jesus' parables of the kingdom plainly state that at the close of the present age all evil persons will be gathered out of the kingdom (Mt 13:41-43; see also Mt 25:31-46).[44] Consequently, the New Testament appears to leave no room for the presence of evil persons within the kingdom in the era beyond the return of Christ.

R. Fowler White notices a related problem surrounding the premillennial understanding of who attains to the millennial era. Premillennialists assert that the nations protected from Satan's deception (Rev 20:1-3) are the survivors of the battle depicted in Revelation 19:19-21. But this is precluded by the context: In 19:18-21, John's narration emphasizes the completeness and finality of Christ's victory by describing his enemies in all-inclusive terms: *all* the nations will have taken up arms against the Divine Warrior and *all* will fall by his sword in the final confrontation (N.B. 19:18, 21; cf. 12:5; 19:15). If any survive the day of Christ's coming (cf. 6:17), they will be able to do so precisely and only because they have been redeemed from among the nations and placed within the Divine Warrior's kingdom-protectorate (5:9-10; cf. 3:10; 20:9).[45]

In addition to problems they note concerning the premillennial understanding of the kingdom and the millennium, critics declare that the complex premillennial chronology does not reflect the simpler expectations for the future presented throughout the New Testament. Nor are the attempts by premillennial apologists to find indications of an interregnum after Christ's return convincing.[46] His comparison of the sequence of events that will climax the church age with that anticipated by premillennialists following the thousand years leads Jay E. Adams to accuse them of "diplopia," or double vision.[47]

For example, premillennialism teaches that there will be at least two resurrections and two judgments. The righteous rise prior to the millennium, but "the rest of the dead" must wait for the end of this era, at which time they face the great white throne judgment. The general conception set forth in the New Testament, however, entails only one resurrection, the general rising of all humankind, critics claim. At the return of Christ, all humans will be resurrected together (Jn 5:28-29), face the one judgment (Mt 13:41-43; 16:27; 25:31-34; 2 Thess 1:9-10) and enter into eternal reward or punishment (Mt 25:31-46).

Another difficult dimension of the premillennial chronology is its conception of the ultimate victory of Christ. According to Paul, the final enemy of Christ is death, and the Lord destroys this last foe at the resurrection of the believers (1 Cor 15:25-26, 50-55). For the ultimate characterization of the cosmic drama, some premillennialists look to the struggle of Christ against Satan—in which the millennium plays a crucial role—rather than his struggle against death. Others agree that death is Christ's final enemy. But because of their loyalty to the premillennial doctrine, they teach that death is not destroyed until the end of the millennial reign.[48] The premillennial chronology, therefore, places the final victory of Christ a full thousand years after the resurrection and thus a thousand years after the event that Paul declares marks the triumph of the Lord.[49]

In the end, amillennialists can find no basis in the eschatology of the New Testament to fit the premillennial golden age between the present era and the age to come.[50] The "third age" that the millennium supposedly comprises is never mentioned in the Gospels, the book of Acts and the Epistles, they argue.[51] But not only is it not explicitly taught, the millennium actually contradicts the theology of these sections of the New Testament.

Because it falls short of the final state of perfection, the thousand years anticipated by premillennialism is, in the words of Anthony Hoekema, "a theological anomaly."[52] He capsulizes the amillennial critique by raising the theological question concerning the necessity of the future millennial, visible expression of Christ's rule:

> Why, for example, should believers be raised from the dead to live on an earth which is not yet glorified and which is still groaning because of the presence of sin, rebellion and death (see Rom. 8:19-22)? Why should the glorified Christ have to come back to earth to rule over his enemies with a rod of iron and thus still have to endure opposition to his sovereignty? Was not this phase of his work completed during his state of humiliation? Is Christ not coming back in the fulness of glory to usher in, not an interim period of qualified peace and blessing, but the final state of unqualified perfection?[53]

In addition to the problem of harmonization, critics of historic premillennialism raise a question concerning the continuity of tradition that premillennialists claim for their position. Apologists declare that they constitute the contemporary expression of the premillennial heritage that dates at least to the second century. A comparison of the view espoused today with that of Irenaeus and Justin, however, indicates that contemporary premillennialism is quite different from the ancient variety. In fact, as sympathetic a historian as D. H. Kromminga concludes that they constitute two distinct views of the end of the age.[54]

The difference between the two viewpoints lies in their respective interpretations of the book of Revelation. Justin and Irenaeus "saw the antichristian power already manifest and at work in persecuting the Christians; to them it was the pagan Roman imperial rule."[55] Hence, when viewed from our perspective patristic premillennialism interpreted the Apocalypse in a preterist fashion, that is, as primarily referring to events transpiring in the first centuries of the church. (Actually, they perhaps exegeted the book in accordance with the continuous-historical view[56]— seeing the Apocalypse as covering the period from the first century to what for them was the present).

In contrast to the patristic understanding of the figures in the book of Revelation, however, modern premillennialism is by necessity futuristic; it places the events of the book in the distant, eschatological future, when viewed from the perspective of the original author. Ancient premillennialists believed that they were living in the time of the end and therefore saw the book of Revelation as referring to events of the first centuries. But today's premillennialists place at least the greater part of the book of Revelation in some yet future period, far removed from its original audience. As Kromminga declares, "this difference makes modern Premillennialism, also that of the moderate type, futuristic in a sense in which ancient Premillennialism can not be called futuristic."[57]

Lying historically between the apparent preterism of the second-century fathers and the futurism of contemporary advocates is a third alternative—the historicist approach—that predominated after the Reformation. In keeping with the Protestant conviction that the pope was the antichrist mentioned in the Bible, Reformation premillennialists interpreted the Apocalypse as a prophecy of the central events of church history. Historicists also viewed the 1,260 days referred to in Daniel as years of church history. In the late nineteenth century, however, a broad shift materialized among premillennialists away from the historicist and toward the futurist position.[58]

Contemporary premillennialism, therefore, lies this side of the transition from preterist to historicist to futurist interpretations of biblical prophecy. Consequently, its claim to the heritage and tradition of the early fathers is not so obvious. Apologists must account for the historical break in the prophetic timeline between the first century and the present, a problem that patristic premillennialists did not need to face. Further, if the events of the Apocalypse were not fulfilled in the events of the early centuries, as patristic premillennialists believed, contemporary adherents of the position of the fathers must suggest in what sense the book of Revelation was meaningful for those to whom it was originally written. These considerations lead Kromminga to conclude that "it may even legitimately be questioned, whether there is such a phenomenon as Historic Premillennialism."[59]

Conclusion

Many observers have noted that premillennialism is basically pessimistic in tone.[60] Human history, its adherents believe, is not progressing toward increasingly higher levels of development. Nor are human nature and human capabilities to be trusted. Consequently, premillennialists generally are wary of human efforts to foster change in the world; human action alone simply can never lead to ultimate success.

This general principle applies even to the role of the church in the world. Christians ought to struggle to advance the kingdom of God, of course. But in the end, despite believers' good intentions, antichrist will emerge, premillennialists declare. Ultimately, only the return of Christ will bring about the era of peace and righteousness—the golden age—on the earth.

The historical pessimism characteristic of premillennialism is readily documented. Ernest Sandeen, for example, summarizes the effects of the rise of this eschatological outlook in nineteenth-century Britain:

> Thus belief in the pre- rather than the postmillennial return of Christ involved much more than a question of the timing of the second advent. Converts to premillennialism abandoned confidence in man's ability to bring about significant and lasting social progress and in the church's ability to stem the tide of evil, convert mankind to Christianity, or even

prevent its own corruption. The premillennial return of Christ presupposed a view of the world in which judgment and demolition were the only possible response from a just God. Christ's return would mean salvation and blessedness for a few but judgment for the world. And it involved most premillennialists in a radical critique of their own churches, which often resulted in complete dissatisfaction if not schism.[61]

Despite the weaknesses its critics see in the details of the premillennial eschatology and the corresponding historical pessimism that characterizes it, this viewpoint has a crucial point to make concerning the shape of the Christian outlook toward the world. Its pessimistic caution must be heard. Premillennialism stands as an important reminder that the eschatological blessings promised by the Bible are ultimately the work of God. They are simply not achievable through human efforts alone.

This realistic reminder is needed in every activist age, lest the people of God become triumphalistic in their approach to life. Christians are to be engaged in the work of the Lord. To this end they carry the promise of the presence of Christ, as postmillennialism so aptly states. At the same time, however, Christian activism must be carried out in the context of the reminder that in the final analysis God alone will bring about the consummation of God's work in the world.

6

A GOLDEN AGE
BEYOND TIME

Amillennialism

*P*remillennialism, divided as it is into dispensational and historic varieties, remains the dominant eschatological viewpoint in evangelicalism. However, if we view the entire Christian heritage, this system must forfeit its pre-eminent ranking to yet another eschatology, amillennialism.

As Justin indicated in the second century, adherents of amillennialism coexisted with premillennialists in the early church. After Augustine, amillennialism came to predominate, so much so that it is the only eschatology that is either expressed or implied in the historic creeds of the Christian tradition.[1] The dominance of amillennialism continued into the Protestant era. The Reformers rejected the millenarian expectations of the "enthusiasts" for the "saner," safer eschatology that had dominated the church since Augustine. And classic Protestantism largely followed their lead. The legacy of the Reformation lives on today among conservatives in the historic Reformed denominations who remain primarily amillennial.[2]

In recent years, amillennialism has gained a more favorable hearing among evangelicals as well. This option has benefitted from the efforts of those who have questioned the validity of dispensationalism in a context in which postmillennialism was perceived as no longer a viable option. Amillennial apologists argue that the hermeneutical principles that lead evangelical thinkers out of dispensationalism logically terminate in this alternative. The eschatological issue within twentieth-century evangelicalism, consequently, has been simply that of—to employ the title of a book by Charles Feinberg published in 1936—"premillennialism or amillennialism?" The overwhelming majority of evangelicals have opted for either dispensational or historic premillennialism. Nevertheless, a small but growing number embrace the amillennial alternative.

The Main Features of Amillennialism

Etymologically, the name "amillennial" means anticipating "no millennium." In keeping with its name, amillennialism asserts that we not interpret the references in Revelation 20 to the thousand years as predicting a literal earthly rule of Christ interjected between the present age and the eschatological judgment, which ushers in the eternal state. Simply stated, amillennialism is an eschatological orientation that awaits no future earthly millennium.

Many amillennialists, however, are not satisfied with this description. They declare that the name is not a happy choice,[3] but a misnomer that is open to misunderstanding. "Amillennial" suggests that proponents of this view ignore Revelation 20:1-6, which indeed affirms a millennial reign. Contrary to what their critics delight to suggest, proponents do not deny the truth or validity of the thousand-year vision of the Apocalypse. What they do deny is that the seer intended this symbol to be interpreted as a literal earthly rule of Christ prior to the judgment.

Amillennialists, therefore, do not want to be labeled as those who hold to a negatively oriented eschatology. Yet in recent decades they have unfortunately tended to focus on responding to the charges leveled at their viewpoint from dispensationalists, especially the charge of infidelity to biblical authority. As a result, amillennial literature has often devoted more attention to launching a counterattack against premillennialism[4] than to setting forth in a clear and positive fashion a complete system of eschatology from the amillennial perspective.[5]

According to Louis Berkhof, amillennialism declares "that the present dispensation of the Kingdom of God will be followed *immediately* by the Kingdom of God in its consummate and eternal form."[6] Rather than an interregnum that will occur between the present age and eternity, the millennium pictured in Revelation 20 is a symbolic description of the church age. It represents the theological truths related to the present rule of Christ: Satan is in some sense already bound, and the saints are already reigning with Christ.

While agreeing that the millennium of Revelation 20 is a symbol of certain present realities rather than a prophecy of a literal future era, amillennialists do not agree among themselves concerning the exact significance of the imagery. The most widely held view interprets the thousand years as a reference to the spiritual reign and blessedness enjoyed by the saints in heaven during the intermediate state. Oswald T. Allis acknowledges that this view is amillennialism in the strictest sense of the term, for it denies that the symbol of the thousand years entails any reference to time.[7] According to Allis, however, it is a relatively recent suggestion, having been proposed by the nineteenth-century German scholar Kliefoth.

An older amillennialism understands Revelation 20 in terms of the spiritual reign of believers on the earth. It is a symbolic description of conversion and the victorious life enjoyed now by believers. This view dates at least to Augustine.

Finally, other amillennialists—notably the Dutch theologian G. C. Berkouwer—emphasize the intention of the Apocalypse to provide us not with a chronology of the end, but with "apocalyptic comfort." The symbol of the millennium, therefore, refers to one aspect of the church in the world. In the midst of tribulation, the people of God experience triumph within the time of the "not yet."[8]

Amillennialists agree that the era depicted by the symbol of the thousand years transpires during the church age, despite variations concerning its exact nature. Consequently, of the major eschatological chronologies, theirs is the simplest.[9] The time between the two advents will be characterized by a mixture of good and evil until the end. At the close of the age, this conflict will intensify as the church completes its mandate of evangelism and the forces of evil coalesce in the appearance of the antichrist. In the midst of a final, intense time of persecution of the church, Christ will appear in the fullness of his glory.

At the Lord's return a conglomeration of events will occur,[10] which complete his redemptive work.[11] These include Christ's victory over the forces of antichrist, the general resurrection, the judgment and the transformation of creation into the eternal state. For the saints of all ages resurrection will mean that they, together with believers on the earth, meet the descending Lord and enter into the eternal kingdom of the new heaven and the new earth. For the wicked, resurrection facilitates their appearance—together with the wicked on the earth—before their judge, followed by banishment into eternal condemnation.

William E. Cox's summary typifies the amillennial expectations concerning the simultaneity of the events surrounding the Lord's return:

When the trumpet sounds, things will take place simultaneously. Our Lord will begin his descent to the earth, the brightness of this event will put down Satan, and all the graves will be opened. . . . All the saints together will go out to meet the Lord and to escort him to the earth. . . . The unsaved . . . will be forced to bow the knee and acknowledge that this is of a certainty the Christ. . . . They will see the suffering Servant of the cross reigning now as Judge of the quick and the dead, and they will seek a place of hiding but will find none (Rev. 1:7).[12]

The Biblical Basis of Amillennialism

Like its rivals, amillennialism arises out of a specific understanding of correct biblical interpretation. The amillennial hermeneutic includes two chief principles: the primacy of the New Testament over the Old and the primacy of clear texts over symbolic.

The first principle of amillennial hermeneutics gives interpretive priority to the New Testament rather than to the Old. Archibald Hughes speaks for all in declaring, "the New Testament is the foremost and final authority in any enquiry, and it is also the interpreter of the Old Testament."[13] The chief implication of this principle is the "spiritualizing" of many Old Testament prophecies, for such an approach is in keeping with the New Testament usage of the Old.

Martin J. Wyngaarden prefers to call this outlook toward the Old Testament "the spiritual interpretation." In his view this exegetical method is chiefly related to the New Testament significance of the Old Testament theocratic kingdom. Consequently, he defines the proper hermeneutic as "the interpretation that the Holy Spirit gives to the various items connected with this kingdom."[14]

In taking their cue from the New Testament interpretation of the Old, amillennialists propose a somewhat complex approach to Old Testament prophecy. Floyd Hamilton's description is typical: The literal interpretation of Old Testament prophecy is to be accepted, he notes, "unless (a) the passages contain obviously figurative language, or (b) unless the New Testament gives authority for interpreting them in other than a literal sense, or (c) unless a literal interpretation would produce a contradiction with truths, principles, or factual statements contained in nonsymbolic books of the New Testament."[15] Wyngaarden offers two questions for determining that the figurative rather than the literal interpretation is to be employed: Does the Scripture itself spiritualize the prophecy? Or does the prophecy fit in organically with the future of the church?[16]

Amillennialists share with historic premillennial interpreters the emphasis on the primacy of the New Testament. Both schools of thought agree that the New reinterprets the Old, including the ancient Hebrew prophets, in terms of Christ.[17] Hence, both assert that the church is now "spiritual Israel."[18]

The amillennialist claim that the church is the new people of God, the new Israel, does not negate the fact that the literal usage of "Israel" continues in the New Testament. But adherents point out that throughout Scripture, alongside the literal there is also a figurative usage. A true Israelite, then, is not merely a physical descendant of the partiarchs, but a person who is right with God (see Gen 32:28: Ps 73:1; 125:5).[19] This figurative use comes into prominence in the New Testament. The Israel of God consists of those who have been regenerated by the Holy Spirit and are new creations in Christ, regardless of whether or not they are Jews (for example, Rom 2:28-29; 9:6-7; Gal 3:29; 6:16; Phil 3:3).

Consequently, the new people of God—the church of Christ comprised of Jew and Gentile—are heirs to the privileges and blessings the Old Testament promised to Israel. Jesus himself indicated that this would be the case (Mt 21:41, 43; 8:11-12; 22:1-14).[20] And the New Testament authors confirmed this truth (for example, Gal 3:7, 29; Rom 4:11, 14; Jas 2:5).[21]

The closing vision of the Apocalypse, in which the church, the bride of Christ, is pictured through the imagery of the new Jerusalem, depicts this same idea. On the gates of the city are written the names of the twelve tribes of Israel and on its foundation the twelve apostles (Rev 21:12, 14). As a conclusion from this observation, William Hendricksen asks the rhetorical question, "Is not this the same as saying that all these blessings are now being bestowed upon the one universal church, the church into which elect from every nation are gathered?"[22]

The New Testament offers many examples of the transference of Old Testament expectations for Israel to the church as the new people of God, amillennialists point out.[23] For example, Zion's tent is enlarged (Is 54:1-3) when the Gentiles accept Christ (Gal 4:27); those whom God termed "not my people" become "my people" (Hos 2:23) through the establishment of the church as the called from both Jew and Gentile (Rom 9:24-26); and the healing waters flow (Ezek 47; compare Is 44:3) through the outpouring of the Holy Spirit on the church (Jn 7:37-39). Hendricksen explains the principle involved in the nonliteral nature of transferences such as these: "When a prophecy is destined to be fulfilled in the new dispensation it is fulfilled according to the spirit of that new era. Hence, the Old Testament prophecies are fulfilled in the Spirit-filled church."[24]

On the basis of the hermeneutical principle of the priority of the New Testament, amillennialists conclude that promises originally given to Israel are fulfilled in the church. As a result of their attempt to apply this principle consistently, amillennialists, in contrast to premillennialists, traditionally are unsympathetic to expectations of a widespread eschatological conversion of Israel. Similarly, they are less willing to find eschatological significance to the restoration of the nation of Israel in the twentieth century. Such expectations, they argue, violate New Testament teaching by assuming that the Jews remain God's specially favored people.[25]

The discussion between amillennialists and premillennialists on the future of Israel often focuses on the Pauline anticipation for Israel as capsulized in the phrase "And so all Israel will be saved" (Rom 11:26).[26] Dispensationalists generally see in this text a reference to the eschatological restoration of the nation of Israel, thereby interpreting "all Israel" in a collective manner. In contrast to this view and in keeping with the spiritualizing hermeneutic, traditional amillennialists tend to find in the phrase a reference to the sum total of the elect from all nations, hence, the church. The word "so" carries the force of "in this manner," they add, and it refers to the previous verse, in which Paul speaks of the ingathering of the full number of the Gentiles. Consequently, the text declares that the coming to faith of the elect of all nations constitutes the fulfillment of the promise of salvation originally given to national Israel but actually referring to the church.

In recent years, many amillennialists have rejected the older view, arriving at a somewhat mediating position. With many dispensationalists, they interpret "all Israel" as a reference to physical descendants of the patriarchs, and not the church of all ages. Yet, in contrast to the standard dispensational interpretation, they claim that the phrase does not refer to the eschatological nation of Israel but to the full number of the elect among the Jews, that is, the remnant.[27]

Proponents who follow the traditional amillennial interpretation claim that the text does not refer to the eschatological future but to the present age. This is indicated by the word "so," which describes the manner, not the time, of the salvation of Israel, namely, by means of the process of grafting into the good olive tree.[28] Hence, the Jews are not saved *after* the full number of Gentiles—that is, immediately prior to or during the millennium—as dispensationalists argue, but concurrent with the Gentiles. Throughout the centuries of the church age, the elect remnant is gathered out of the people of Israel by the preaching of the gospel. Rather than a future national restoration, therefore, these expositors anticipate what they term a *remnant* conversion.

A few Reformed thinkers have gone beyond even this exegesis.[29] Arguing for a "hermeneutic of progressive fulfillment"[30] not unlike that of certain progressive dispensationalists,[31] they accept the claim that a distinct place must be accorded Israel in the historical plan and purposes of God.[32] Because the benefits of Christ are both material and spiritual,[33] the future for Israel may include even the enjoyment of "the times of refreshing" in the land of Palestine, just as the church enjoys both spiritual and material blessings—"the 'tokens' of the times of refreshing on earth."[34] The church's hope, they argue, includes a hope that God's promises to Israel will be realized, although the manner of this fulfillment may be hidden from us.[35]

Despite such movement in the direction of dispensationalism, the newer view retains a basic amillennial flavor. It affirms but one covenant, one covenant people, one salvation and one Savior.[36] It does not envision that the promises to Israel await fulfillment in a future millennium, but lie rather in the present messianic era and in the new heavens and the new earth that mark the consummation of the kingdom.[37] And the newer view acknowledges that the New Testament proclamation calls on Jews to enter into a salvific relationship with Jesus the Messiah, so that they, together with the Gentiles, can enjoy the messianic era in this age and in the age to come.[38] Consequently, it is the "remnant" of Israel who constitute "the people."[39]

The newer Reformed interpretation of the phrase "all Israel" in Romans 11:26 approaches the understanding favored by most contemporary scholars.[40] According to this view Paul is referring to a future event at which time the nation of Israel will be saved. Hence, he anticipates a conversion of the eschatological Israelite nation. This exegesis, however, raises the question of the means of the anticipated national conversion. Some contemporary thinkers offer an answer not too dissimilar from what critics found objectionable in the older dispensationalism, namely, a salvation of Israel that is not dependent on faith in Christ.[41] This suggestion, however, has come under heavy attack. Evangelicals who agree that the text is best understood as a reference to an eschatological event argue that according to Paul ethnic Israel will be saved but on the same basis as the Gentiles—only through faith in Christ and because of God's mercy.[42]

Amillennialism asserts that in some way the church enjoys the benefits that come through being the new Israel. However, the transference of focus from Israel to the church that amillennialists find in the New Testament also carries unpleasant consequences. Like historic premillennialism, amillennialism anticipates that the church, not Israel, will experience the eschatological tribulation. Actually, many amillennialists argue that the era of tribulation began with the first advent, as Christ entered the earthly arena to fight his cosmic foe. We therefore can anticipate that Satan's persecution of the church will grow progressively worse until it culminates in the appearance of the antichrist. But even this is within the plan of God. Cox explains: "The *fact* of tribulation is self-evident; its *nature* is primarily spiritual; its *purpose* is to refine; and its end will be the appearing the second time unto salvation by the Lord Jesus Christ."[43]

The priority of the New Testament is crucial in the amillennial system. The employment of this principle results in the elimination of the necessity of a millennium. No future earthly golden age is required for God to fulfill his promises to Israel. All promises to the nation either were already fulfilled in the Old Testament era or are now being fulfilled during the church age, whether to the church or to the remnant of Israel.[44]

If the first hermeneutical principle, the priority of the New Testament, undercuts the need for a millennium, the second undercuts the claim that any expectation of a future thousand years lay at the heart of the eschatology of the New Testament. The amillennial eschatology is built on a second hermeneutical assertion, namely, that the New Testament as a whole takes precedence over Revelation 20. Again Hamilton articulates the principle: "The clearest New Testament passages in nonsymbolic books are to be the norm for the interpretation of prophecy. . . . In other words, we should accept the clear and plain parts of Scripture as a basis for getting the true meaning of the more difficult parts of Scripture."[45]

On the basis of this principle, amillennialists argue that we must understand the vision of the millennium in terms of the simple eschatological chronology they find clearly taught throughout the New Testament (such as 2 Pet 3:10-13). The present age will climax in the return of the Lord in triumph and judgment, followed immediately by the inauguration of the eternal state. Whatever conclusions are gleaned from Revelation 20, therefore, can neither contradict nor supersede but rather must be understood in light of this general New Testament eschatological position.

The simple chronology taught by the Bible means, for example, that there will be but one eschatological rising of all humankind from the grave. Amillennialists support this assertion by appeal to several types of biblical material. Some texts represent the resurrection of believers and unbelievers as occurring together (for example, Dan 12:2; Jn 5:28-29; Acts 24:14-15).[46] Other texts indicate that the righteous and the wicked remain together throughout the age until they are separated at the judgment (Mt 13:30, 39, 49-50), at which time death itself will be abolished (1 Cor 15:26).[47] Finally, the New Testament declares that this judgment will occur at Christ's Second Coming, which time is called "the last day" (Jn 6:40; Mt 25:31; 2 Thess 1:7-10).[48]

Amillennialists claim that we must understand the mention of a first resurrection prior to the thousand years of Revelation 20:4-5 in a manner that harmonizes with the New Testament teaching of the one general resurrection. In fact, amillennialists are convinced that the vision of the seer is but a symbolic restatement of the eschatological expectations presented elsewhere in the New Testament.[49]

While they agree concerning this basic approach, adherents are divided as to the exact meaning of the text. Some propose that the coming to life following the millennium (v. 5) refers to the general, physical resurrection, whereas the first resurrection is spiritual in nature. Proponents of this view claim that the text itself indicates this exegesis. The interpretive key lies in the crisscrossing pattern of two pairs present or implied in the text, most significantly the link the seer makes between the first resurrection and the second death (v. 6).[50] The second death, most exegetes declare, is a spiritual rather than a physical reality, for it refers to the eternal punishment of the wicked. In the same way, the first resurrection, which frees an individual from the power of the second death (that is, which frees the believer from eternal damnation), must also be a spiritual reality. Otherwise the point of the verse would be lost.[51]

Amillennialists offer two different possibilities as to the meaning of this spiritual event. Some find in it a reference to the new birth,[52] or perhaps the experience of baptism as it relates to conversion.[53] The validity of this view, they argue, is indicated by those New Testament passages that refer to conversion as a rising from death (Eph 2:5-6; Col 2:13; 3:1; Rom 6:4-5, 13). But the most crucial support comes from the Lord himself. In John 5:24-29, Jesus contrasts two resurrections (see also Jn 11:25-26). One is present; the other is future. One is spiritual; the other is physical. One is restricted to believers; the other includes all humankind. The first, consequently, is conversion that results in spiritual life for those who are dead in sin; the second is the eschatological physical resurrection.[54] Revelation 20:4-6, adherents of this viewpoint argue, presents in symbolic form these truths about the new birth and eternal life.

More widely held is another interpretation of the spiritual significance of the symbol of the first resurrection. Proponents find in the text a reference to the intermediate state of the dead in Christ, namely, that the righteous dead are reigning with Christ in heaven.[55] As Benjamin Warfield explains, it is a vision of the peace of those who have died in the Lord: "The picture that is brought before us here is, in fine, the picture of the 'intermediate state'—of the saints of God gathered in heaven away from the confused noise and garments bathed in blood that characterized the war upon earth, in order that they may securely await the end."[56]

This interpretation arises both from the broader context of the Apocalypse as a whole and from certain clues in the text itself. The argument from the broader context focuses on one of the central purposes of the book, namely, to give assurance to believers in the face of the onslaught of Satan.[57] Consequently, the imagery of the first resurrection intends to encourage the Lord's people to be "overcomers," reminding them that faithfulness unto the end is not in vain, but brings victory and blessedness. The vision, therefore, is in keeping with the emphasis of the book, which focuses on faithfulness, or "the beatitude of the Christian dead," to use Meredith Kline's phrase.[58] Hence, Revelation 20:4 forms a striking parallel to the vision of the cry of the martyrs under the altar that God avenge their blood (Rev 6:9-11). In response, they are given white robes and told to rest a little longer. The millennium text declares that these resting martyrs are also reigning in heaven with Christ.[59]

The internal argument builds from the seer's use of certain significant terms. The most important clue is the fact that he saw the souls, not the bodies, of the martyrs.[60] This, coupled with the temporally limited length of their reign, indicates that the first resurrection cannot refer to a physical coming to life. In contrast to the millennial era, during which time the dead in Christ enjoy blessedness as disembodied souls, in the eternal state the righteous will reign in their resurrected bodies forever.[61] Further, those given authority to judge were seated on thrones, suggesting that the scene is in heaven, not on earth.[62]

Finally, some amillennialists find significance in the fact that both verbs in verse 4 ("lived" and "reigned") are in the aorist tense. Because both verbs are in the same tense, both must be translated in a parallel manner. And because they are aorist, a verb form that rarely refers to the inception of an action, they do not speak of an action that occurs at the beginning of the thousand years. Rather, the entire period is in view. Consequently, it is incorrect to interpret the first verb as indicating an event occurring at the beginning of the millennium and the second as a state of being throughout the era, as demanded by the premillennial eschatology. Rather, the best translation of the text is simply "they lived and reigned with Christ a thousand years."[63]

Acknowledging the validity of both positions concerning the nature of the spiritual resurrection, Hamilton offers a mediating interpretation that combines the two alternatives. He declares, "The first resurrection is the new birth of the believer which is crowned by his being taken to heaven to be with Christ in His reign during the interadvental period."[64] The point of the vision of the seer, therefore, is that for the believer eternal life is a present possession that is not interrupted by physical death.

Not all amillennialists believe that the first resurrection is spiritual and the second physical. Some take a different tack, interpreting both occurrences of "they lived" as references to a spiritual reality.[65] Proponents agree with those amillennialists who argue that verse 4 is a reference to believers in the intermediate state. The point at issue is the interpretation of the statement "The rest of the dead did not come to life until the thousand years were ended" (v. 5). This verse is commonly interpreted to mean that those not resurrected at the beginning of the thousand years were resurrected at its conclusion; hence the second resurrection is physical. The alternative view claims that this exegesis is faulty. The Greek verb in the text means "they did not live." Were a physical resurrection in view, the sentence would require a different Greek verb, meaning "they did not live again." And the word "until" does not itself imply that a change occurs after the point to which it refers, as is assumed in the standard exegesis; rather it is used to indicate that no change occurs for the duration of the time period and beyond.[66] Consequently, the intent of the statement is to declare that the wicked never join the disembodied righteous in the intermediate state.

In addition to its importance for the exegesis of the figure of the millennium, the priority of the plainer texts over Revelation 20 is visible as well in the amillennial interpretation of the symbol of the binding of Satan. The proper understanding of the millennial vision, amillennialists claim,

demands a return to the assertion found elsewhere in the New Testament
that in his ministry Jesus bound his enemy.[67] The Lord himself indicated
that such an act was necessary in order for him to release Satan's captives
(Mt 12:24-29). This claim, in turn, forms the basis for the *Christus Victor*
theme found repeatedly in the Gospels and Epistles. In his life, death and
resurrection Jesus has triumphed over the power of evil (Mt 4:1-11; Lk 9:1;
10:17-20; Jn 12:31-33; Col 2:14-15; Heb 2:14; 1 Jn 4:8). The Apocalypse itself
also gives evidence to the correctness of this interpretation, for the twelfth
chapter, which forms the center of the book, depicts Christ's coronation
as bringing about the ejection of Satan from heaven.[68]

Premillennialists argue that the binding of Satan must be future because the devil is obviously active in the world (1 Pet 5:8). Amillennialists
point out, however, that the imagery of Satan's binding does not mean total
powerlessness, but refers to the controlling of Satan's activities with a
view toward the advance of God's program.

A case in point is Jude's statement concerning certain fallen angels who
are kept in chains awaiting the judgment (Jude 6). Many commentators
suggest that these fallen angels are demons. But demons are not completely powerless in the world, even though they have been defeated by Christ
and therefore are now under his control. Just as the demons in chains are
not totally powerless, but restricted in activity, so also the binding of Satan
entails restriction rather than total incapacitation.

Restriction, rather than total powerlessness, is likewise indicated by the
text itself, proponents of this view claim. The devil is cast into a pit for
the duration of the thousand years and not into the lake of fire, the place
of absolute separation from the affairs of humanity.[69]

But what is the meaning of the symbol of the binding of Satan? In a
manner somewhat similar to that of postmillennialists, amillennial interpreters find the answer in the text itself: Satan is bound so as not to
deceive the nations. That is to say, the devil is unable to stop the spread
of the gospel throughout the world.[70]

Adherents are quick to point out the important change Christ's ministry
inaugurated. During the Old Testament era all the nations, with the ex-

ception of Israel, were under the dominance of Satan and in ignorance of the truth (Eph 2:11-12). The New Testament era, in contrast, is the time of the worldwide proclamation of the gospel, so that all nations can hear the truth. The vision of the binding of Satan provides a picture as to how this is possible. The devil can no longer deceive the nations as he once did. Of course, hearers of the gospel can refuse to accept its message. But Satan must yield to the working of the proclamation of the good news.

Consequently, amillennialists view Revelation 20:1-2 as a symbolic commentary on the Great Commission (Mt 28:19-20). Christ, and not the devil, possesses kingly authority. As a result, his followers, acting as his agents, can be bold in proclaiming the good news and discipling the nations of the world.

As is already evident, amillennialism interprets Revelation 20 as a vision of the present age, the time between Christ's two advents,[71] not some future era. The opening verses of the chapter declare the cosmic victory won by Christ at his first advent. Verses 4-6 speak of the resultant victory of his faithful witnesses, despite apparent defeat, whether that victory be in the heavenly realm of the intermediate state or the earthly realm of Christian living.

Amillennialists claim that their simple chronology reflects the biblical expectation of only one eschatological conflict between good and evil.[72] A comparison of Ezekiel 38—40 with the New Testament texts that speak of the final conflict suggests that the "battle of Armageddon" and the "battle of Gog and Magog" are alternative designations of the one event that immediately precedes the return of Christ[73] (which premillennialists separate by the thousand years). According to Ezekiel the destruction of Gog, the enemy of the ancient people of God, occurs prior to God's bringing Jacob back from captivity (Ezek 39:25). Revelation 20:8, however, places this battle after the millennium. Likewise, the terminology Ezekiel employs in describing this battle (see 39:17-20) re-emerges in the Apocalypse in the description of the triumph of the rider on the white horse (Rev 19:11-21), which is another reference to the battle of Armageddon (Rev 16:16). But if Revelation 16:16 and 19:11-21 describe the same battle, then obviously we cannot view the book as progressing purely in chronological order.[74] Amillennialists capitalize on this observation, for it provides further support for the thesis that the thousand years correspond to the time between Christ's two advents.

According to many amillennial interpreters, the Apocalypse is structured into seven sections that roughly parallel each other, recapitulating the time from the first to the second advent but evidencing what William Hendricksen terms "progressive parallelism."[75] As Warfield explains,

> the structure of the book is such that it returns at the opening of each of its seven sections to the first advent, and gives in the course of each section a picture of the whole interadventual period—each successive portraiture, however, rising above the previous one in the stress laid on the issue of the history being wrought out during its course.[76]

The most obvious indication of parallelism comes in chapter 12, which returns to the first advent of Jesus rather than following chronologically after chapter 11. Revelation 1—11, proponents explain, describes the struggle on earth, picturing the church persecuted by the world. The second half of the book provides the deeper spiritual background, namely, the conflict between Christ and the dragon. Given the book's parallel structure, it comes as no surprise that the events of chapter 20 do not follow those of chapter 19, but likewise mark a return to the first advent.

As a vision of the age between Christ's two advents, the thousand years are a symbolic presentation of the great New Testament declaration that the risen Lord is reigning now (Rev 1:6, 9; 3:21; 5:10; 1 Cor 15:24-28). His rule constitutes a present reality that believers enter at the time of conversion (Col 1:13; Mk 1:15; Lk 17:20-21). Because Christ reigns throughout the church age, the biblical declaration of his rule does not necessitate that a future millennial era be inserted between the present and the eternal state.

Despite the roar of the devil who seeks to intimidate the believers through deceit and persecution, Christ is reigning over history, and he has given his church the mandate to preach the gospel in all the world. Their faithfulness is rewarded beyond death, and one day it will be rewarded as the king returns in vindication and judgment to inaugurate the eternal state. This is the message of the Bible as read by amillennialists.[77]

The Critique of Amillennialism

Although amillennialism in its various forms has been the dominant eschatology in Christian theological history, among evangelicals it comprises the minority position. Hence, like the other viewpoints, its tenets have been the object of intense scrutiny by proponents of competing eschatologies.

Because of its closer affinity to postmillennialism, adherents of this persuasion have been relatively mild in their critique of amillennialism. The main point of contention between them is the meaning of the rider on the white horse (Rev 19:11-21). Because they view this as a symbol of the Second Coming of Christ, amillennialists must see in the twentieth chapter of the Apocalypse a return to the beginning of the church age. Postmillennialism, in contrast, which interprets the rider in terms of the victory of the Word in history, sees the millennium of chapter 20 as following this victory, and hence as a yet future golden age in history, a Christianized world.[78]

Historically there has always been a certain fluidity between the two views. A twentieth-century expression of this is the "realized millennialism" of Jay Adams,[79] which is his conscious attempt to combine the best of postmillennialism with certain strands of amillennialism.

Adams agrees with pre- and postmillennialism that Revelation 20 follows chapter 19 chronologically. But in contrast to expositors who place these visions in the eschatological future, he interprets nearly the entire Apocalypse as having been fulfilled in early Christian history. Chapters 6—19, he argues, refer to the two major persecutions—the Jewish and the Roman—faced by the early church. The visions of chapter 19 predict the victory of the church over its persecutors, a victory that from our perspective, however, lies in the past. Consequently, his understanding of Revelation 20 reflects to some degree the older Augustinian understanding, which equated the thousand years with the church age. Because the victory of Revelation 19 is behind us, we live in the era symbolized by the thousand years, that indefinite period of time in which the church is relatively free from persecution and the gospel spreads throughout the world. The millennial era, Adams speculates, is now drawing to a close. Soon Satan will be loosed, and his activity will bring a short time similar to "the days of Noah." Then the Lord will return to bring judgment on the enemies of the church and to establish the eternal state.

While amillennialism has received rather mild treatment at the hand of postmillennialists, it has been subjected to intense criticism by premillennialists, especially those of the dispensational variety. The focus of their attack is almost invariably the question of hermeneutics.

Dispensationalists criticize the amillennialist approach to the prophecies of the Old Testament. While acknowledging that a literal interpretation of these texts leads to the future messianic reign anticipated by dispensationalists,[80] amillennialists, rather than accepting the plain meaning of the texts, introduce another principle of exegesis. One problem with this approach, critics argue, is that it leads to hermeneutical inconsistency. Charles Ryrie, for example, is amazed that conservative amillennialists can find the literal principle sufficient for all biblical exegesis except for the interpretation of prophecy, at which point they suddenly introduce spiritualizing. Ryrie wonders if this is not a case of "the conclusions determining the means"; his opponents introduce spiritualizing in order to provide the hermeneutical basis for their eschatological system.[81]

But even more serious is another problem. Dispensationalists are concerned that spiritualizing of any sort in scriptural interpretation gives unbelievers strong leverage in rejecting Christianity. It opens the door to the rejection of the plain teaching of the Bible on all subjects.[82] Hence, any approach that moves beyond simply accepting the plain meaning of the text runs the danger of denying scriptural authority.

Historic premillennialists are largely in agreement with the amillennial interpretation of the Old Testament, and consequently do not join dispensationalists in criticizing the spiritualizing hermeneutic at this point. However, they echo their premillennial cousins in accusing amillennialists of unwarranted spiritualization when Revelation 20:1-6 is at issue. All premillennial critics, therefore, speak with one voice in rejecting the amillennial exegesis of certain figures of the seer's vision.[83]

Amillennialists are correct in finding the general charge of inappropriate spiritualizing wide of the mark. There seems to be no overriding categorical reason to interpret the symbols of the text in accordance with their literal meanings. Amillennial exegetes are quick to note that all interpretations of prophecy and apocalyptic literature must by necessity be nonliteral at points,[84] and their basic conclusion has been echoed even by dispensationalists of the newer progressive variety.[85]

Further, amillennial apologists point to the symbolic intent of the Apocalypse as a whole (such as Rev 5:6), which ought to put the interpreter on notice not to insist on a literal explanation at every place,[86] but to look for interpretive keys in the clear New Testament eschatological texts. Like the book as a whole, chapter 20 is highly symbolic. It speaks of Satan being bound with a chain and cast into a bottomless pit, and it anticipates a second death that lasts forever. The author obviously intended that none of these be interpreted in a purely literal manner, as such an interpretation would be nonsensical—that is, a spiritual being bound with a physical chain and confined in a physical pit with no bottom. Consequently, it is possible that other figures in these verses, including the thousand years, are likewise to be understood symbolically.

The intention of the amillennialist hermeneutic, therefore, is not to get around the plain meaning of the text, but to interpret the text literally—that is, as the author intended—albeit not in what proponents would see as a "woodenly literal" manner that fails to take into consideration the symbolic significance of the figures of speech employed by the biblical author. Thus amillennialists claim that they successfully deflect the negative implications implied in the charge of spiritualizing that their opponents so readily level at them.

More problematic than the general charge of spiritualizing is the question of the actual meaning of the millennium text. Premillennialists are unhappy with the amillennial understanding at several points. For example, they do not agree that the binding of Satan accomplished in Jesus' ministry is the same as that represented in Revelation 20:1. Ladd explains, "The former meant the breaking of the power of Satan that individual men and women might be delivered from his control. The latter binding meant that he should deceive the nations no more."[87] Amillennialists, of course, find such distinctions to be unwarranted hairsplitting.

Most participants in the discussion agree that the crux of the issue lies with the meaning of the seer's reference to the first resurrection. Amillennialists find in the Bible only one literal event, the eschatological resurrection of all humankind at Jesus' return, and they demand that Revelation 20 be understood in terms of this finding. Premillennialists argue that any understanding of the references to "coming to life" and "resurrection" in these verses that does not interpret them in the physical, bodily sense is a gross violation of sound hermeneutics.[88] The plain meaning of the text, they argue, teaches two eschatological events—the resurrection of the righteous at Christ's appearing and that of the unrighteous after the millennium. When amillennialists raise the problem of harmonization with the rest of the New Testament, premillennialists respond by appealing to the principle of progressive revelation,[89] or by declaring that the Apocalypse provides fuller information. Herman Hoyt, for example, argues that the other New Testament passages do not assert that there will be a general judgment, but only "that both wicked and righteous will be raised." Revelation 20 adds the details concerning the time element.[90]

Regardless of how we resolve the issue of hermeneutical priority—Revelation 20 or the rest of the New Testament—the vision of the resurrections is problematic in one way or another for all parties in the debate. A major difficulty focuses on who participates in the first resurrection and the millennium. This problem arises whether these symbols are interpreted as the eschatological rising of the righteous to participate in the earthly rule of Christ (historic premillennialism) or as the reign of departed believers in the intermediate state (amillennialism).

Among those who lived and reigned with Christ a thousand years, the author specifically includes only "the souls of those who had been beheaded because of their testimony for Jesus and because of the word of God," those who "had not worshiped the beast or his image and had not received his mark on their foreheads or their hands" (v. 4). Hence, participation in the first resurrection and the enjoyment of millennial blessings is the specific prerogative only of the tribulation saints. If the seer explicitly connects the first resurrection and the reigning with Christ only with those who are martyred for the cause of the gospel, then, regardless of what we are led to conclude that the author actually intended by this vision, the blessings that the millennium brings simply cannot be extended to all Christians. The involvement of all believers in the first resurrection and the millennium that expositors of varying eschatological orientations presuppose is at best an inference derived from the text; it is not expressly stated.[91]

In contrast to the post-tribulational resurrection of all the righteous anticipated by historic premillennialists and amillennialists, the classical dispensational chronology includes a restricted martyr resurrection at Christ's Second Coming (for the saints of all ages rise to meet their Lord prior to the tribulation). Although this more complicated timetable eliminates the problem of the exclusive nature of the resurrection of Revelation 20:4, it introduces another difficulty, that of the actual number of resurrections. Premillennial critics point out the difficulty the allusion to two resurrections in Revelation 20 poses for the simpler chronology of amillennialism; their eschatological timetable appears to have too few resurrections. For dispensationalists the problem is reversed; they appear to anticipate too many. The pretribulation rapture means that there are actually three resurrections, not two. The first occurs prior to the tribulation, when those who have died in Christ are raised to life. The resurrection of tribulation saints (Rev 20:4-5) marks a second resurrection, not the first as the text indicates. Then after the millennium comes yet a third resurrection, that of the wicked. This problem is not solved by the ploy that the pretribulational and post-tribulational resurrections form two parts of one event.

Considerations such as these suggest that the debate over the meaning of the first resurrection in the Apocalypse is inconclusive. Thus, we cannot reject amillennialism on the basis of its interpretation of this symbol. The amillennial eschatology, however, is beset by other, more significant problems.

Some of these difficulties focus on the book of Revelation. For example, amillennialists are rightly challenged for their general approach to the Apocalypse, which understands the book as a series of progressive parallels. Several of the visions of the book may indeed parallel each other, as amillennialists suggest, and the vision that begins in Revelation 12:1 does indeed take the reader back to the first advent of Christ.[92] Nevertheless, the suggestion by some that the book consists of seven divisions, all of which cover the time between the first and second advents, appears contrived and is ultimately unsatisfying.[93]

Of the parallels proposed by amillennial expositors, the break between chapters 19 and 20, demanded by this eschatological system, is most problematic. Such a break seems to be unwarranted by the text. The simplest reading places the events of the latter chapter after those of the former. Christ first overcomes the beast and the false prophet (19:19-21), and then he turns his attention to the one who had inspired their diabolical actions (20:7-10). Between these two struggles lies the thousand years of tranquility.

The correctness of this understanding is suggested by Revelation 20:10, which indicates that the beast and the false prophet are present in the lake of fire at the time when the devil is confined to a similar fate. R. Fowler White proposes that "20:10 need only imply that at the second coming the devil is cast into the lake of fire shortly after the beast and the false prophet are cast there."[94] The argument, while plausible, simply lacks the ring of truth enjoyed by the millenarian interpretation of the verse.

In the final analysis, no presentation of the relation between Revelation 20:1-10 and the preceding chapter has proved itself to be without difficulties and therefore able to command universal allegiance.[95]

Another problem concerning the amillennial understanding of Revelation focuses more directly on the meaning of the thousand years. Amillennialism has simply not been able to present a fully satisfying understanding of the actual nature of the millennium. Apart from whether or not they are correct, both the post- and premillennial expectations of a golden age on earth carry with them a sense of plausibility. The amillennial picture of souls reigning in the intermediate state or of believers reigning over the world, the flesh and the devil in the present age pales in comparison to the concrete future age of peace and righteousness anticipated by the millenarians.

Other difficulties move beyond the Apocalypse to other theological issues. One such problem concerns the future of Israel. Amillennialists tend to minimize or even eliminate any future role for national Israel in God's program on the basis of the principle that Israel has been superseded by the church. Paul, however, held out hope that "all Israel will be saved" (Rom 11:26), and he was diligent in his ministry among the Gentiles in an attempt thereby to make Israel envious (see Rom 11:11).

The contemporary amillennial interpretation of the Pauline expectation that anticipates a conversion of the remnant throughout the church age forms a welcomed move beyond the older exegesis, which relegated even Romans 11:26 to the church. Yet even this understanding fails to give sufficient place to the eschatological reference point of the Pauline hope. Concerning Israel's rejection of Christ, Paul declares, "if their transgression means riches for the world, and their loss means riches for the Gentiles, how much greater riches will their fullness bring!" (Rom 11:12). The apostle clearly anticipates a future conversion of Israel on a grand scale, an event that would usher in a glorious day for the entire world.

Of course, we ought not to read into this expectation more than is there. The Pauline exclamation does not demand that we separate Israel and the church as comprising two peoples of God, for Paul apparently understood the future salvation of Israel in terms of a great ingathering of Jews into the one fellowship of those who acknowledge Jesus as the Messiah. Nor does his hope require an earthly millennial reign of Christ, for the conversion of Israel could just as easily prepare for the inauguration of the eternal state as for an earthly golden age. Nevertheless, the Pauline expectation demands that more be made of the continuing existence of the Jews as a people than amillennialists have traditionally tended to admit.

Finally, although there are signs of a shift in thinking among certain contemporary amillennial thinkers,[96] when taken as a whole the dominant eschatological tradition of the church has tended to remove the reign of God from human history. This tendency is a natural outworking of the spiritualized understanding of the kingdom of God, which theologians derived from Augustine. As a result, they tend to relegate the realm of God's reign to a heavenly sphere beyond the world. Where the kingdom does intersect time, the intersection is generally not understood in terms of the realm of human affairs. Rather, the focus of the kingdom rests on either the sacramental community or the human heart. Either the kingdom is God's ruling in the hearts of his people, or it is a heavenly reality reflected in the earthly ecclesiastical copy, the sacramental life of the church.

One consequence of the amillennial spiritualizing of the kingdom is a too close connecting of the kingdom of God and the church of Jesus Christ. Oswald T. Allis reflects the typical understanding. Although acknowledging that "the kingdom is a broader concept than the Church," he nevertheless concludes that "the two institutions are co-existent and largely co-extensive." He therefore asserts that the kingdom and the church "are so closely related, so nearly identical, that it is impossible to be in the one and not in the other."[97]

The tendency to remove the kingdom from temporal history is evident in the amillennial interpretation of the thousand years. The saints reign with Christ beyond the world and beyond the realm of human history. And even the picture of the eternal state lacks real connection with the world as we know it.

Conclusion

The difficulties in the amillennial position ought not to be overlooked. Yet in spite of the problems that beset it, on the whole amillennialism does offer certain advantages. For example, of the several eschatological systems, it is perhaps the most reflective of the simple chronology presented by the New Testament as a whole. Consequently, its adherents generally refuse to speculate concerning the minute details of the end or be caught up in the end-times fever that has been known to infect segments of the church from time to time. Although millennialists criticize them for being indifferent to "the signs of the times" or uninterested in prophecy and the end times, amillennialists articulate a simple, biblical hope concerning the future.[98]

The hope set forth by amillennialism combines the optimistic tone of postmillennialism and the more pessimistic message found in premillennialism into a realistic world view. Hamilton, for example, speaks for all when he declares,

> From New Testament times to the present, the Church of Christ has been a hopeful church. Pessimism has no place in the Christian consciousness. No matter how dark the days or how discouraging the outlook of the world, Christians, who understand the teaching of the Word of God, and believe it to be true, have universally been optimists. Optimists, not because they believed that man was becoming better and better and making the world constantly a better place in which to live, or because they shut their eyes to the evils that surrounded them in the world, but because they knew the God in whom they trusted, and knew that His promises can never fail of fulfillment.[99]

Amillennialism is a realist outlook, therefore, in that it sees the presence of two tendencies—evil and good—in the world throughout the age, but emphasizes the final triumph of good. The gospel will be proclaimed, but Satan will seek to thwart the work of the church, until Christ comes in victory.[100] As Hoekema explains: "Though we must always recognize these two lines of development in history—that of the kingdom of God and the kingdom of evil—faith will always see the former as controlling, overruling, and finally conquering the latter."[101] On the basis of this realism, the amillennialist can confidently engage in the Lord's work, knowing the outcome is assured, but knowing as well that only partial, albeit real, success will come about in human history short of the Lord's return.

7

OPTIMISM—
PESSIMISM—
REALISM

The Theological Significance of the Millennium Issue

*D*uring the last two centuries, evangelicals have hotly debated the question concerning the nature and time of the thousand-year reign of the saints with Christ envisioned by the seer of the Apocalypse. As the previous chapters indicate, each of the major historical positions concerning the millennium carries importance beyond the obvious question concerning the placement of the thousand years in the chronology of history.

One dimension of this importance lies in the area of hermeneutics, or biblical interpretation. The understanding of Revelation 20 that each of the major eschatologies advocates is in part the result of the crucial hermeneutical principles its proponents employ. The issue of the millennium, therefore, raises these deeper questions of the proper approach to the Bible in general and to literature that speaks of the Second Coming in particular.

Beyond these issues, an even more decisive difference separates the various positions on the millennium question. Embedded in each scenario is a broader world view, an outlook toward the course of history and the role of humankind in that history that is bigger than the issue concerning the correct meaning of the vision of the Apocalypse. And the world views reflected in the major contemporary conservative eschatologies crop up repeatedly in theological history, even among theologies espoused by non-evangelical thinkers.

Before attempting to chart a way out of the impass the current discussion of the millennium has produced among evangelicals, we must therefore summarize the hermeneutical issues the debate poses and then set forth more explicitly the broader world-view perspectives evident in the major positions.

The Millennium Debate and Hermeneutics

As previous chapters indicate, the way in which a reader of Revelation 20:1-8 understands this text will in part be determined by the principles of hermeneutics the interpreter brings to it. The millennium debate, in other words, triggers a debate over hermeneutics. It is left to us now to summarize this discussion in terms of the issues of interpretation that form the essence of the debate.[1]

The central disagreements that have direct bearing on the question of the millennium are, of course, the interpretive issues surrounding Revelation 19 and 20. Scholars simply do not agree concerning the meaning of many of the features of these chapters.

One crucial point of disagreement is how the two chapters are related. Does chapter 20 follow chronologically after chapter 19, or does Revelation 20:1 begin a new cycle, another recapitulation of the book's sweep from the first to the second advents? As we have already noted, the recapitulation understanding favors amillennialism, whereas the chronological tends toward some type of millenarian view. If chapter 20 takes the reader back to the first advent, then however they are to be understood the thousand years parallel the church age. Such parallelism adds credence to the suggestion that the reign of the saints with Christ is either a spiritual reality in the lives of believers or transpires in heaven. But if chapter 20 follows the events of chapter 19, then the millennium may be a specific period of earthly history.

Closely tied to the question of chronology is the interpretation of the details of Revelation 20:1-8, especially the binding of Satan and the first resurrection. Does the former refer to a control over Satan's activities won by Christ through his ministry and hence is an event that occurred at Christ's first advent (amillennialism)? Is it rather a reference to the freedom of the church to advance the gospel set forth at some point in church history (postmillennialism)? Or does this imagery await a complete state of Satanic inactivity that will commence only at the second advent (premillennialism)? In the same way, is the first resurrection either the translation of the martyr to heaven to enjoy the intermediate state or a spiritual reality experienced by the believer in this life? Is it instead a renewal of the martyr spirit in the church at some point in history? Or is it a purely future event, referring to a physical resurrection of believers at the Lord's return?

Answering the question of chronology does not immediately solve all the interpretive problems of these chapters, however. The millenarian thesis that chapter 20 follows chronologically after chapter 19 raises a further question: How are we to interpret the rider on the white horse, and what historical point corresponds to this symbol? Contemporary postmillennialists and premillennialists agree that the event is yet future. But for the former its fulfillment occurs somewhat imperceptibly, the rider being a symbol of the triumph of the gospel, whereas the latter understand it to be a vision of Christ's second advent.

These two options, however, do not exhaust the possible interpretations of the symbol. Some thinkers, including many among the Reformers and the Puritans, place the coming of the rider, and with this event the advent of the millennium, at some point in past church history. In their view, the thousand years are already completed or nearly completed.

The attempt to find unambiguous answers to interpretive questions such as these taxes our best exegetical skills. These texts raise the deeper issue concerning the proper approach to figurative biblical language—the old question of literal versus spiritual interpretation. Must we find in historical situations and events literal correspondence to biblical figures? Or ought we to remain open to the possibility that biblical imagery is intended to correspond instead to deeper spiritual realities?

Not only do the exegetical problems surrounding the correct interpretation of the imagery of Revelation 19 and 20 raise this deeper hermeneutical question in terms of these two chapters, they also ask the question concerning the entire book of Revelation. Foundational to any attempt to understand the meaning of the specific visions of the seer is the question as to how the author intends that the reader approach the book as a whole. Hence we must ask, What is the nature of the Apocalypse itself? In the history of the church several major responses to this question have been defended.[2]

One of the oldest and most widely held methods of interpreting the book of Revelation is the historicist view. This approach assumes that the Apocalypse sets forth in symbolic form the entire course of church history from the writing of the book to the end of time, that is, from the period in which the seer lived to the final consummation of the divine program. Therefore, the several series of sevens—the seals, the trumpets and the bowls—represent specific historical events. Regardless of when they lived, historicists have generally placed their own day somewhere within the later chapters of the book.

In a sense, the early church leaders such as Irenaeus and Justin read Revelation in the historicist manner.[3] They believed that the seer was describing the situation of the recent past and of their day. They were convinced that they were living in the time of the antichrist—the persecuting Roman emperor—whose power would soon be destroyed by the victorious Lord.

The historicist view was likewise the dominant approach of the Reformers and their heirs. Like the early Christians they believed that theirs was the struggle against antichrist depicted in the Apocalypse, a struggle now seen, however, as waged against the Roman pope. The historicist view remained the nearly universal position of Protestants in England and America—even among premillennialists—until well into the nineteenth century.[4]

As the time between the writing of the Apocalypse and the present lengthened, the span represented by the book's symbols by necessity lengthened as well. Second-century Christians found fulfillment in recent history for all the events predicted by the seer, short of the Lord's triumphal return. For subsequent interpreters, in contrast, for whom the fulfillment of the prophecy was occurring over a greater length of time, the task became more difficult. The finite number of symbols in the seer's visions of history (for example, the total of twenty-one seals, trumpets and bowls) forced exegetes to be increasingly more selective concerning which of the great events of history could serve as the reference points for the book's prophecy of the ongoing stream of history. Unfortunately, this necessity, coupled with the desire to maintain the sequence portrayed in the book, produced many strained and far-fetched interpretations.

Since the close of the nineteenth century, the loyalties of evangelicals have largely shifted away from the historicist position. In its place many have embraced the futurist view. This approach dates at least to the Middle Ages, but was set forth in earnest by Jesuit thinkers in their attempt to exonerate the pope against the charges of the Protestants.

Futurists assume that the bulk of the book of Revelation—perhaps even everything beginning in the fourth chapter—refers to the period immediately surrounding the second advent of Christ. In this way they claim to follow the seer's distinction between "what is now" and "what will take place later" (Rev 1:19). The futurist view also allows for a more literal interpretation of the various happenings in the book, if for no other reason than because it relegates these events to the not-yet-realized future.

But for this advantage, the futurist approach pays a price. It cannot provide a satisfactory understanding of the importance of the Apocalypse for, and application of, its prophecy to its original readership. If the happenings presented by the seer speak solely of events experienced by the generation that witnesses the climax of the age, then why did the angel leave John with the command, "Do not seal up the words of the prophecy of this book, because the time is near" (Rev 22:10; compare Dan 12:9)? The futurist interpretation likewise provides a less than satisfactory understanding of the dramatic picture that sets the stage for the opening of the seals by the Lamb (Rev 5:1—6:1). Our most natural inclination is to assume that the ascension marks the point at which the Lamb is invested with authority to take the sealed book. Futurists, however, must place this event in the future.

The problems of the historicist and futurist views have made two other alternatives—the preterist and the idealist—attractive to some interpreters. Preterists argue that the main part of the Apocalypse refers to, or was fulfilled during, the early Christian era. The book provides a sketch of the conditions experienced by Christians in the Roman Empire at the time when it was written. The seer's vision, consequently, presents in apocalyptic form the struggle of the early church against the organized opposition of the political system (Roman and/or Jewish). While focusing on the descriptive elements of Revelation, preterists do find a predictive element in the book as well, for it also prophesies the final triumph of the people of God over their foes through the power of Christ.[5]

In contrast to the other three, the idealist view lifts Revelation out of any one historical context. It looks for the timeless message of the book, rather than a historical fulfillment to its symbols. The Apocalypse, idealists assert, is a dramatic presentation of the basic Christian message concerning the conflict between God and Satan, good and evil, the people of God and the forces of persecution, which rages in every age. The book affirms that God will ultimately be victorious, and that knowing this, the believing community ought to take comfort and be exhorted.

Today nearly all interpreters are preterists to the extent that they agree that the Apocalypse, being addressed as it was to the early church, must be interpreted in a way that will give it meaning for its original audience. Nearly all are also idealists insofar as they agree that the book does have a message for believers in every age. Many evangelicals, however, find themselves compelled to say more about a future reference point for the details of the prophecy. Not only does the book offer assurance of God's ultimate victory, it also provides specific details concerning the chronology of that victory. The point at issue among them is how these details fit together.

The question of hermeneutics raised by the millennium issue, however, moves beyond the book of Revelation. In its most comprehensive scope, of course, it encompasses the proper approach to the Bible as a whole. But more specifically, the millennium debate raises hermeneutical questions concerning Old Testament prophecy, literalism and the relation of the Old Testament to the New.

Simply stated, millennialists pour the Old Testament anticipations of a future, messianic age into the mold of the thousand years of Revelation 20. Of course, differences exist among them. Dispensationalists argue that the millennial messianic age will entail the fulfillment of promises concerning the land of Palestine and prosperity to the nation of Israel in accordance with a somewhat literal hermeneutic. Others envision the golden age in terms of the church or the spread of the Christian gospel. Postmillennialists anticipate that the golden age will open the way for the Lord's Second Coming; premillennialists cannot conceive of its arrival apart from the physical return of Christ. Yet all millennialists find in the Old Testament the prophecy of an earthly, historical golden age.

Nonmillennialists, in contrast, question the validity of such an understanding. They declare instead that the visions of the ancient Hebrew prophets find their reference point in the church, in the intermediate state or in the eternal kingdom that lies beyond the consummation of history.

Those who do not anticipate an actual historical messianic age question the hermeneutic of literalism that underlies millennialism, especially its dispensationalist variety. In this they are joined to greater or lesser extents by proponents of other types of millennialism. These interpreters reject the demand that prophecies articulated under the terms of the old covenant be fulfilled as they were given. The order of the fulfillment, they argue, may be higher than the order of the promise. This principle means that we must be open to the possibility that prophecies couched in physical, earthly terms and given to the old people of God, national Israel, may find their fulfillment in spiritual realities connected with the new people of God, the church of Jesus Christ. The prosperity God promised to Israel may indeed find its fulfillment in the expansion of the church.

These issues point finally to another. In the end, the millennium question raises a fundamental query concerning the nature of the kingdom of God proclaimed throughout the Bible: What kind of reality is the reign of God, and when is it present on the earth? Will the kingdom of God express itself in a future messianic age within history?[6] Or is the kingdom primarily a transcendent reality, lying above or beyond history but also present in the world wherever the rulership of God through Christ is acknowledged?

The question concerning the kingdom of God was debated with new vigor in the first half of the twentieth century. The older view tended to equate the kingdom on earth with the church or to see it in terms of the society of people of good will founded by Jesus. This understanding was shattered by the rediscovery of the apocalyptic element in the Bible. As scholars came to see that the apocalyptic vision of the world was a central feature of the New Testament writings, they came to the parallel realization that the biblical portrait of the kingdom was in one sense that of a catastrophic act of God breaking into history.

Although differences of opinion remained as to how the two dimensions fit together, by the middle of the twentieth century scholars had reached an uneasy consensus. Jesus and the New Testament writers envisioned the kingdom as both a present and a future reality. This kingdom was inaugurated by Jesus himself through his proclamation of the rulership of God, his decisive battle against the forces of evil and his provision of reconciliation and life for human beings. Yet the consummation of the reign of God remains future. Although the power of the "age to come" has broken into history and is therefore present, its fullness will not be our experience until the end of the age.

Since mid-century the older consensus has given way to a newer understanding that has developed from the older view.[7] The phrase "the kingdom of God" points to the self-disclosure of God, "God in strength,"[8] or the
sovereign activity of God.[9] It is the ultimate intervention of God in human
affairs. The coming of the kingdom, consequently, creates a new way of
life in the present.

The kingdom, therefore, is related to Christ's first advent. In a sense it
is a reality that people can enter (Mk 9:47; Mt 21:31-32). It is the kingly
power of God.[10] Hence, the kingdom is a "sphere of existence" in which
people are called to live. It is an incorporation into God's powerful invasion
of our world; as such it consists in doing the will of God (Mt 6:10; 7:21-
23) and demands a radical decision (Mt 13:44-46). To enter the kingdom
means to participate in "the already inaugurated explosion of God's power
into the world," to employ the words of Joel Marcus.[11] Nevertheless, its
consummation awaits the glory surrounding Christ's second advent.

Here and there we detect the reign of God in the midst of the present
age. Some people come to acknowledge the lordship of Jesus; for them the
kingdom is a reality. In certain situations of life the desires of God—the
principles of his rulership—are followed; in them the kingdom breaks into
our world. One day, however, what is now partial and incomplete will be
universal and perfect. Then Christ will be publicly recognized as Lord
(Phil 2:10-11); then God will in fact be sovereign over all creation.

On the surface, the millennium debate focuses on how the thousand-
year vision of the Apocalypse fits into the overarching program of the
coming of the reign of God. Is the millennium a further stage after the
second advent that contributes to the transition from the present age to
the age to come (premillennialism)? Is it a further dimension of the advance of the kingdom during the present age that will lead to the age to
come (postmillennialism)? Or is the thousand-year symbol to be understood as a spiritual realm that believers enjoy during the present age,
whether in their spiritual experience or beyond death (amillennialism)?

Such questions are, of course, important. They call to the fore our often
undeveloped or unarticulated understandings as to how we are to approach

the Scriptures and what they teach concerning God's program. But they raise a further question as well, the fundamental question of world view, to which we now turn.

World View and Traditional Millennialism

During the last two centuries, the multiplicity of positions concerning the thousand years have crystalized into three basic alternatives: postmillennialism, premillennialism and amillennialism. Beyond the position each takes concerning the actual interpretation of the vision of the millennium, the viewpoint each of the three articulates as to the nature of the thousand years illustrates a deeper conviction concerning the flow of history. Simply stated and no doubt somewhat oversimplified, they embody three foundational theological moods: optimism (postmillennialism), pessimism (premillennialism) and realism (amillennialism).

Postmillennialism, which was the dominant eschatology of the eighteenth and nineteenth centuries, sets forth a basically optimistic outlook toward history and our role in the attainment of God's program. Despite the attempts of the evil one to thwart the onward movement of the divine purposes through seduction, treachery or persecution, the people of God will be successful in the completion of their mandate, postmillennialism joyously proclaims. Christ will reign over the world through his obedient church, and as a result the world will enjoy an era of peace and righteousness prior to the conclusion of history.

In keeping with this basic optimism concerning world history, postmillennial theologies emphasize the continuity between the present order and the kingdom, and they highlight those present realities that offer hope for the immediate future. The future kingdom comes as a heightening of forces already at work in the present. Whatever it may be, the "golden age" is the product of concursive action, as human agents cooperate with the divine Spirit in bringing God's goals to pass.

In its various forms, postmillennialism forms a constant reminder that before the people of God can become the church triumphant they must be the church militant. En route to the dawning of the golden age battles must be won. And because the divine power is now at work through the church, that golden age may be "just around the corner." As a result of this expectation, postmillennialists tend to focus their attention on the present situation, finding in it only a few, albeit challenging, impediments to the full realization of the blessed society. And they are hopeful that the soon overcoming of these remaining problems might just mark the dawning of the reign of God.

At its best, then, the postmillennial world view leads to engagement in the world. In this sense it forms a positive counterbalance to the tendency toward disengagement that often characterizes premillennialism. It is no historical accident that by and large the great thrusts toward worldwide evangelistic outreach and social concern in the modern era were launched by a church imbued with the optimism that characterizes postmillennial thinking.[12]

In contrast to the optimism of postmillennialism, premillennialism displays a basic pessimism concerning history and the role we play in its culmination. Despite all our attempts to convert or reform the world, prior to the end antichrist will emerge and gain control of human affairs, premillennialism reluctantly predicts. Only the catastrophic action of the returning Lord will bring about the reign of God and the glorious age of blessedness and peace.

In keeping with this basic pessimism concerning world history, premillennial theologies emphasize the discontinuity, or even the contradiction between, the present order and the kingdom of God, and they elevate the divine future over the evil present. The kingdom is the radically new thing God will do. However it may be conceived, the "golden age"—the divine future—comes as God's gracious gift and solely through God's action.

Premillennialism in its various forms, therefore, is a constant reminder that we must always retain what H. Richard Niebuhr termed a sense of the broken relation between the present and the coming kingdom.[13] The loss of just this sense of discontinuity is the special temptation of all varieties of postmillennialism. Partially for this reason, the nineteenth-century expression of that eschatology so readily gave way to theological liberalism with its increasingly secular orientation. No wonder premillennialism came to be the dominant eschatology among fundamentalists and evangelicals during the twentieth century. It offered a formidable protest to the direction being charted by mainline Christianity. And this eschatology provided a way of making sense of the world, as conservatives came to view themselves as an embattled remnant in an increasingly liberal-dominated ecclesiastical context and as a minority relegated to the fringes of life in an increasingly hostile, secular environment.

The difference in mood between these two millennial views as it impacts the believer's outlook toward the church in the world is evidenced in an autobiographical confession by Puritan scholar Iain H. Murray. Murray recounts the difference in focus between his prayers as a new believer and those of his father:

> Our difference concerned the extent to which the success of the kingdom of Christ is to be expected in the earth. My father would pray for its universal spread and global triumph, for the day when "nation shall not lift up sword against nation, neither shall they learn war any more," and when great multitudes in all lands will be found numbered among the travail of Christ's soul. According to the teaching with which I was then in contact these petitions were misguided, the product of a theological liberalism which believed in the upward progress of man and in the coming of a better world. Evangelical belief, so I thought, bound one to a contrary persuasion, namely, that growing evil must dominate the world-scene until Jesus Christ comes again in power and glory. Until then the gospel must be preached as a testimony unto all nations, though not with anticipation that large numbers of the human race will receive it.[14]

Standing between the two millenarian expectations is amillennialism, which repudiates every hope for a golden age on earth at some future point in world history. If a millennial hope is to have any validity, it must find its focal point above the present age (in the heavenly repose of martyred believers) or in the hearts of individual believers (in the experience of spiritual victory over evil). No golden age will come to humankind on earth, except perhaps as the partial triumph now enjoyed by the church in the midst of tribulation.

Unlike the millenarian outlooks, the amillennial world view cannot be derived from an expectation of a thousand years in history, whether beyond the catastrophic end of the present age (premillennialism) or as the result of the success of the gospel within this age (postmillennialism). Instead of finding a historical focus for the millennial hope, it is forced to relegate that hope to a sphere beyond time, whether in the heavenly abode of the righteous dead or in the inner spiritual life of the believer. Convinced of the truths found in pre- and postmillennialism but lacking their historical focal point, amillennialism is drawn to the ethos of each of the millenarian positions, while in the end rejecting both. It seeks to balance and blend the two into an ultimately nonmillenarian outlook.

The result is a world view characterized by realism. Victory and defeat, success and failure, good and evil will coexist until the end, amillennialism asserts. The future is neither a heightened continuation of the present nor an abrupt contradiction to it. The kingdom of God does not come by human cooperation with the divine power currently at work in the world, but neither is it simply the divine gift for which we can only wait expectantly.

Consequently, both unchastened optimism and despairing pessimism are illegitimate, amillennialism declares. Rather, the amillennialist world view calls the church to "realistic activity" in the world. Under the guidance and empowerment of the Holy Spirit the church will be successful in its mandate (postmillennialism); yet ultimate success will come only through God's grace (premillennialism). The kingdom of God arrives as the divine action breaking into the world (premillennialism); yet human cooperation brings important, albeit penultimate, results (postmillennialism). Therefore, the people of God must expect great things in the present; but knowing that the kingdom will never arrive in its fullness in history, they must always remain realistic in their expectations.

World View and Twentieth-Century Theologies

The discussion of eschatology among conservative theologians as delineated in the question of the millennium gives evidence to three basic out-looks toward the world—pessimism, optimism and realism. But this inter-play of moods is not limited to conservative theology. On the contrary, the basic orientations toward history and human involvement in history char-acteristic of the three millennial viewpoints—pessimism, optimism and realism—may be found in the movement of contemporary theology as well, even though all recent theologies would disavow the approach to Revela-tion 20 that lies at the basis of the argument among conservative thinkers.

In nineteenth-century America optimism flourished not only in the theological world dominated by evangelical postmillennialism, but also in society in general. This optimism was originally grounded in a theology of history, articulated by Puritan thinkers such as the eighteenth-century postmillennialist Jonathan Edwards, that anticipated a new day for the renewed church which in turn would spill over into the world.

As the nineteenth century unfolded, however, this church-centered op-timism was replaced by an optimism that focused on society. The dream for the truly reformed church was transformed into a blueprint for a new world order. What emerged was a secularized myth of redemptive history that viewed the American nation—the special beneficiary of God's prov-idential care—as the tutor of the family of nations in the pilgrimage to-ward the golden age on earth. When theological liberalism exchanged original sin for human perfectibility and replaced Christ as our substitute with Jesus as the model of the new human, the triumph of this-worldli-ness was complete and the way was open for the church to join the sec-ularized millennial vision.

The flowering of the utopian optimism of theological liberalism came with the social gospel movement. The salvation of souls gave way to the salvation of society. Hope for a better life beyond the grave was lost in the call for a better life in the here-and-now. Proponents of the social gospel were confident that the kingdom of God would soon dawn as the outwork-ing of their efforts to transform society. In effect, history had become self-redemptive.

After World War 1, however, a major shift in thinking occurred. As a result of the horrors of a war that by nineteenth-century expectations should not have occurred, the realism characteristic of amillennialism replaced the optimism of the previous century as the dominant mood in theology.

One example of the postwar emergence of amillennial realism lies in the widespread use of existentialist categories by many prominent theologians beginning in the 1920s and continuing for half a century. Although New Testament studies had rediscovered the centrality in the teaching of Jesus of the apocalyptic outlook toward history, many thinkers followed Rudolf Bultmann's lead and reinterpreted the futurist categories of the synoptic Gospels in existentialist terms. As a result Jesus' proclamation of a catastrophic action of God marking the climax of history was dehistoricized. His message was transposed from a word concerning the future of the world to a declaration about the private realm of the inner spirit of the individual believer. For Bultmann, "the end of the world" no longer could be understood in terms of human history. Instead the phrase meant the change from inauthentic existence to faith within the heart of the hearer of the proclamation.

In a sense, then, existentialist theology is a twentieth-century reformulation of the realism of classic amillennialism. Amillennialism transposes the millennial hope—the expectation of a golden age for humankind as a specific stage in world history—into a hope for the individual believer, whether beyond history in the intermediate state or as a spiritual victory enjoyed in the present. In the case of Bultmann and his followers, the millennial hope is sublimated into the experience of authentic living in each present moment of decision.

The realism of the amillennial world view is evident as well in the theology of Reinhold Niebuhr, who has been hailed as the most prominent American theologian of the twentieth century. Like that of other post-World War 1 theologians, Niebuhr's thinking grew out of a rejection of liberal optimism. Throughout his career he assailed the two articles of liberal faith: the idea of progress and the idea of the perfectibility of humankind.[15]

In reponse to what he saw as the naive optimism of liberalism, Niebuhr set forth what for him was a more balanced appraisal concerning the human situation in the world, which he termed "Christian realism." Regardless of our good intentions, we will never reach perfection in any dimension of life, he declared. In the realm of the real, the ideal always remains "the impossible possibility."[16] Hence, we ought not believe that our efforts will inaugurate the just human society; we can only hope to foster a more just situation.

Niebuhr's caution was based on what he saw as the realistic picture of human nature found in the Bible. In keeping with the Scriptures, he sought to emphasize the two-sidedness of the present human situation, which forms the human contradiction. We are created in the image of God but have fallen into sinfulness.

In the midst of the contradictions of the real situations of life Niebuhr found meaning in Christian eschatology, especially the symbol of the kingdom of God.[17] By standing over against history, God's kingdom forms a check on the human tendency toward self-assertion and pride. At the same time, this symbol discloses the meaning of history in the present, and consequently "eternity will fulfill and not annul" the present. This disclosure, in turn, forms the basis for a positive Christian witness in the world.[18]

Niebuhr's realism resembles that of amillennialism insofar as both are devoid of any expectation of a perfect human social order within history. Instead they relegate the ideal to the realm that transcends the historical. For both, the ideal always remains an impossible possibility. The realm of perfection lies beyond the world, in the kingdom of God above history.

After the middle of the twentieth century the realism of the theologies influenced by neo-orthodoxy began to give way to other moods. A momentary resurgence of optimism occurred in the secular theology popularized by Harvey Cox in the mid-1960s. However, of more lasting importance were certain themes set forth by several European thinkers, especially Jürgen Moltmann, under the rubric "theology of hope."

The most important discovery of Moltmann's early work was the orientation of the Bible to history—specifically, to the future, to eschatology—and its crucial implications for theology. According to Moltmann, modern theology had misunderstood this central biblical theme. In contrast to the claims of the existentialists, eschatology is not directed toward the sphere of individual existence, but proclaims a God who will do a new work on behalf of the world in the future, and thereby inspires hope in the present. This is the central orientation of the Bible, which is "the history book of God's promises," he argued.[19]

Theology, in turn, arises out of hope in the promises of the one Moltmann terms "the coming God."[20] Consequently, theology is an interpretation of the promissory history found in the Bible in order to provide an understanding of the present-day mission of the church in the world.

Despite the optimism that we could anticipate from this emphasis on hope, Moltmann's view actually displays dimensions of the basic pessimism that characterizes premillennialism. In fact, in one sense we could view Moltmann's theology of hope as marking a rejection of the realism of thinkers such as Bultmann and Niebuhr in favor of a type of premillennial pessimism. Of course, his is not a pessimism that foresees only doom and gloom in the future. Just as classic premillennialism looks beyond the horrors of the tribulation to the golden age to follow, the theology of hope looks beyond the present to the future of the "coming God."

However, Moltmann's theology was pessimistic in its understanding of the relationship of the divine future to the present. The future comes to us out of the divine reality and as the divine gift, he asserted. It does not arise from possibilities already inherent in the present.[21] The future, he pointed out, is not "that which is already pregnant in the present."[22] It cannot be derived simply by extrapolating from current realities. Rather than move from the present to the future, we must look from the future to the present and anticipate the future in the midst of our present existence.

We can perhaps understand Moltmann's point by observing how he conceives of the future as already present. Two examples—the divine promises and the divine reality—illustrate the movement from future to present so prominent in Moltmann's thinking. "A promise," he writes, "is a pledge that proclaims a reality which is not yet at hand."[23] The promise concerning God's future is present as the proclaimed word about the future. This word anticipates a new future and thereby commends us to seek that future.[24] God is likewise already present, yet not in the same way that the things in the world are, but only as the "coming one," as "future." God is present "in the way in which his future in promise and hope empowers the present," Moltmann declares.[25]

Moltmann's theology, therefore, resembles premillennialism in that it is basically pessimistic in its understanding of the relationship of the present to the future. Rather than being its fulfillment, the future contradicts the present. The kingdom of God does not arise as the completion of forces already at work in the present world. Rather, it comes from beyond and negates the present evil situation.

On the basis of his emphasis on the future, Moltmann did develop a theology for involvement in the present. In fact, he and his colleagues launched an activist approach that is often referred to as "political theology." Nevertheless, the activism spawned by Moltmann's thinking arises on basically premillennial (pessimistic) rather than postmillennial (optimistic) terms. Although we ought not simply to wait passively for the arrival of the future, according to Moltmann, we dare not confuse the glorious future of God with the fruit of our labors.[26] The promise of the future ought to motivate us to action in the present; yet in the final analysis the future does not come as the result of our doing. Instead, the future must break into the present and transform it. Only then does the reign of God, the "golden age," arrive.

Moltmann summarizes the relationship between present and future with this poignant description:

> One does not move to another country to find freedom and God. One remains where one is in order to correspond to the conditions of the coming kingdom of God through the renewal of the heart and by practical transformation of social circumstances. The front line of the ex-

odus is not emigration, but liberation through the transformation of the present. For in the present, where we always are, the powers of the past wrestle with the powers of the future, and fear and hope struggle for domination. By changing ourselves and the circumstances around us, by anticipating the future God, we emigrate out of the past into the future.[27]

In reaction to the pessimistic note sounded by the European theology of hope, the 1970s brought a bold reaffirmation of optimism. However, just as the rebirth of pessimism in contemporary theology sprang unexpectedly from Moltmann's emphasis on hope, so the return to optimism came from an unanticipated source. In the midst of a social situation that gave little cause for optimism—the poverty of the South American peasantry—arose liberation theology with its reassertion of the optimistic world view of the older postmillennialism.

Liberation theology was spawned as an attempt to meet a perceived theological crisis. Its early architects found that the European theology in which they had been schooled—even the political theology of Moltmann and other new lights—was unable to meet the challenges posed by the dire social and economic situation of Latin America.

The theologians of liberation agreed with the basic categories of the theology of hope. They shared its emphasis on world history as the realm of God's saving activity and its focus on the future as a constant overcoming of the present. But despite agreement on fundamental theological orientation, they lambasted their mentors for what the Latin Americans perceived to be the historical pessimism of the Europeans. The Continental theology with its philosophical orientation, liberationists argued, translated merely into a concern for right thinking, rather than into a zeal for right living. And in the end it produced no genuine commitment to working for radical change in society.

The basis for liberation theology's critique lies in the radical break from classical theological methodology it entails. The new approach declares that the theological enterprise rightly focuses not on questions of correct belief (orthodoxy) in the "ivory tower" of intellectual reflection, but on issues of correct activity (orthopraxis) in the "real world" context of the oppressed and their social situation. Theology is not the quest for correct thinking about the nature of ultimate reality in response to the challenge of unbelief. Rather, it is the explication of the nature of God in the light of the oppressed people of the world with the goal of alleviating their miserable plight. Its purpose is to transform the world, specifically, to humanize the oppressed by changing those economic, social and political shackles that keep them in servitude to the oppressor.[28]

In this sense liberation theology constitutes a revival of the historical optimism of postmillennialism. Of course, theologians of liberation readily acknowledge the truth found in the basic tenet of premillennialism, namely, that the kingdom of God stands in judgment on the present situation in the world and in that sense the future ideal contradicts the present reality. Nevertheless, their vision of the kingdom as the realm of full liberation and humanization causes them to move beyond seeing the future only as a contradiction to the present. Rather, liberation theologians focus on the presence of the liberating power of God in the world today. And they invite the church to stand together with God, to become involved in God's liberating activity by joining forces with movements of liberation now happening in the world.

With its employment of Marxist categories as a grid for understanding the Latin American situation, liberation theology is wedded to the political left. Postmillennial optimism, however, has also been expressed in newer, theologically conservative movements as well. Among Pentecostals this rebirth of postmillennialism has carried the banner of the "kingdom now" theology. Perhaps more significant, however, has been the politically conservative social-theological movement, which emerged in the 1970s and 1980s under the banner of "Christian reconstructionism," or "dominion theology," described in chapter three. Just as liberation theology arose in part as a response to the European theology of hope, reconstructionism came in part as a response to the dominance of dispensationalism within American evangelicalism.

These contemporary examples illustrate the importance and resiliency of the deeper theological moods that lie at the foundation of the designations pre-, post- and amillennial. Beyond the academic question concerning the proper exegesis of the vision of the thousand years found in Revelation 20 is the more practical question concerning the mood or world view that ought to characterize the church of Jesus Christ as it seeks to fulfill its mandate in the world. As we look for an answer to this question, we must turn our attention, in a final chapter, to the nature and purpose of eschatology.

8

OUR PRESENT
IN THE LIGHT
OF GOD'S FUTURE

The Significance of
Corporate Eschatology

*T*hroughout church history the question of the chronology of the
end—especially as it relates to the nature and placement of the millennium—has been a major point of debate in eschatology. However, the actual
order of the events associated with the Lord's return is not, in and of itself,
the most significant dimension of the biblical teaching concerning the
consummation. Underlying the major millennial positions is a disagreement concerning fundamental world view or attitude toward history. Consequently, the question of the chronology of the end ought not to be given
center stage in theological reflection, for it simply does not deal with the
deeper issue of theological mood that is at stake.

Not only does the focus on chronology not address the crucial issue of attitude toward history, it does not reflect the fundamental nature and purpose of corporate eschatology. Eschatology, the doctrine of the inauguration of the kingdom and the consummation of history in the reign of God, is more than an outline of the scenario of the end. Often unfortunately overshadowed by the discussion of "the correct order" of future events is a deeper reality to which eschatology seeks to point. To this deeper level of the message of eschatology we now must turn.

Eschatology as Insight into the Present

To assist us in understanding what constitutes a truly biblical eschatology and consequently to draw some conclusions as to what eschatological orientation ought to characterize our outlook, we must raise the question of the actual purpose of biblical eschatology. What does the Bible intend to teach by the orientation toward the future that flows through its pages?

One basic thrust of the eschatological orientation of the New Testament as it builds from that of the Old seeks to mediate to the people of God insight into the significance of the age in which we are living. Such insight arises as the present is viewed in the light of the God who is sovereign over history. Biblical eschatology offers this insight in that it speaks of the consummation of the kingdom of the triune God. In fact, eschatology is closely linked to the consummation of the kingdom of God. At its center is the message concerning the coming into being of the fullness of God's rule. A panorama of the nature of the biblical teaching concerning the reign of God may bring this aspect of eschatology into clearer focus.

When viewed from the perspective of the Bible, one central theme of history is the question of ultimate sovereignty. Is the Creator Lord over creation? Or is the universe self-existing and autonomous? The first human attempt to answer this question, which came in the Fall, offered a negative response. Adam and Eve acted in willful defiance of divine command, thereby denying God's sovereignty. To this day humans continue the attempt to manage their own lives apart from God, that is, to affirm themselves, rather than God, as lord of their own destinies.

In salvation history, however, God moves to reassert divine rulership in the face of human rebellion and estrangement. According to the Bible, the focal point of God's action is the Christ event. At his first advent, Jesus of Nazareth proclaimed through his life, death and resurrection the sovereign rulership of God. Yet the story remains incomplete. The conclusion of the drama of salvation history must speak of the consolidation of the universal rule of God on earth.

The final chapter demanded by the narrative is broad in scope. While focusing on the participation of individual humans, the climax of God's historical activity moves beyond the purely individual dimension to include society. And it must also entail the consummation of the divine victory over the cosmic powers of the universe and even the power of death itself.

According to the New Testament the consummation of the divine program for history—the climax to the story—lies still in the future, specifically, at the return of Jesus as the triumphant Lord of history. That event will establish the universal rulership of God, in that it will entail the public display of the lordship of Jesus, the Son, who came as the bearer of the claim of God the Father to universal sovereignty. However, the future display of Christ's lordship—the yet future conclusion of the story—has already been declared in history before the end, specifically through the resurrection of Jesus from the dead. Knowing this, we can boldly assert that, although its consummation remains future, the reign of God has indeed broken into human history.

Since the coming of Christ, therefore, we have been living in the in-between age, the time between the inauguration of the kingdom and its consummation. Our age—the present chapter in the history of the world—lying as it does between the two advents of Christ, points toward the consummation of the already inaugurated kingdom.

Eschatology articulates this understanding of our present in the light of God's future. Because it proclaims the truth that one day the now incomplete universal rule of God will arrive in its fullness, the message of eschatology is a hope-producing promise that provides insight into the nature of our age. We are living in the time of the already and the not-yet. The reign of God has broken into our world in a decisive fashion. Yet the consummation of the divine rule lies still in the future. For that day we wait expectantly, and in the light of that day we seek to fulfill our divinely given mandate in the world.

Because of their awareness of the significance of the present in the light of the future, those who acknowledge the lordship of Christ seek throughout this epoch to proclaim in word and action by the power of the Holy Spirit the good news about the reign of God. Thereby they participate in the expansion of the rule of God on earth. But there is more to come. This present age will one day reach its climax in the consummation of the kingdom, the complete reign of God over the redeemed and transformed creation. This expectation is the theme of eschatology.

By providing insight into the significance of the present age, eschatology sets forth a special understanding of the significance of history. One fundamental outlook toward the flow of time widely held in religious traditions declares that the historical process is an unending cycle of meaningless repetition, so that meaning can be found only through an escape from history to the realm of timelessness above the sequence of events. Biblical eschatology, in contrast, asserts that history is meaningful because it is directed toward an end, a goal that lies at its conclusion and gives meaning to the whole.

In addition to declaring that history is meaningful, the Christian faith boldly asserts the unparalleled claim that this climactic goal of history is already known, for it has been disclosed before the end in Jesus of Nazareth. Jesus—this historical life—belongs to the eternity of God and is the key to the meaning of history. The future consummation, therefore, is nothing else but the public disclosure of Jesus of Nazareth as the focal point of the historical process.[1] Once again we are led to conclude that the present era is the in-between time, the age between his first coming and the public acknowledgment of his glory as the center of history (the Logos).

As a result of its declaration of this theme, eschatology—the word concerning the consummation of the already inaugurated divine rule at the return of Christ—is a message of hope for the Christian. Because it proclaims that faith in Jesus as the meaning of history (the Logos, or the Word) will one day be publicly confirmed, this message means that the people of faith are rightfully a people of hope. We live with assured confidence concerning the outcome of history and our participation in the eternal reign of God.

In the same way, eschatology declares that not only for the world but also for the faith community the present age is the era of the already and not-yet. The Christian has tasted the goodness of the eternal kingdom and even now participates in the reign of God. For this reason the disciple is called to offer joyful obedience to the God of the future. At the same time, the church has not entered into the fullness of God's universal rule. Therefore, the community of the faithful must avoid all triumphalism.

The New Testament takes this matter one step further. As the in-between time, the present era is the last days. In fact, since the ascension of Jesus the world has been living in the last days, an age characterized by two opposite tendencies. On the one hand, ours is the time of tribulation and antichrist. As John declares, "You have heard the antichrist is coming, even now many antichrists have come. This is how we know it is the last hour" (1 Jn 2:18; see also 2 Jn 7). But in the midst of tribulation, the church of Jesus Christ moves forth triumphantly under the banner of the cross. Because the church acts under mandate from the risen Lord (Mt 28:19-20), the very gates of Hades cannot prevail against it (Mt 16:18), and the gospel works like leaven in the world (Mt 13:33).

Eschatology provides the world-view framework, insight into the nature of the present age in the light of God's future, for the proclamation and spread of the gospel in the world today.

Eschatology as a Call in the Present

The purpose of eschatology is to provide insight into the significance of the present age in the light of God's action in Christ and in the light of God's future. As such it issues a multifaceted call in the present. This call arises insofar as looking to the future consummation of the kingdom of God leads to authoritative speaking in the present situation. Believers who understand God's future intentions for the world both hear and proclaim God's word in the present, for they realize that God's future has implications for life now.

The dimension of eschatology as call in the present in the light of God's future may be illumined by an understanding of the nature of Old Testament prophecy, out of which New Testament eschatology arose. Among the ancient Hebrews, prophecy was a twofold activity. The prophet would foretell future events and "forthtell" the message of God. These two dimensions did not stand on equal footing, however, for the predictive component was subservient to the declarative. That is, the focus of the prophetic ministry lay in the proclamation of the message of God in the present, not in the prediction of the future. In fact, true prophets of God never foretold future events simply in order to tickle the imagination of Israel. Rather, their disclosure of the coming actions of God served always to form the basis for the issuance of a call to action and obedience in the present.

In its essence, then, prophecy is the utilization of a word concerning God's future in order to speak God's call (the word of God) to the present. The message of the prophet followed a familiar pattern: "Because God is going to do this, you must now respond to God in this way."

In the same way the purpose of biblical eschatological declarations is not merely to speak about the details of the future. Rather, eschatology is the attempt to employ the truth concerning the future consummation in order to issue God's call (the Word of God) in the present. As G. C. Berkouwer has rightly said, "Eschatology is not a projection into the distant future; it bursts forth into our present existence, and structures life today in the light of the last days."[2]

This purpose, employing the word concerning the future consummation of the inaugurated kingdom in order to speak the word of God in the present, clarifies the task of eschatology. Its goal is not the discovery of those events which must come to pass in the end times, in order thereby to satisfy our human curiosity. Rather, eschatology's task is to challenge the hearts of people today in the light of God's future and the destined future of the world.

Jesus is the greatest example of this manner of speaking. According to Mark the central thrust of his message focused on the proper response of his hearers in view of the action of God: "The kingdom of God is near. Repent and believe the good news" (Mk 1:15). In essence Jesus was declaring, "We are now at a crucial junction of history. God is acting to assert his claim to rulership. Therefore, turn from your sins and accept the good news." In keeping with the pattern of Jesus and the prophets, eschatology issues a call to response in the present in the light of God's future.

One dimension entailed in the eschatological message is a call to zeal in worldwide evangelism. Jesus' own proclamation is crucial in this context: "And this gospel of the kingdom will be preached in the whole world . . . and then the end will come" (Mt 24:14). The purpose of this prophecy is not to encourage the Lord's disciples to enter into discussions of questions of time and chronology. Rather, this word from the Lord intends to instill confidence in us as we fulfill our mandate under the authority of Christ. The church will complete its task of carrying the good news throughout the world, Jesus has promised. Knowledge of this ought to produce in us zealous involvement in the evangelism mandate (see also Mt 28:19-20; Acts 1:8). We can commit ourselves to the proclamation of the gospel because we know full well that this task will be accomplished before the end comes.

The ministry of the apostle Paul offers a vivid example of this principle. His expectation of the eschatological salvation of Israel motivated Paul to zealous engagement in evangelism. In fact, this eschatological perspective formed a basis for Paul's entire philosophy of missions (Rom 9:1-3; 10:1; 11:13-14, 25-32). The apostle was zealous for the gospel in part because he believed that his mission to the Gentiles would result in the salvation of his people, Israel, before the return of Christ. Likewise, this vision formed the basis for his admonition to the Gentiles to avoid arrogance (Rom 11:17-22). God was allowing salvation to come to them, Paul said, in order that the Jews might become jealous. Therefore, rather than become puffed up, they ought humbly to accept God's salvation.

In addition to being a call to zealous evangelism in the light of the end, eschatology is a call to holiness and right living. Repeatedly the New

Testament sounds the alarm concerning the end of history and the eschatological judgment. This message, however, is not intended so much to offer data for charts depicting the chronology of future events as to produce proper conduct in the present.

Jesus himself linked eschatological truth to the importance of right living. In the parables of readiness in the Mount Olivet Discourse, for example, he clearly declared that the future coming of the Son of man demands prepared watchfulness on the part of his disciples (Mt 24:45— 25:46). And in their preaching and writing his disciples followed his lead.

Peter describes the proper response to the message concerning the consummation of history in terms of "sane and sober living" in the present: "The end of all things is near. Therefore be clear minded and self-controlled so that you can pray." He then elaborates concerning the meaning of such living in view of the end. It includes love for other believers, the practice of hospitality, and the use of spiritual gifts (1 Pet 4:7-11). Paul employs imagery from light and darkness in his admonition to the Roman believers to "understand the present time." Because "the night is nearly over" and "the day is almost here," Christians are to live accordingly. They should "put aside the deeds of darkness and put on the armor of light" (Rom 13:11-14). According to John, knowledge of the soon return of Jesus forms a call to purity: "What we will be has not yet been made known. But we know that when he appears, we shall be like him, for we shall see him as he is. Everyone who has this hope in him purifies himself, just as he is pure" (1 Jn 3:2-3).

In addition to encouraging zealous evangelism and demanding holiness and preparedness in the lives of believers, as the message concerning God's future, eschatology issues a call to courage and steadfastness. To this end it reports both encouraging and discouraging news. In this era the church will continually face tragedy, persecution and false prophets. This dark message means steadfast loyalty to Christ is required; those who belong to the Lord must stand firm despite persecution and apostasy in the world, because he will one day return in judgment (Mt 24—25; 2 Thess 2:13-17). But eschatology also enjoins steadfast loyalty through the joyous events it reports. It speaks of future resurrection and victory over death. This news provides motivation to courageous involvement in the tasks given us by the Lord.

Paul's great chapter on the resurrection forms an example of the employment of the message concerning the future to issue a call to steadfastness in the present. After discussing the nature of the resurrected body and presenting proofs concerning its reality, Paul concludes with a resounding call for action in the present: "Therefore, my beloved brethren, be steadfast, unmovable, always abounding in the work of the Lord for you know that your labors in the Lord are not in vain" (1 Cor 15:58 KJV). Hence, Paul does not articulate the grand promise concerning our future resurrection to stimulate curiosity about dates and places. Rather, his intent is to encourage steadfast involvement in the work of the Lord, for he knows that present action carries eternal consequences. This is eschatology at its biblical best: the message concerning God's future becomes the vehicle for the proclamation of the word of God in the present.

Eschatology as Chronology Plus Message

The fundamental intent of eschatology is to provide insight into the present age in view of God's future and on that basis to issue a call in the present. But this primary purpose does not necessarily negate the desire sensed throughout Christian history to establish from the Bible the correct chronology of the end. On the contrary, the expansion of God's program throughout the church age raises the question of its final, future consolidation. But how are we to evaluate this desire in view of the primary task of eschatology?

That the future expectation in biblical eschatology leads to some sense of chronology is undeniable. The authors of Scripture do set forth events that must transpire in the future. Such discourse is not surprising, for it arises naturally out of both the New Testament conception of the eschatological nature of the present era and the confession of Christ's lordship.

Lying behind the writings of the New Testament is the presupposition that the world has entered a special, eschatological era. This age is bounded on the one side by the Christ event (the advent, life, death, resurrection and ascension of Jesus of Nazareth and the outpouring of the Holy Spirit) and on the other side by the consummation (the return of Christ in victory and judgment). When viewed from the Old Testament perspective of promise, this is the time of fulfillment, the New Testament argues (for example, 1 Pet 1:10-12). It is "the last days," the final era before the consummation of God's activity in the world.

The presupposition of the importance of the age between the ascension and the consummation leads to certain expectations concerning what must characterize these years. The Bible presents this as a two-sided time period. One dimension is discouraging. Our age will witness a regrouping of the forces of evil. Persecution, heresy, deception and seduction will increase as the Evil One mounts an onslaught against the message of God's universal rule. The enemy will seek to resist the advancement of the church into the domain of darkness and to neutralize the ranks of the church. The marshaling of the forces of evil will not be without effect, for many will fall away, be deceived or lose heart. At the same time, however, the biblical characterization is a cause for hope. This era will be marked by the progress of the gospel. The Spirit-empowered church will complete its mandate before the end comes.

The New Testament indicates that the early Christians believed that the two basic dimensions that will characterize the entire era between the advents were already visible. The forces of evil were already regrouping, and the gospel was progressing throughout the world. According to the New Testament authors, these events constitute signs that the special eschatological age has indeed dawned. Because they believed that the last days were already upon the world (1 Jn 2:18-19), the early Christians were filled with expectations concerning the future. Certain events were soon to transpire, they knew. These events formed some sort of chronological sequence. The expectation concerning future events that characterized the outlook of the early church arises likewise from the confession of the universal lordship of Christ. The New Testament sets forth the significance of that fundamental Christian affirmation. If Jesus is Lord, then he must be Lord over every power in the universe. But this means that the eschaton must be a real historical event. The day must come when Jesus acts to vindicate those who now proclaim his lordship and to exercise dominion over every cosmic power. One day he must bring victory not only over those who persecute the church but also over every power hostile to humankind, including our great cosmic enemy, death. Because of their hope for this victory, the apostles viewed the return of Christ to raise the dead as *the* crucial future event.

The presence of this future expectation in New Testament eschatology suggests that we may legitimately speak of an eschatological timetable. Central to the biblical chronology are events such as a final onslaught of evil and the victorious return of Christ, together with our resurrection and eternal presence with him.

But any construction of a future chronology demands that we understand properly the nature of all eschatological language. We must understand eschatological events in the context of the New Testament emphasis on eschatology as insight into the present in the light of God's future. They are not isolated incidents that together form a time line, a series of mileposts that the flow of history passes one after the other and that therefore form an "end-times checklist." One cannot simply look at the events of history and thereby determine what part of the distance from the first coming to the second has been traversed. On the contrary, the New Testament says the end is always at hand.

In short, all eschatological events must be understood in the context of sound biblical theology. They are not mere brute facts of a not yet attained history (history written before the time). Instead, they are expressions of hope. In Greek, the original language of the New Testament documents, hope entails expectation and certainty. Hence, as expressions of hope— that is, of anticipation concerning what must certainly transpire—eschatological assertions are fundamentally statements of grounded expectation, based on an understanding of the nature of reality, history and present experience.

The future expectation in biblical eschatology allows the believer to speak of future events as expressions of hope. But in so doing we must not overlook the dimension of contingency present in world events. It is certain that the Lord will return and the eschatological consummation will be realized. At the same time, the future is to some degree open. God has a program for the world, but many details are not fixed. Consequently, we may see creation as in some sense an experiment guided by God. It includes risks. War may lead to a doomsday holocaust, for example; or our misuse of the environment may usher in an ecological disaster.

Perhaps the experimental nature of creation provides insight into the nature of God and God's relationship with creation. For example, it may form in part the basis for the divine joy. Some do respond to God's love. In their lives, the experiment is successful. And all heaven celebrates this success: "There will be more rejoicing in heaven over one sinner who repents than over ninety-nine righteous persons who do not need to repent" (Lk 15:7).

But in the same way, the experimental nature of creation opens a window on the divine sorrow. Some people choose not to be gathered into the kingdom. The suffering of the Christ who in life and death revealed to us the heart of God displays the divine sorrow that arises when sinful humans reject the love of God. Just as the failure of some of God's creatures to respond to Jesus' ministry resulted in his suffering and death (see Mt 23:37-39), so also God grieves over all those who reject his love (Is 65:2).

The openness of the future carries another important implication. Human beings are called to participate in the future. God's future will surely come, but we are invited to be involved in that coming future and in God's historical work in bringing it into the present. This theme is evident, for example, in Peter's admonition to his readers to hasten the day of the Lord (2 Pet 3:12).

Our involvement in the work of consummation is motivated by eschatologically inspired hope. God has set before us a vision of the coming kingdom. Evangelism is a key aspect of this program, for alienated sinners must hear the good news of God's reconciliation so that they too can participate in his reign. Because the kingdom of God is a society of love, righteousness and justice, social action must also be a part of the church's agenda. In all of this, our knowing that God stands in the future beckoning us onward provides a source of hope. In hope we can direct our efforts— which include our prayers[3] and our actions—toward the advance of God's reign on earth. We can be steadfast in our efforts at each step en route to the consummation (1 Cor 15:58).

In the final analysis, this is the message that stands at the foundation of the millennial debate.

Eschatological Living and the Millennial Debate

The question of the nature and time of the millennium envisioned by the seer of the Apocalypse has been debated, rehashed and rehearsed *ad nauseam* within evangelicalism. Having grown tired of the disagreements and speculations about matters that only the future will resolve, many believers are disdainful of eschatology in its entirety. How often have Christians repeated the glib, even ignorant, response: "I'm a panmillennialist. I believe it will all pan out in the end." Such simplistic dismissal of the discussion merely fails to understand the importance of the world-view issues at stake.

Which position, then, is the correct one? The answer to this question is dependent on the level of the discussion of the millennium that we are querying. As long as our focus remains solely on the quest for the correct interpretation of the thousand years of Revelation 20, it is unlikely that we will ever reach unanimity. We can at best only offer educated conjectures as to what exactly the seer was envisioning, none of which is likely to win universal agreement.

Throughout its history, the church as a whole has displayed true wisdom in consistently refusing to endow any one millennial view with the status of orthodoxy. Those within evangelicalism who are tempted to break fellowship with believers with whom they disagree on this matter or to make one millennial view a standard for congregational membership ought to take heed to the counsel of the Christian tradition at this point.

But we have seen that there is a deeper level of discussion beneath the surface of the millennial issue. More important than speculation concerning the chronology of the end time is the question of how we as the church of Jesus Christ understand ourselves and our mission in the present age. In this matter we can be instructed by all participants in the debate about the millennium.

Apart from whether or not it is a correct theological system, dispensationalism has made a crucial contribution by emphasizing the importance of eschatology. In the words of George Eldon Ladd, "To all intents and purposes it revived the doctrine of the Second Advent of Christ and made it a meaningful truth in the churches."[4] This reminder developed at a time when much of the church had directed its attention away from the "blessed hope" and toward the progress that appeared to be resulting from human attempts to better the world. Dispensationalism has resolutely refused to allow the people of God to forget that they remain at all times a pilgrim people and that the ultimate hope for the world rests with the return of the risen Lord.

In this sense dispensationalism has more nearly paralleled developments in modern theology than have its evangelical alternatives. Beginning in the late nineteenth century, when liberalism interpreted the biblical concept of the kingdom of God in terms of the fellowship of the ethically minded, modern biblical scholarship rediscovered the apocalyptic dimension of the biblical outlook, even though it took theology nearly three-fourths of a century to digest the implications of this discovery. In a somewhat parallel manner, at a time when evangelicals were interested in settling in while living on the earth, dispensationalism reintroduced the evangelical community to the apocalyptic literature of the Bible and the apocalyptic view of history, and it prodded evangelicals to take seriously the biblical expectations concerning the consummation of history.

With its emphasis on the restructuring of the world in the millennium, dispensationalism has offered an implicit and sometimes overlooked reminder that the vision of the kingdom of God has a social as well as an individual dimension. The dispensational scenario anticipates a time when the nation of Israel will be renewed according to the biblical model and thereby become a light to the nations, who will worship the God of the patriarchs under the shepherding of the reigning Christ. Although the details of this vision are open to debate, the hope for a day when all human society will be ordered according to the principles of the reign of Christ is surely not misplaced.

In addition to reintroducing apocalyptic, dispensationalism has reopened the question of the future role of Israel in God's program. This important reminder shattered the brash conclusion of most Christians that because the church is the new Israel God had forever forgotten the old Israel. Dispensationalists, however, set forth the bold thesis that the church and Israel remain two distinct entities in God's program. Consequently, they held out a hope for a renewal of the importance of Israel in the divine program for history. The older dispensationalism may have gone too far in the direction of proposing two distinct peoples and two distinct programs of salvation, as some of its contemporary adherents have come to admit,[5] but its proponents were the harbingers of things to come in theology.

In reopening the issue of the continuing role of the Jews in God's program, dispensationalism anticipated a mood that developed in modern theology during the final third of the twentieth century. A broad spectrum of thinkers—architects of Jewish-Christian dialogs, Christian Zionists[6] and mainline theologians[7]—all came to articulate a thesis that resembled the teaching of dispensationalism concerning the Old Testament people of God: The church has not replaced Israel to the extent that the Jews are no longer to be spoken of as God's chosen people. Rather, the Jews— perhaps even the state of Israel—have lasting theological significance. Christian theology, therefore, must take the continued existence of this older covenant people of God with greater seriousness than they have often done in the past.[8]

More important for evangelicals, dispensationalism's central tenet of a distinction between Israel and the church reopened the discussion of Israel even among amillennialists.[9] Many have come to the conclusion that the apostle Paul himself did indeed anticipate a great eschatological conversion of Jews to their Messiah. Under the prodding of dispensationalists, therefore, evangelicals have gained a new hope for Israel. Many nondispensationalists now anticipate an ingathering of Jews into the church, the stage for which is perhaps being set before our eyes through the rebirth of the state of Israel and the ongoing tensions in the Middle East. Even if we must conclude that a biblically inspired hope for Israel only can be focused on their inclusion into the church of Yeshua Messiah, we must be grateful to dispensationalism for refusing to allow us to discount Israel.

Beyond the contributions of dispensationalism lay the insights mediated by the other participants in the millennial debate. These theological discussions have been fruitful in that from them a basic consensus concerning corporate eschatology has emerged. Most scholars now agree that eschatology focuses primarily on the kingdom of God. They also speak of this kingdom as in some sense both a present and a future reality. Consequently, many biblical scholars characterize ours as the time of the already and the not-yet. The millennial views all have important points to make concerning this eschatological living.

As we live in the in-between time—the era between the two advents of Christ—we need to listen to each of the three major millennial views, for each voice comprises a dimension of "what the Spirit is saying to the churches." On the one hand, each speaks a word of caution. Historically, the self-perception of the people of God has been an important factor in determining which millennial view would predominate among them. As Stanley N. Gundry notes, "Time and again there seems to be a connection between eschatology and the Church's perception of itself in its historical situation," so much so that "eschatologies have been a reflection of the current mood or *Zeitgeist*."[10] We must be cautioned by the various voices, lest our eschatological view be nothing more than a reflection of the mood of the times in which we live.

On the other hand, beyond being a cautionary word each position sets forth a world view worthy of incorporation into life. In fact, it is imperative for us as Christians to sense the heartbeat of these foundational theological moods. Each offers insight into the mind of the Spirit that transcends them all.

Postmillennialism is the voice of the Spirit calling us to confident engagement. The mood of optimism with which this eschatological orientation oozes drives us ever onward as we realize that our efforts are linked with the program of God.

The optimism of postmillennialism derives from two foundational truths. First, in the final analysis, God is sovereign over history and is actively engaged in bringing his sovereign goal to pass. Our knowledge of this truth should encourage us, for we know that in the cosmic battle we have joined the cause that will in the end be victorious. But second, this same God has invited us—through Christ has even *commissioned* us—to participate in the advance of the divine reign. Knowing that we act under the authority of the King himself we ought to be motivated to redouble our commitment to work and pray, in order that his kingdom indeed come, his will be done on earth as it is in heaven.

Postmillennialism invites us to look beyond what may from time to time appear to be the downward spiral of events and perceive the grander, heavenly reality that forms the context for our ongoing mission in the world. In the words of John Jefferson Davis, "In the postmillennial framework the key to the church's hope is faith in the sovereignty of God and the power of the Spirit, not in world conditions as such."[11] This courage-producing message is the admonition that the Spirit is speaking to the church today through postmillennial eschatology.

As nineteenth-century American theological history so aptly demonstrates, left unbridled, postmillennial optimism runs the risk of separating itself from its proper source and thereby degenerating into blind utopianism. The awareness of our role in cooperating with the God of history can easily lead to a sense that we are the determiners of our history. And the proclamation of the kingdom of God as the goal of historical activity can unfortunately be transformed into efforts to produce the kingdom of God within history.

Consequently, in the midst of our confident acceptance of our mandate, we need to hear what the Spirit is saying to the churches through the pessimistic tone of premillennial eschatologies. Simply stated, premillennialism reminds us that ultimately it is God, and not our feeble actions, who is the hope of the world.

Finally, amillennial realism lifts our sights above the merely historical future to the realm of the eternal God. It reminds us that the kingdom of God is a transcendent reality that can be confused with no earthly kingdom prior to the final transformation of creation. No earthly city can ever hope to become the New Jerusalem, except through a radical transformation both of human nature itself and of the universe that through the Fall unwillingly participates in the human predicament. Not only "we ourselves, who have the firstfruits of the Spirit," but even creation itself groans, longing to "be liberated from its bondage to decay and brought into the glorious freedom of the children of God" (Rom 8:20-23).

Because of the cosmic dimensions of the vision of corporate eschatology, our ultimate goal is not a golden age on earth, whether preceding or following the return of Christ. Rather, we await with eager anticipation a glorious eternal reality, the new heaven and new earth. This alone forms the complete fulfillment of the promises of land and physical blessings given to the ancient people of God and the promise of the fullness of our participation in eternal life proclaimed in the New Testament. Only with the coming of the gloriously re-created cosmos will God make his dwelling with us. And only on the redeemed and transformed creation will we experience full community with nature, with each other and, most important, with God our Creator and Redeemer.

This radically transcendent kingdom is at the same time radically immanent.[12] God has broken into our world. And he has brought us into participation in his already inaugurated explosion into the earthly realm. Therefore, in the midst of the brokenness of life we can celebrate the new life of the Spirit.

Early in the twentieth century, the great Southern Baptist theologian E. Y. Mullins admonished his readers to maintain a balanced perspective. On the one hand, we should cultivate the New Testament attitude of expectancy, Mullins said, always looking for the Lord "because he commanded it, and because we love him and trust him, and because all the future would be blank without him." At the same time, he cautioned against becoming "absorbed in apocalyptic calculations and speculations. We should not be so assured of the program of the unrevealed future that we 'begin to beat our fellow servants' because they do not accept our particular interpretation. We should not attempt to fix dates or insist too greatly upon detailed programs." Rather than following either extreme, the theologian enjoined believers to faithfulness in every dimension of our Christian duty:

> We should ever watch against temptation and pray for divine strength. We should cultivate a passion for righteousness, individual and social. We should work while it is day, knowing that the night cometh when no man can work. We should be so eager for the coming of our Lord, that if he should come to-morrow we would not be taken by surprise. We should so hold ourselves in restraint, that if his return should be delayed a thousand or ten thousand years, we would not be disappointed. And our hearts should be ever filled with joy at the prospect of his coming and the certain triumph of his kingdom.[13]

The eternal reign of God has dawned, is dawning and will one day dawn in its consummated fullness. The God who has reconciled us to himself through Christ will one day bring us into full participation in the grand eschatological community of his divine reign. This is the vision that should inspire us in this in-between era to seek to be a kingdom people now and to proclaim now in word and deed the good news of the coming eternal reign of God.

Corporate eschatology, with its vision of God's glorious program for history, confronts the church with a grave question: Will we as the church be motivated by the vision of God's ultimate future to be about the Lord's business in the present era until Christ comes in glory and splendor?

Notes

Introduction

[1]"Fifty Quitting Jobs, Getting Ready to Be Lifted to Heaven June 28," *Winnipeg Free Press*, June 3, 1981.

[2]"The Faithful Fall for Another Far-fetched Fable," *Christianity Today* 25/6 (March 27, 1981): 54, 56.

[3]"Prepare for Messiah, Lubavitch Sect Says," *Vancouver Sun*, August 30, 1991, p. E5.

[4]D. H. Kromminga, *The Millennium in the Church* (Grand Rapids, Mich.: Eerdmans, 1945), p. 117.

[5]Ernest R. Sandeen, *The Roots of Fundamentalism: British and American Millenarianism, 1800—1930* (Chicago: University of Chicago Press, 1970), p. 59.

Chapter 1: The Nearness of the End

[1]Christopher Lasch, *The Culture of Narcissism: American Life in an Age of Diminishing Expectations* (New York: Norton, 1978), p. 3.

[2]As quoted by Robert Jewett, "Coming to Terms with the Doom Boom," *Quarterly Review* 4/3 (Fall 1984): 9, who cites the *Chicago Sun-Times*, October 29, 1983.

[3]See, for example, Ernest Lee Tuveson, *Millennium and Utopia*, Harper Torchbooks edition (New York: Harper and Row, 1964), p. 1.

[4]Klaus Koch, *The Rediscovery of Apocalyptic* (London: SCM, 1972), pp. 67-68.

[5]Many thinkers have noted this characteristic of the contemporary *Zeitgeist*. See, for example, Paul D. Hanson, "Introduction," in *Visionaries and Their Apocalypses*, ed. Paul D. Hanson, Issues in Religion and Theology, number 4 (Philadelphia: Fortress, 1983), p. 3. See also Hanson's article, "Old Testament Apocalyptic Reexamined," p. 37.

[6]Robert Jay Lifton, *Boundaries: Five Talks for CBC Radio* (Toronto: Miracle Press, 1967), p. 43. See also Henri Nouwen, *The Wounded Healer: Ministry in Contemporary Society* (Garden City, N.Y.: Doubleday, 1972), pp. 12-14.

[7]Lasch, *Culture of Narcissism,* p. 7.

[8]For a succinct overview of the development of scholarship concerning apocalyptic, see Hanson, "Introduction," pp. 4-6.

[9]For a recent discussion, see Koch, *Rediscovery of Apocalyptic,* pp. 18-35. This chapter is reprinted as Klaus Koch, "What Is Apocalyptic? An Attempt as a Preliminary Definition," in *Visionaries,* pp. 16-36.

[10]For a recent discussion of certain of these themes, see Koch, *Rediscovery of Apocalyptic,* pp. 28-33.

[11]H. H. Rowley, *The Relevance of Apocalyptic,* 2d edition (London: Lutterworth, 1947), p. 165.

[12]Ibid., p. 151.

[13]See, for example, the *Book of the Secrets of Enoch,* an Egyptian-Jewish apocalyptic writing of the first century A.D. This work may have been the first to use the "creation-day world-age" theory as the basis for conceiving of the messianic kingdom as lasting a thousand years. R. H. Charles, *Eschatology: The Doctrine of a Future Life in Israel, Judaism and Christianity,* revised edition (New York: Schocken, 1963), p. 315; 2d edition originally published in 1913.

[14]Rowley, *Relevance of Apocalyptic,* p. 155.

[15]Ibid., p. 35.

[16]Ibid., p. 170.

[17]See, for example, the conclusion of Jonathan Z. Smith, "Wisdom and Apocalyptic," reprinted in *Visionaries,* p. 115. Michael E. Stone also states this conclusion in "New Light on the Third Century," reprinted in *Visionaries,* p. 99.

[18]See, for example, Gerhard von Rad, *Old Testament Theology,* 2 vols. (New York: Harper and Row, 1965), pp. 301-8.

[19]Smith, "Wisdom and Apocalyptic," p. 115.

[20]Hanson attributes the genesis of this thesis to the work of Friedrich Luecke in 1832. Hanson, "Introduction," p. 5. See also Charles, *Eschatology,* pp. 173-206; Rowley, *Relevance of Apocalyptic,* pp. 13-14, 35.

[21]Hanson, "Introduction," p. 6.

[22]Rowley, *Relevance of Apocalyptic,* p. 14.

[23]Hanson, "Old Testament Apocalyptic Reexamined," p. 58.

[24]See, for example, Charles, *Eschatology,* pp. 247-48.

[25]See ibid., pp. 209-10, 245-51.

[26]Ibid., pp. 210, 245.

[27]Ibid., pp. 248, 250-51.

[28]Ibid., pp. 289-90.

[29]For a window into the current discussion of this issue, see T. Francis Glasson, "The Temporary Messianic Kingdom and the Kingdom of God," *Journal of Theological Studies* 41/2 (1990): 517-25.

Chapter 2: Anticipating the End

[1]This is the teaching, for example, of the apocalyptic books IV Ezra and II Baruch.

[2]As cited by Eusebius *Ecclesiastical History* 3.39 (London: G. Mill, 1636), pp. 11-12.

[3]Jean Danielou, *The Theology of Jewish Christianity,* vol. 1 of *A History of Early Christian Doctrine Before the Council of Nicaea,* trans. John A. Baker (Philadelphia: Westminster, 1964), pp. 400-403.

[4]Peter Toon, "Introduction," in *Puritans, the Millennium and the Future of Israel: Puritan*

Eschatology 1600 to 1660, ed. Peter Toon (Greenwood, S.C.: Attic, 1970), p. 11.

⁵Justin Martyr *Dialogue with Trypho, A Jew, 80,* in *The Ante-Nicene Fathers: Translation of the Fathers Down to A.D. 325,* ed. A. Roberts and J. Donaldson (Grand Rapids, Mich.: Eerdmans, 1975), 1:239. Works from *The Ante-Nicene Fathers* will be cited as ANF, followed by volume and page number.

⁶Irenaeus *Adversus Haereses* 5.30.4; ANF 1:560.

⁷See Norman Cohn, *The Pursuit of the Millennium* (London: Secker & Warburg, 1957), p. 11.

⁸Irenaeus *Adversus Haereses* 5.33; ANF 1:563. The word *metretes* is an archaic English measurement. A *metrete* was equivalent to nine gallons. Tertullian, the North African church father who later joined the heretical Montanist movement, presented a similar picture. He taught that the millennium will be a pleasant reward for faithfulness, for the resurrected saints retain physical characteristics such as sex and digestion.

⁹Irenaeus *Adversus Haereses* 5.32.1; ANF 1:561. *Epistle of Barnabas* 15; ANF 1:146-47.

¹⁰D. H. Kromminga, *The Millennium in the Church* (Grand Rapids, Mich.: Eerdmans, 1945), pp. 30-40. In fact, Kromminga even suggests that Barnabas is the father of the amillennial understanding of the Bible (p. 37).

¹¹*Epistle of Barnabas* 15.

¹²Danielou, *Jewish Christianity,* p. 397.

¹³Kromminga, *Millennium in the Church,* pp. 35-36.

¹⁴Danielou, *Jewish Christianity,* pp. 397-98.

¹⁵Ibid., p. 399.

¹⁶Kromminga, *Millennium in the Church,* p. 33.

¹⁷Ibid., pp. 36-38.

¹⁸Lactantius *Divine Institutes* 7.24; ANF 7:219.

¹⁹Ibid., 7.22; ANF 7:217.

²⁰Ibid., 7.24; ANF 7:219.

²¹Cyprian *An Address to Demetrianus* 3; ANF 5:458.

²²Ernest Lee Tuveson, *Millennium and Utopia,* Harper Torchbook edition (New York: Harper and Row, 1964), p. 14.

²³See, for example, Eusebius *The Ancient Ecclesiastical Histories of the First Six Hundred Years after Christ,* trans. Meredith Hammer, 4th edition (London, 1636), p. 50.

²⁴Augustine *The City of God,* trans. Marcens Dods, Modern Library edition (New York: Random House, 1950), 20.7 (p. 719).

²⁵Toon, "Introduction," p. 13.

²⁶Augustine *City of God* 20.6 (p. 716).

²⁷Ibid. 20.7 (pp. 719-20).

²⁸Augustine concludes *The City of God* with a brief reference to the seven ages of human history; 22.30 (p. 867).

²⁹Ibid. 20.7 (p. 720).

³⁰This understanding seemed to be the natural import of Augustine's own statements. See especially *City of God* 20.8 (pp. 722-23).

³¹Richard Kenneth Emmerson, *Antichrist in the Middle Ages* (Manchester, England: Manchester University Press, 1981), pp. 50-54.

³²Ibid., p. 51.

³³Augustine *City of God* 20.9 (pp. 725-27).

³⁴Thomas Aquinas *Treatise on the Last Things, Supplement to the Summa Theologia* 91.5. Found

in *The Summa Theologia of St. Thomas Aquinas,* trans. Fathers of the English Dominican Province (London: Burns, Oates and Washbourne, 1922), 21:66-69.

[35]Emmerson, *Antichrist,* p. 57.

[36]Toon, "Introduction," p. 17.

[37]Emmerson, *Antichrist,* pp. 54-56.

[38]Ibid., p. 58.

[39]Ibid., p. 7.

[40]Ibid., p. 58.

[41]For a statement of Joachim's teachings and their impact, see Marjorie Reeves, *Joachim of Fiore and the Prophetic Future,* Harper Torchbook edition (New York: Harper and Row, 1977).

[42]Ibid., pp. 6-7.

[43]Ibid., p. 13.

[44]Ibid., p. 58.

[45]Ibid., p. 72.

[46]Ibid., p. 79.

[47]Ibid., p. 63.

[48]See ibid., pp. 116-35.

[49]Tuveson, *Millennium and Utopia,* pp. 20-21.

[50]See, for example, John Laird Wilson, *John Wycliffe: Patriot and Reformer* (New York: Funk and Wagnalls, 1884).

[51]Ibid., p. 147.

[52]This is the opinion of Tuveson, *Millennium and Utopia,* p. 24, who cites John Wyclif, "De Pontificum Romanorum Schismate," in *Select Works of John Wyclif,* ed. Thomas Arnold (Oxford: Clarendon, 1871), 3:245-51.

[53]Emmerson, *Antichrist,* p. 71.

[54]See ibid., p. 207.

[55]Ibid., p. 219.

[56]This was the case even in Puritan England, where millennial viewpoints abounded. See Bryan W. Ball, *A Great Expectation: Eschatological Thought in English Protestantism to 1660,* vol. 12 of *Studies in the History of Christian Thought,* ed. Heiko A. Oberman (Leiden, the Netherlands: Brill, 1975), p. 71.

[57]*The Works of Martin Luther* (Philadelphia: Muhlenberg, 1932), 6:480-88.

[58]Reeves, *Joachim of Fiore,* p. 141.

[59]See, for example, Philip Schaff, "The Second Helvetic Confession, A.D. 1566, *The History of Creeds,* vol. 1 of *The Creeds of Christendom* (New York: Harper and Brothers, 1922), pp. 390-420.

[60]For the medieval foundation of this contention, see Emmerson, *Antichrist,* p. 46.

[61]Thus, concerning the two alternatives to the historicist approach, Ball notes that futurism "made even less impression on English Protestant thought than did preterism." Ball, *Great Expectation,* pp. 74-75.

[62]Peter Toon, "The Latter Day Glory," in *Puritans, the Millennium and the Future of Israel,* pp. 26ff. See also Ball, *Great Expectation,* p. 172.

[63]Toon, "The Latter Day Glory," pp. 38-39.

[64]See R. G. Clouse, "The Rebirth of Millenarianism," in *Puritans, the Millennium and the Future of Israel,* pp. 48-54.

[65]Ball finds three basic categories represented among the seventeenth-century English Prot-

estant thinkers broadly analogous to the later classifications of amillennialism, premillennialism and postmillennialism. Ball, *Great Expectation,* pp. 160-61.

[66]Ibid., p. 157.

[67]Clouse, "Rebirth of Millenarianism," p. 60.

[68]Ibid., pp. 60, 64.

[69]Ball, *Great Expectation,* pp. 164, 168.

[70]Ibid., p. 171.

[71]Ibid., p. 181.

[72]Ibid., p. 134.

[73]Peter Toon, "Conclusion," in *Puritans, the Millennium and the Future of Israel,* p. 126.

[74]Ball, *Great Expectation,* pp. 181, 185-87.

[75]B. S. Kapp, "Extreme Millenarianism, in *Puritans, the Millennium and the Future of Israel,* pp. 73-74.

[76]Ibid., p. 76.

[77]See Ball, *Great Expectation,* p. 202.

[78]Ibid., p. 169, citing John Cotton, *The Churches Resurrection or The Opening of the Fift and Sixt Verses of the 20th Chap. of the Revelation* (London: Printed by R. O. & G. D. for Henry Overtone, 1642), pp. 7-9.

[79]H. Richard Niebuhr argues this concept in *The Kingdom of God in America,* Harper Torchbook edition (New York: Harper and Row, 1959), pp. 45-87.

[80]Ibid., p. 143.

[81]See the discussion in ibid., pp. 143-46.

[82]For a discussion of Isaac Backus's view, see Stanley J. Grenz, *Isaac Backus—Puritan and Baptist,* NABPR Dissertation Series, number 4 (Macon, Ga.: Mercer University Press, 1983), pp. 226-32.

[83]Sydney E. Ahlstrom, *A Religious History of the American People* (New Haven, Conn.: Yale University Press, 1972), p. 311.

[84]Ernest R. Sandeen, *The Roots of Fundamentalism: British and American Millenarianism, 1800—1930* (Chicago: University of Chicago Press, 1970), p. 42.

[85]Edward Beecher, "The Scriptural Philosophy of Congregationalism and Councils," *Bibliotheca Sacra* 22 (April 1865): 312. As quoted by Niebuhr, *Kingdom of God,* p. 157.

[86]See Niebuhr, *Kingdom of God,* pp. 161, 183.

[87]Many historians have noted this development. See, for example, the characterization in ibid., pp. 179-84.

[88]For a discussion of the demise of this system, see James H. Moorhead, "The Erosion of Postmillennialism in American Religious Thought, 1865—1925," *Church History* 53/1 (March 1984): 61-77.

[89]Timothy P. Weber, *Living in the Shadow of the Second Coming,* enlarged edition (Grand Rapids, Mich.: Zondervan, 1983), p. 15.

[90]Komminga, *Millennium,* pp. 204-6.

[91]See, for example, Weber, *Living in the Shadow,* p. 17.

[92]See, for example, John Darby, "The Apostasy of the Successive Dispensations," *Collected Writings* 1:190; "God, Not the Church," *Collected Writings* 4:366, 379. Cited in ibid., p. 170.

[93]Sandeen, *Roots of Fundamentalism,* pp. 26-27.

[94]This is Sandeen's conclusion in ibid., pp. 64-65.

[95]For a discussion of the role of dispensationalists within the broader fundamentalist camp and

the millenarian-conservative alliance, see ibid., pp. 132-207.

[96]See Weber, *Living in the Shadow,* pp. 160-69.

[97]For a discussion of the important role of the Bible institutes, see Sandeen, *Roots of Fundamentalism,* pp. 240-43.

[98]This thesis was reasserted as late as 1984 by the president of Dallas Theological Seminary, John F. Walvoord, "Russia—King of the North," *Fundamentalist Journal* 3/1 (January 1984): 34-38.

[99]For a fuller account of the rise of dispensationalism in the United States, see Weber, *Living in the Shadow.*

[100]Ibid., p. 231.

[101]Weber supports this conclusion in ibid., pp. 241-42.

Chapter 3: Bringing in the Kingdom

[1]Hal Lindsey, *The Late Great Planet Earth,* Bantam edition (New York: Bantam Books, 1973), pp. 164-65.

[2]Alexander Reese, *The Approaching Advent of Christ* (London: Marshall, Morgan and Scott, 1937), p. 306.

[3]J. Dwight Pentecost, *Things to Come* (Findlay, Ohio: Dunham, 1958), p. 386.

[4]Lindsey, *Late Great Planet,* p. 164.

[5]For a postmillennialist rebuttal of Lindsey's statement, see David Chilton, *Paradise Restored* (Tyler, Tex.: Reconstruction Press, 1985), pp. 226-35.

[6]"History of Opinions Respecting the Millennium," *American Theological Review* 1 (1859): 655, as cited in James H. Moorhead, "The Erosion of Postmillennialism in American Religious Thought, 1865—1925," *Church History* 53/1 (March 1984): 61.

[7]John Jefferson Davis of Gordon-Conwell Theological Seminary is perhaps the most prominent of recent evangelical proponents of postmillennialism. He participated in the Christianity Today Institute discussion of this issue. See "Our Future Hope: Eschatology and Its Role in the Church," *Christianity Today* 31/2 (February 6, 1987): 1/I-14/I. For his articulation of this eschatology, see John Jefferson Davis, *Christ's Victorious Kingdom* (Grand Rapids, Mich.: Baker, 1986).

[8]A Christianity Today Institute survey conducted in the mid-1980s suggested that about nine per cent of the magazine's readers held to a postmillennial view. See "Our Future Hope," p. 9/I.

[9]See, for example, Shirley Jackson Case, *The Millennial Hope* (Chicago: University of Chicago Press, 1918), pp. 229-30, 237-41.

[10]For example, Davis, *Christ's Victorious Kingdom,* pp. 12-16.

[11]Loraine Boettner, *The Millennium* (Philadelphia: Reformed, 1957), p. 4.

[12]Boettner, for example, writes, "Among Postmillennialists should be mentioned first of all the great Augustine, whose eminently sound interpretation of Scripture set the standard for the Church for nearly a thousand years." *Millennium,* p. 10.

[13]"Postmillennialism" is a somewhat fluid category today. Some thinkers who classify themselves as postmillennialists follow Augustine in equating the millennial era with the kingdom established by Christ at his first coming, thus making it coterminous with the church age itself. See, for example, Chilton, *Paradise Restored,* pp. 228-29. We can call this position "postmillennialist" in that it places the Second Coming after the millennium/church age. This chapter, however, focuses on that postmillennial eschatology that anticipates a golden age still

in the future.

[14]For a helpful discussion of postmillennial ideas among the English Puritans, see Iain H. Murray, *The Puritan Hope* (Edinburgh: Banner of Truth, 1971).

[15]See, for example, Dwight Wilson, *Armageddon Now! The Premillenarian Response to Russia and Israel since 1917* (Grand Rapids, Mich.: Baker, 1977), p. 18; Lewis Sperry Chafer, *Systematic Theology* (Dallas: Dallas Seminary Press, 1948), 4:280-81.

[16]On this see, for example, Davis, *Christ's Victorious Kingdom*, pp. 16-18.

[17]Jonathan Edwards, *The History of Redemption* (Marshallton, Del.: The National Foundation for Christian Education, n.d. [1773]), p. 305.

[18]For Edwards's description of this prosperity, see ibid., pp. 319-25.

[19]Ibid., pp. 325-28.

[20]Augustus Hopkins Strong, *Systematic Theology* (Philadelphia: Griffith and Rowland, 1909), 3:1008.

[21]J. Marcellus Kik, *An Eschatology of Victory* (Philadelphia: Presbyterian and Reformed, 1974), p. 4. For similar summaries of the postmillennial viewpoint, see Boettner, *Millennium*, pp. 14-15, and Davis, *Christ's Victorious Kingdom*, pp. 10-11. Kik's own position is complex. On the one hand, like Augustine and unlike modern postmillennialists, he interprets the thousand years as referring to the period from the first to the second advents *(Eschatology,* p. 205). On the other hand, similar to other postmillennialists he anticipates an increase in spiritual blessings on the earth sometime in the future (p. 235).

[22]See Loraine Boettner, "Postmillennialism," in *The Meaning of the Millennium: Four Views,* ed. Robert G. Clouse (Downers Grove: InterVarsity Press, 1977), p. 117.

[23]Ibid.

[24]Strong, *Systematic Theology* 3:1014.

[25]Boettner, *Millennium,* pp. 19-20.

[26]Boettner, "Postmillennialism," pp. 132-33; *Millennium,* pp. 58-62.

[27]Strong, *Systematic Theology* 3:1010.

[28]Boettner, "Postmillennialism," p. 117.

[29]See Boettner, *Millennium,* pp. 63-66, who cites Warfield, Kuyper and Calvin.

[30]Ibid., p. 19.

[31]Ibid., p. 56.

[32]Boettner, "Postmillennialism," p. 130; *Millennium,* pp. 48-53. This theme forms a basis for the increasingly popular movement often called "prosperity theology," which because of this link may be seen as in some sense an expression of the contemporary resurgence of postmillennialism.

[33]Boettner, "Postmillennialism," p. 131.

[34]Ibid., p. 121.

[35]Hence, for example, Strong, *Systematic Theology* 3:1008.

[36]Ibid., p. 1009; for a lengthier discussion of this question, see Boettner, *Millennium,* pp. 67-76. The expectation of a final apostasy is not universally held among postmillennialists.

[37]Kik, *Eschatology,* p. 238.

[38]For example, Jay Adams, *The Time Is at Hand* (Philadelphia: Presbyterian and Reformed, 1974), pp. 86-88.

[39]Boettner, *Millennium,* p. 30.

[40]Benjamin B. Warfield, *Biblical Doctrines* (Edinburgh: Banner of Truth, 1988), pp. 647-48, 662. See also Boettner, *Millennium,* pp. 31-34; Kik, *Eschatology,* p. 250.

[41]Davis, *Christ's Victorious Kingdom,* p. 93.

[42]Warfield offered this understanding in *Biblical Doctrines,* pp. 647-48.

[43]Strong, *Systematic Theology* 3:1011.

[44]Davis, *Christ's Victorious Kingdom,* p. 98.

[45]Alexander Archibald Hodge, *Outlines of Theology* (London: Nelson and Sons, 1870), pp. 458-59.

[46]James H. Snowden, *The Coming of the Lord: Will It Be Premillennial?* (New York: Macmillan, 1919), pp. 178-79.

[47]Strong, *Systematic Theology* 3:1013.

[48]Ibid., p. 1014.

[49]For a treatment of these parables, see Snowden, *Coming of the Lord,* pp. 72-84.

[50]Chilton, *Paradise Restored,* pp. 73-75.

[51]Snowden, *Coming of the Lord,* p. 98.

[52]Millard J. Erickson, *Contemporary Options in Eschatology: A Study of the Millennium* (Grand Rapids, Mich.: Baker, 1977), p. 64.

[53]Kik, *Eschatology,* p. 196.

[54]Davis, *Christ's Victorious Kingdom,* p. 49.

[55]Boettner, *Millennium,* p. 22.

[56]Ibid., p. 35.

[57]William G. T. Shedd, *Dogmatic Theology,* Classic Reprint edition (Grand Rapids, Mich.: Zondervan, n.d.), 2:745.

[58]Boettner, "Postmillennialism," p. 124.

[59]For a discussion of this point, see Boettner, *Millennium,* pp. 22-27; Kik, *Eschatology,* pp. 16-29.

[60]Charles Hodge, *Systematic Theology,* 3 vols. (New York: Scribner, Armstrong and Co., 1872), 3:800.

[61]See, for example, Davis, *Christ's Victorious Kingdom,* pp. 28-44.

[62]Kik, *Eschatology,* p. 5.

[63]Boettner, "Postmillennialism," p. 136.

[64]Boettner, *Millennium,* pp. 82-83.

[65]Ibid., p. 86.

[66]Ibid., p. 85.

[67]Ibid., p. 101.

[68]Ibid., p. 89.

[69]Davis, *Christ's Victorious Kingdom,* p. 34.

[70]Ibid.

[71]For example, Chilton, *Paradise Restored,* pp. 125-31. Whitby also articulated this hope.

[72]Boettner, *Millennium,* pp. 95, 104.

[73]Davis, *Christ's Victorious Kingdom,* pp. 65-82; Boettner, *Millennium,* pp. 38-47.

[74]Boettner, "Postmillennialism," p. 126.

[75]Greg L. Bahnsen, *Theonomy in Christian Ethics* (Nutley, N.J.: Craig, 1979), p. xv.

[76]Rousas John Rushdoony, *The Institutes of Biblical Law* (Tyler, Tex.: Craig, 1973), pp. 8-9.

[77]Bahnsen, *Theonomy,* p. xvi. Elsewhere Bahnsen denies that he advocates that God's law be imposed on a society by force. Greg L. Bahnsen, *By This Standard: The Authority of God's Law Today* (Tyler, Tex.: Institute for Christian Economics, 1985), p. 9.

[78]James B. Jordan, *The Law of the Covenant* (Tyler, Tex.: Institute for Christian Economics,

1984), pp. 26-27.

79While drawing inspiration from Calvin, reconstructionists do not hesitate to indicate those points at which the Geneva reformer failed to go far enough. See, for example, Rushdoony, *Institutes,* pp. 651, 653-54, 659.

80Bahnsen, *By This Standard,* pp. 34, 398-400. See also David Chilton, *Productive Christians in an Age of Guilt Manipulators,* 3d edition (Tyler, Tex.: Institute for Christian Economics, 1985), pp. 31-33.

81Bahnsen, *By This Standard,* p. 279.

82Ibid., p. 445.

83Ibid., pp. 34, 486-87.

84Ibid., pp. 424-25.

85Ibid., p. 428.

86Ibid., p. 448. See also Chilton, *Paradise Restored,* p. 12.

87Chilton, *Paradise Restored,* p. 53.

88Ibid., pp. 10-11.

89Ibid., p. 54.

90Ibid., p. 11.

91Ibid., p. 55.

92For a recent response to reconstructionism, see William S. Barker and W. Robert Godfrey, eds., *Theonomy: A Reformed Critique* (Grand Rapids, Mich.: Zondervan, 1990).

93For example, Gary North, in his foreword to the third edition of Chilton's *Productive Christians,* pp. ix-x, bemoans the ignoring of reconstructionism by the broader evangelical community in the person of Ronald J. Sider.

94For a discussion of the relationship of reconstructionism with the Christian Right, see Fred Clarkson, "Hardcore," *Church and State* 44/1 (January 1991): 9-12.

95See Moorhead, "Erosion of Postmillennialism," pp. 76-77.

96Hal Lindsey, for example, presents "world conditions and the accelerating decline of Christian influence today" as sufficient arguments against postmillennialism *(Late Great Planet,* p. 165). Certain other critics, however, employ the argument from world conditions in a more nuanced manner. Erickson, for example, cites its unrealistic optimism as a shortcoming of postmillennialism, but then declares that an argument from Scripture is more damaging. *Contemporary Options in Eschatology,* pp. 71-72. Hoekema likewise asserts that the postmillennialist sketch of world conditions is "seriously out of date." Anthony A. Hoekema, "An Amillennial Response," in *Meaning of the Millennium,* p. 151.

97Even as careful an articulator of dispensationalism as E. Schuyler English characterizes postmillennialism as proposing "that through the preaching of the Gospel the world will get progressively better." *A Companion to the New Scofield Reference Bible* (New York: Oxford, 1972), p. 148 note.

98Boettner, "Postmillennialism," pp. 125-33.

99Chilton, *Paradise Restored,* pp. 234-35.

100Davis, *Christ's Victorious Kingdom,* p. 127.

101Hoekema, "Amillennial Response," p. 151.

102Herman A. Hoyt, "A Dispensational Premillennial Response," in *Meaning of the Millennium,* p. 146.

103Ibid.

104Various authors cite the presence of the pessimistic theme in the New Testament against postmillennialism. See, for example, Erickson, *Contemporary Options in Eschatology,* p. 72. See also Hoyt, "Dispensational Premillennial Response," pp. 146-47.

[105]Boettner raises this point, but can answer the objection only by suggesting that the implied answer need not be the "no" that objectors assume. *Millennium,* p. 47.

[106]Snowden, *Coming of the Lord,* as cited by Boettner, *Millennium,* p. 47.

[107]Even certain premillennialists acknowledge this contribution. See, for example, Erickson, *Contemporary Options in Eschatology,* p. 70.

Chapter 4: A Future Kingdom for Israel

[1]George E. Ladd, *Crucial Questions about the Kingdom of God* (Grand Rapids, Mich.: Eerdmans, 1952), p. 49. Actually dispensationalist writers themselves often sought to equate their view with premillennialism and thereby make claim to standing in continuity with the theology of the patristic era. See, for example, Charles C. Ryrie, *The Basis of the Premillennial Faith* (New York: Loizeaux Brothers, 1953), pp. 17ff.

[2]For example, Herman Hoyt, "Current Trends in Eschatological Beliefs," in *Understanding the Times,* ed. William Culbertson and Herman B. Centz (Grand Rapids, Mich.: Zondervan, 1952), pp. 147-51.

[3]Clarence B. Bass, *Backgrounds to Dispensationalism* (1960; reprint, Grand Rapids, Mich.: Baker, 1977), p. 9.

[4]Some scholars see this as the most important explanation for the ongoing acceptance of dispensationalism by conservative Christians. See, for example, David Edwin Harrell, Jr., "Dispensational Premillennialism and the Religious Right," in *The Return of the Millennium,* ed. Joseph Bettis and S. K. Johannesen (Barrytown, N.Y.: New ERA Books, 1984), p. 14.

[5]For example, John F. Walvoord, "Russia—King of the North," *Fundamentalist Journal* 3/1 (January 1984): 34-38. As late as 1991, Walvoord continued to advocate this thesis. See John F. Walvoord, "Is a New World Order in the Prophetic Future?" *Kindred Spirit* 15/1 (Spring 1991): 5.

[6]Dwight Wilson, *Armageddon Now! The Premillenarian Response to Russia and Israel Since 1917* (Grand Rapids, Mich.: Baker, 1977), p. 123.

[7]See, for example, Arthur W. Kac, *The Rebirth of the State of Israel* (Chicago: Moody, 1958). In contrast to most dispensationalists, Kac argued that Iraq, not Russia, was the prophetic king of the north (pp. 327-30).

[8]See, for example, Charles C. Ryrie, *Dispensationalism Today* (Chicago: Moody, 1965), p. 74. For a discussion of Darby's views and influence, see Ernest R. Sandeen, *The Roots of Fundamentalism: British and American Millenarianism, 1800—1930* (Chicago: University of Chicago Press, 1970), pp. 59-80.

[9]The dispensationalism that crowds the airwaves of the electronic church remains largely that of the older classical variety. This is evident in the 1988 publication of the Radio Bible Class, "What Can We Know About the Second Coming?" which argues that Israel and the church "have different places in God's prophetic plan" (p. 4), and that the church "has been given a hope that is to be realized more in heaven than on earth" (p. 5).

[10]Ryrie, *Dispensationalism,* pp. 24-25.

[11]Ibid., p. 16.

[12]C. I. Scofield, The Scofield Reference Bible (New York: Oxford, 1909), note to Genesis 1:28, heading. For an alternative definition, see Ryrie, *Dispensationalism,* p. 29.

[13]See The Scofield Reference Bible, note to Genesis 1:28. For an earlier alternative enumeration,

see C. I. Scofield, *Rightly Dividing the Word of Truth* (New York: Loizeaux Brothers, 1896), pp. 12-16. Scofield's followers eventually renamed the dispensation of grace, preferring to call it the dispensation of the church, in that grace was not limited to the present era but was available in all dispensations. See the New Scofield Reference Bible, note to Genesis 1:27, heading. Ryrie, however, continued the older nomenclature. Ryrie, *Dispensationalism*, pp. 50-52.

[14]Such as Kenneth L. Barker, "The Scope and Center of Old and New Testament Theology and Hope," in *Israel and the Church: Essays in Contemporary Dispensational Thought*, ed. Craig A. Blaising and Darrell L. Bock (Grand Rapids, Mich.: Zondervan, 1992), pp. 293-328 [all citations from page proofs].

[15]See Ryrie, *Dispensationalism*, p. 33.

[16]E. Schuyler English, *A Companion to the New Scofield Reference Bible* (New York: Oxford, 1972), p. 54.

[17]Ibid., p. 152.

[18]Ryrie, *Dispensationalism*, p. 31.

[19]For the precursors claimed by contemporary dispensationalists, see ibid., pp. 71-73.

[20]Augustine *City of God* 22.30.

[21]Richard Kenneth Emmerson, *Antichrist in the Middle Ages* (Manchester, England: Manchester University Press, 1981), pp. 17-18.

[22]This is the judgment of former dispensationalist Clarence Bass, *Backgrounds to Dispensationalism*, p. 17.

[23]Even though the exact labels may vary, classical dispensationalists generally follow Scofield in enumerating seven epochs. See, for example, Ryrie, *Dispensationalism*, pp. 50-52.

[24]Ryrie echoes this conclusion in ibid., pp. 43-44.

[25]Progressive dispensationalists themselves are not sure what constitute the *sine qua non* characteristics of their system of thought.

[26]For a similar characterization, see John F. Walvoord, "Dispensational Premillennialism," *Christianity Today* 2/24 (September 15, 1958): 13. This portrayal differs from that set forth by Ryrie, *Dispensationalism*, pp. 44-47.

[27]For the characterization of classic dispensationalism as positing a *metaphysical*, as opposed to a merely historical, distinction between Israel and the church, see Michael D. Williams, "Where's the Church? The Church as the Unfinished Business of Dispensational Theology," *Grace Theological Journal* 10/2 (1989): 165-82.

[28]For a discussion of this tenet, see Ryrie, *Dispensationalism*, pp. 132-55.

[29]See, for example, William F. Kerr, "Tribulation for the Church—But Not *The Tribulation*," in *Understanding the Times*, pp. 102-3.

[30]For a delineation of this position, see Bruce A. Ware, "The New Covenant and the People(s) of God," in *Israel and the Church*, pp. 68-97.

[31]Even progressive dispensationalists affirm this point. See, for example, Barker, "Scope and Center."

[32]For a recent argument against that thesis, see W. Edward Glenny, "The Israelite Imagery of 1 Peter 2," in *Israel and the Church*, pp. 156-87.

[33]Ryrie, *Dispensationalism*, p. 137.

[34]Scofield had already set forth this distinction at the end of the nineteenth century in *Rightly Dividing*, pp. 5-12.

[35]Darrell L. Bock, "The Reign of the Lord Christ," in *Israel and the Church*, p. 65.

[36]Ibid, p. 66.

[37]Robert L. Saucy, "The Church as the Mystery of God," in Blaising and Bock, *Israel and the Church*, p. 151.

[38]Scofield, *Rightly Dividing*, p. 3.

[39]Ryrie, *Dispensationalism*, pp. 95-96.

[40]Bock, "The Reign of the Lord Christ," in *Israel and the Church*, pp. 60-61.

[41]See J. Dwight Pentecost, *Things to Come* (Findlay, Ohio: Dunham, 1958), pp. 219-28.

[42]For a presentation of this position, see Gleason L. Archer, "The Case for the Mid-Seventieth-Week Rapture Position," in *The Rapture: Pre-, Mid-, or Post-tribulational* (Grand Rapids, Mich.: Zondervan, 1984), pp. 113-45.

[43]Donald Burdick, for example, long-time professor of New Testament at Denver Conservative Baptist Seminary, claimed to be a dispensationalist while holding to a post-tribulational rapture.

[44]Dallas Seminary theologian Robert P. Lightner summarizes the classical dispensationalist scenario in the column "Dallas Seminary Faculty Answer Your Questions," *Kindred Spirit* 15/1 (Spring 1991): 3.

[45]Pentecost, *Things to Come*, p. 358. For detailed dispensationalist descriptions of the military intrigue at the end of the tribulation, see Pentecost, pp. 318-58; See also Hal Lindsey, *The Late Great Planet Earth*, Bantam edition (New York: Bantam Books, 1973).

[46]See, for example, Pentecost, *Things to Come*, pp. 508-11.

[47]Ibid., pp. 547-83.

[48]For an exhaustive treatment of this hermeneutic and its relation to dispensationalism, see ibid., pp. 1-64.

[49]Ryrie, *Dispensationalism*, p. 96.

[50]Ibid., p. 86.

[51]Sandeen, *Roots of Fundamentalism*, p. 109.

[52]Ryrie, *Dispensationalism*, pp. 87-88.

[53]For example, David L. Turner, "The New Jerusalem in Revelation 21:1—22:15: Consummation of a Biblical Continuum," in *Israel and the Church*, pp. 275-77.

[54]Ryrie, *Dispensationalism*, p. 89.

[55]The attempt to apply a literal method to Old Testament prophetic texts did not arise first with dispensationalism. On the contrary, such ideas were proposed as early as the Puritan era in England. For example, in a book published in 1621 under the auspices of the influential Presbyterian clergyman William Gouge, Sir Henry Finch proposed a literal interpretation of Old Testament references to "Israel," "Judah," "Zion" and "Jerusalem." Because such terms always relate to the physical and not the spiritual descendants of Abraham, Finch and Gouge argued, texts that predict Israel's return to their homeland, their conquest of their enemies and their primacy over the nations must be taken literally and not seen as fulfilled in the church. Peter Toon, "The Latter Day Glory," in *Puritans, the Millennium and the Future of Israel: Puritan Eschatology 1600 to 1660*, ed. Peter Toon (Greenwood, S.C.: Attic, 1970) pp. 32-33.

[56]See, for example, the four-part series by John F. Walvoord, "Interpreting Prophecy Today," *Bibliotheca Sacra* 139/553-56 (1982): 3-12, 111-28, 205-15, 302-11.

[57]Pentecost, *Things to Come*, pp. 512-31.

[58]Harold L. Willmington, "Let Earth Receive Her King: Life in the Millennium," *Fundamentalist Journal* 4/1 (January 1985): 35.

[59]See, for example, Saucy, "The Church as the Mystery of God." See also Barker, "Scope and Center."

[60]Even progressive dispensationalists remain adamant on this point. See Glenny, "Israelite Imagery," p. 186.

[61]Ryrie, *Dispensationalism*, pp. 138-40; Pentecost, *Things to Come*, pp. 88-89.

[62]See, for example, Bock, "Reign of the Lord Christ." See also Saucy, "Church as Mystery."

[63]Pentecost, *Things to Come*, pp. 134-38.

[64]Saucy, "Church as Mystery," pp. 149-50.

[65]Ibid, p. 151.

[66]For the dispensationalist use of this prophecy, see Pentecost, *Things to Come*, pp. 239-50.

[67]One interesting alternative sees the prophecy in terms of Cyrus and the antichrist. Thomas Edward McComiskey, "The Seventy 'Weeks' of Daniel Against the Background of Ancient Near Eastern Literature," *Westminster Theological Journal* 47 (1985): 18-45.

[68]See, for example, Ronald W. Pierce, "Scriptural Failure, Postponement, and Daniel 9," *Trinity Journal* 10 NS (1989): 211-22.

[69]See, for example, Archibald Hughes, *A New Heaven and a New Earth* (London: Marshall, Morgan and Scott, 1958), pp. 166-74; Oswald T. Allis, *Prophecy and the Church* (Philadelphia: Presbyterian and Reformed, 1945), pp. 113-14.

[70]See, for example, Edward J. Young, *The Prophecy of Daniel* (Grand Rapids, Mich.: Eerdmans, 1949), pp. 191-221.

[71]Lewis Sperry Chafer, *Systematic Theology* (Dallas: Dallas Seminary Press, 1948), 4:265-67; Pentecost, *Things to Come*, pp. 446-66.

[72]Pentecost, *Things to Come*, pp. 472-75.

[73]Carl B. Hoch, Jr., "The New Man of Ephesians 2," in Blaising and Bock, *Israel and the Church*, p. 126.

[74]Ryrie, *Dispensationalism*, pp. 158-59.

[75]For the classical position, see, for example, Eric Sauer, *The Triumph of the Crucified*, trans. G. H. Lang (Grand Rapids, Mich.: Eerdmans, 1951), pp. 145-46.

[76]See, for example, Chafer, *Systematic Theology* 4:364-67; Pentecost, *Things to Come*, pp. 194-98, 237-39.

[77]English, *Companion*, p. 140; Kac, *Rebirth of Israel*, pp. 321-22.

[78]For a fuller delineation of this thesis, see Paul D. Feinberg, "The Case for the Pretribulation Rapture Position," in *Rapture: Pre-, Mid-, or Post-tribulational?* pp. 50-63.

[79]English, *Companion*, p. 137; Kerr, "Tribulation for the Church," pp. 98-106.

[80]For a summary of the biblical argument for this point, see Feinberg, "Case for Pretribulation Rapture," pp. 50-72.

[81]Chafer, *Systematic Theology* 4:367-68; Pentecost, *Things to Come*, pp. 202-4.

[82]See, for example, Feinberg, "Case for Pretribulation Rapture," pp. 80-86.

[83]Ibid., p. 80.

[84]English, *Companion*, p. 136.

[85]Ibid., p. 139.

[86]Hal Lindsey, *There's a New World Coming* (Santa Ana, Calif.: Vision House, 1973), p. 78.

[87]See, for example, ibid., pp. 75, 78.

[88]English, *Companion*, p. 138; Chafer, *Systematic Theology* 4:371-72; Alva J. McClain, "The Pretribulation Rapture and the Commentators," in Culbertson and Centz, *Understanding the Times*, pp. 198-207; Pentecost, *Things to Come*, pp. 201-9, 251-58.

[89]Feinberg argues this in a detailed manner in "Case for Pretribulation Rapture," pp. 63-72.

[90]Chafer, *Systematic Theology* 4:369.

[91]Chafer argues that the restrainer is the Holy Spirit. But he nevertheless comes to the same conclusion: Because "the believer can never be separated from the Holy Spirit . . . when the Spirit, the Restrainer, is 'taken out of the way,' the Church will of necessity be removed with Him." *Systematic Theology* 4:372. See also Pentecost, *Things to Come*, pp. 204-5, 259-63.

One need not be a dispensationalist to interpret the restrainer as the Holy Spirit. The amillennialist William E. Cox argues the same position in *In These Last Days* (Philadelphia: Presbyterian and Reformed, 1964), p. 44.

[92]English, *Companion*, p. 138, representing the editorial committee of the New Scofield Reference Bible.

[93]See Ryrie, *Dispensationalism*, pp. 159-60; Pentecost, *Things to Come*, p. 193.

[94]For a dispensationalist response to this argument, see Kac, *Rebirth of Israel*, pp. 366-67.

[95]See, for example, the discussion of Cox, *These Last Days*, pp. 12-16.

[96]Craig A. Blaising, "Development of Dispensationalism by Contemporary Dispensationalists," *Bibliotheca Sacra* 145 (July-September 1988): 278

[97]See Ware, "New Covenant and People(s) of God," pp. 91-93, 96-97.

[98]Barker, "Scope and Center," pp. 325-27.

[99]See Pentecost, *Things to Come*, pp. 275-85.

[100]George E. Ladd, *The Blessed Hope* (Grand Rapids, Mich.: Eerdmans, 1956), pp. 72-73.

[101]Ibid., p. 146.

[102]Ibid., pp. 148-49.

[103]Ibid., pp. 73-75, 94-95.

[104]H. E. Dana and Julius Mantey, *A Manual Grammar of the Greek New Testament* (New York: Macmillan, 1927), p. 147, cite the following definition of the Granville Sharp rule:

When the copulative *kai* connects two nouns of the same case, if the article *ho* or any of its cases precedes the first of the said nouns or participles, and is not repeated before the second noun or participle, the latter always relates to the same person that is expressed or described by the first noun or participle; i.e., it denotes a farther description of the first-named person.

[105]Ladd, *Blessed Hope*, pp. 92-94.

[106]Ibid., p. 144.

[107]Ibid., p. 158.

[108]Ibid., pp. 96-98.

[109]Norman B. Harrison, *The End: Rethinking the Revelation* (Minneapolis: Harrison, 1941), p. 65; see also Theodore H. Epp, *Practical Studies in Revelation* (Lincoln, Neb.: Back to the Bible Broadcast, 1969), p. 67.

[110]Ladd, *Blessed Hope*, pp. 85-86.

[111]Feinberg, "Case for Pretribulation Rapture," p. 68. For his complete discussion, see pp. 63-72.

[112]D. H. Kromminga, *The Millennium* (Grand Rapids, Mich.: Eerdmans, 1948), p. 40.

[113]Ladd, *Blessed Hope*, pp. 99-100.

[114]Ibid., p. 165.

[115]Hughes, *New Heaven and New Earth*, p. 68.

[116]Ibid., pp. 115-27.

[117]Ibid., pp. 116-17. This tactic actually may have been the invention of Herman Bavinck, who

in 1930 declared against premillennialism, "not the New Testament, but the Old Testament is a parenthesis." Bavinck, *Reformed Dogmatics* 4:643, as cited in Willem A. VanGemeren, "Israel as the Hermeneutical Crux in the Interpretation of Prophecy (II)," *Westminster Journal of Theology* 46/2 (1984): 262.

[118]Hughes, *New Heaven and New Earth,* pp. 116-17.

[119]See, for example, Ryrie, *Dispensationalism,* pp. 162-65. For the charge of de-emphasis on the cross, see Bass, *Backgrounds to Dispensationalism,* p. 33; Allis, *Prophecy and the Church,* pp. 74-75, 234-35.

[120]For example, Saucy, "Church as Mystery,"p. 155.

[121]Ware, "New Covenant," pp. 96-97.

[122]See, for example, the conclusion of W. R. Wallace, "Shadows of Armageddon," in Culbertson and Centz, *Understanding the Times,* p. 189.

[123]Sandeen, *Roots of Fundamentalism,* p. 185.

[124]Timothy Weber, *Living in the Shadow of the Second Coming* (Grand Rapids, Mich.: Zondervan, 1983), pp. 234-38.

[125]Wilson, *Armageddon Now!* p. 17.

[126]Sandeen, *Roots of Fundamentalism,* p. 41.

[127]Weber, *Living in the Shadow,* p. 232.

[128]Ibid., p. 241.

[129]Bass, *Backgrounds to Dispensationalism,* p. 148.

[130]For this criticism, see David Chilton, *Paradise Restored* (Tyler, Tex.: Reconstruction Press, 1985), p. 53.

[131]See Roy Aldrich, "A New Look at Dispensationalism," *Bibliotheca Sacra* 120/477 (January 1963): 42-49.

[132]See Ryrie, *Dispensationalism,* pp. 192-205. See also Allis, *Prophecy and the Church,* pp. 15, 159-64.

[133]See Harold Lindsell, "Changes in the Scofield Reference Bible," *Christianity Today* 11/14 (April 14, 1967): 31-32.

[134]For an indication of this newer state of affairs, see Robert Saucy, "Dispensationalism and the Salvation of the Kingdom," *TSF Bulletin* 7/5 (May-June 1984): 6-7.

[135]This is evidenced by two articles that appeared in a major evangelical scholarly publication during the 1980s: Kenneth L. Barker, "False Dichotomies between the Testaments," *Journal of the Evangelical Theological Society* 25/1 (March 1982): 3-16; Mark W. Karlberg, "Legitimate Discontinuities between the Testaments," *Journal of the Evangelical Theological Society* 28/1 (March 1985): 9-20.

[136]See Robert Saucy, "Contemporary Dispensational Thought," *TSF Bulletin* 7/4 (March-April 1984): 10-11. See also Barker, "False Dichotomies," p. 4.

[137]See Barker, "False Dichotomies," pp. 12, 10.

[138]Ibid., pp. 4, 12-15.

[139]Ryrie, *Dispensationalism,* pp. 17-18, 98-105.

[140]Hence, Bass, *Backgrounds to Dispensationalism,* pp. 43-45; Allis, *Prophecy and the Church,* pp. 242-48. To this question Sauer provides what would appear to be the only consistent dispensationalist answer: glorified believers belong to the heavenly world, but are able to make appearances on the earth. See Sauer, *Triumph of the Crucified,* pp. 167-68.

[141]Bass, *Backgrounds to Dispensationalism,* p. 28. See also the serious criticism of Allis, *Prophecy and the Church,* p. 262.

[142]In the words of E. Schuyler English, "Salvation has always been by God's grace through faith in the work of Christ in His death and resurrection, for even in Old Testament times salvation was prospective of Christ's atoning sacrifice." *Companion,* p. 53. For this conclusion he cites the New Scofield Reference Bible, notes at Exodus 29:33 and Leviticus 16:6.

[143]One such problem is the interesting dilemma concerning the placement of the tribulation among the dispensations. Typically moderate dispensationalists, such as Charles Ryrie, place it as the final seven years of the sixth dispensation. Employing Scofield's categories, it comes at the close of the dispensation of "grace" (Ryrie maintains this terminology; *Dispensationalism,* pp. 55-57). But to avoid the charge that the other dispensations employ a means of salvation that differs from justification through faith by grace, moderate dispensationalists changed the designation of the dispensation of "grace" to "church." But the tribulation no longer can be a part of this dispensation, because the church is raptured out of the world prior to the tribulation, and the task of evangelism is undertaken by the 144,000 Israelite witnesses.

[144]Robert L. Saucy, "A Rationale for the Future of Israel," *Journal of the Evangelical Theological Society* 28/4 (December 1985): 433-42.

[145]Peter Beyerhaus, "Evangelization: Preparing the Kingdom of Glory," *Christianity Today* 118/16 (May 10, 1974): 17-18 [925-26].

[146]Karlberg raises this question in "Legitimate Discontinuities," p. 19.

[147]This issue is raised by Mark W. Karlberg, "The Significance of Israel in Biblical Typology," *Journal of the Evangelical Theological Society* 31/3 (September 1988): 257-69.

[148]This point is argued by Arthur H. Lewis, "Israel in New Testament Prophecy," *The Standard* (August-September 1982): 36-40.

Chapter 5: Millennial Blessings for the Church

[1]See, for example, Clarence B. Bass, *Backgrounds to Dispensationalism* (1960; reprint, Grand Rapids, Mich.: Baker, 1977), p. 17.

[2]Millard Erickson, *Contemporary Options in Eschatology: A Study of the Millennium* (Grand Rapids, Mich.: Baker, 1977), pp. 91-92.

[3]Ibid., p. 97.

[4]For an explication of the premillennialist understanding of the millennium, see, for example, ibid., pp. 101-2.

[5]See, for example, D. H. Kromminga, *The Millennium* (Grand Rapids, Mich.: Eerdmans, 1948), p. 66.

[6]Bass, *Backgrounds to Dispensationalism,* p. 152.

[7]George E. Ladd, "Revelation 20 and the Millennium," *Review and Expositor* 57 (1960): 169-70.

[8]Kromminga, *Millennium,* p. 48.

[9]Robert H. Gundry, *The Church and the Tribulation* (Grand Rapids, Mich.: Zondervan, 1973), p. 49.

[10]Erickson, *Contemporary Options in Eschatology,* p. 152; Douglas J. Moo, "The Posttribulation Rapture Position," in *The Rapture: Pre-, Mid-, or Post-tribulational* (Grand Rapids, Mich: Zondervan, 1984), pp. 172-76.

[11]Moo, p. 175.

[12]Erickson, *Contemporary Options in Eschatology,* pp. 154-56.

[13]Moo, pp. 176-78. Dispensationalists, of course, dispute this thesis. Concerning the rapture in the Olivet Discourse, see, for example, John F. Walvoord, "Is a Posttribulational Rapture

Revealed in Matthew 24?" *Grace Theological Journal* 6/2 (1985): 257-66.

[14]Moo, pp. 177-78.

[15]Erickson, *Contemporary Options in Eschatology,* pp. 156-57.

[16]See, for example, Moo, pp. 178-82.

[17]Ibid., pp. 185-202.

[18]George Eldon Ladd, "Historic Premillennialism," in *The Meaning of the Millennium: Four Views,* ed. Robert Clouse (Downers Grove: InterVarsity Press, 1977), pp. 17-18.

[19]George E. Ladd, *Crucial Questions about the Kingdom of God* (Grand Rapids, Mich.: Eerdmans, 1952), p. 141.

[20]Erickson, *Contemporary Options in Eschatology,* pp. 98-99.

[21]Ladd, *Crucial Questions,* p. 146.

[22]Ibid., p. 149.

[23]George R. Beasley-Murray, "The Revelation," in *The New Bible Commentary: Revised,* ed. Donald Guthrie and J. A. Motyer (Grand Rapids, Mich.: Eerdmans, 1970), p. 1306.

[24]Henry Alford, *The New Testament for English Readers,* 2 vols. (1863—1866; reprint, 2 vols. in one, Chicago: Moody, n.d.), pp. 1928-29.

[25]Erickson, *Contemporary Options in Eschatology,* pp. 100-101.

[26]See G. H. Lang, *The Revelation of Jesus Christ* (London: Oliphants, 1945), pp. 339-40; Kromminga, *Millennium,* p. 84; Ladd, *Crucial Questions,* pp. 178-79; Millard Erickson, *Christian Theology* (Grand Rapids, Mich.: Baker, 1983—1985), 3:1217.

[27]Kromminga, *Millennium,* p. 105.

[28]See Ladd, "Historic Premillennialism," pp. 20-27.

[29]See, for example, Kromminga, *Millennium,* p. 65.

[30]Ibid., pp. 65-66.

[31]Ladd, "Historic Premillennialism," p. 27.

[32]Ibid., pp. 29-32.

[33]George E. Ladd, *The Presence of the Future* (Grand Rapids, Mich.: Eerdmans, 1974), p. 218.

[34]Moo, "The Posttribulation Rapture Position," p. 207.

[35]Ladd, "Historic Premillennialism," p. 39.

[36]George Eldon Ladd, "Israel and the Church," *Evangelical Quarterly* 36 (1964): 206-13; Erickson, *Contemporary Options in Eschatology,* p. 103.

[37]For example, Ladd, "Historic Premillennialism," pp. 18-29.

[38]For example, Ladd, *Crucial Questions,* pp. 136-41.

[39]Archibald Hughes, *A New Heaven and a New Earth* (London: Marshall, Morgan and Scott, 1958), pp. 83-105; Floyd Hamilton, *The Basis of Millennial Faith* (Grand Rapids, Mich.: Eerdmans, 1952), pp. 63-64.

[40]Ladd, *Crucial Questions,* pp. 66-74.

[41]Erickson, *Contemporary Options in Eschatology,* p. 91.

[42]Hughes, *New Heaven and New Earth,* pp. 75-79.

[43]Hamilton, *Basis of Millennial Faith,* pp. 46-51.

[44]Ibid., pp. 60-66, 71-80, 100-102.

[45]R. Fowler White, "Reexamining the Evidences for Recapitulation in Rev. 20:1-10," *Westminster Theological Journal* 51 (1989): 324.

[46]See, for example, Vos's response to the premillennial exegesis of 1 Corinthians 15:24, Geerhardus Vos, *The Pauline Eschatology* (1930; reprint ed., Grand Rapids, Mich.: Eerdmans, 1972), pp. 243-46. See also Hamilton, *Basis of Millennial Faith,* pp. 95-98.

[47]Jay Adams, *The Time Is at Hand* (Philadelphia: Presbyterian and Reformed, 1974), pp. 17-40.

[48]For example, Ladd, "Historic Premillennialism," pp. 17-18.

[49]Hughes, *New Heaven and New Earth*, pp. 103-5; Vos, *Pauline Eschatology*, p. 245; Hamilton, *Basis of Millennial Faith*, pp. 93-102.

[50]Anthony Hoekema, *The Bible and the Future* (Grand Rapids, Mich.: Eerdmans, 1979), pp. 185-86.

[51]For a summary treatment of the Epistles, see Hamilton, *Basis of Millennial Faith*, pp. 91-112. The classic amillennial study of Paul is Vos, *Pauline Eschatology*.

[52]Hoekema, *Bible and the Future*, p. 186.

[53]Anthony Hoekema, "Historic Premillennialism: An Amillennial Response," in *Meaning of the Millennium*, p. 59. For a similar critique, see Louis Berkhof, *The Second Coming of Christ* (Grand Rapids, Mich.: Eerdmans, 1953), p. 93.

[54]D. H. Kromminga, *The Millennium in the Church* (Grand Rapids, Mich.: Eerdmans, 1945), p. 242.

[55]Ibid., p. 253.

[56]Ibid., pp. 313-14.

[57]Ibid., p. 253.

[58]Dwight Wilson, *Armageddon Now! The Premillenarian Response to Russia and Israel Since 1917* (Grand Rapids, Mich.: Baker, 1977), p. 29.

[59]Kromminga, *Millennium in the Church*, p. 253.

[60]For example, Wilson, *Armageddon Now!*, p. 17.

[61]Ernest R. Sandeen, *The Roots of Fundamentalism: British and American Millenarianism, 1800—1930* (Chicago: University of Chicago Press, 1970), pp. 13-14.

Chapter 6: A Golden Age Beyond Time

[1]Louis Berkhof, *Systematic Theology*, revised and enlarged edition (Grand Rapids, Mich.: Eerdmans, 1953), p. 708.

[2]Millard Erickson, *Contemporary Options in Eschatology: A Study of the Millennium* (Grand Rapids, Mich.: Baker, 1977), p. 76.

[3]See, for example, Anthony Hoekema, *The Bible and the Future* (Grand Rapids, Mich.: Eerdmans, 1979), p. 173.

[4]Erickson has noted this tendency in *Contemporary Options in Eschatology*, p. 73.

[5]One notable attempt to delineate an eschatology from the amillennial perspective is Hoekema, *The Bible and the Future*. See also Stephen Travis, *I Believe in the Second Coming of Jesus* (Grand Rapids, Mich.: Eerdmans, 1982).

[6]Berkhof, *Systematic Theology*, p. 708.

[7]Oswald T. Allis, *Prophecy and the Church* (Grand Rapids, Mich.: Baker, 1972), p. 5.

[8]G. C. Berkouwer, *The Return of Christ* (Grand Rapids, Mich.: Eerdmans, 1972), pp. 314-15.

[9]For the typical amillennial scenario, see Floyd Hamilton, *The Basis of Millennial Faith* (Grand Rapids, Mich.: Eerdmans, 1952), pp. 35-37.

[10]See, for example, William E. Cox, *In These Last Days* (Philadelphia: Presbyterian and Reformed, 1964), pp. 59-67.

[11]Louis Berkhof, *The Second Coming of Christ* (Grand Rapids, Mich.: Eerdmans, 1953), p. 83.

[12]Cox, *These Last Days*, pp. 80-81.

[13]Archibald Hughes, *A New Heaven and a New Earth* (London: Marshall, Morgan and Scott,

1958), p. 44.

[14]Martin J. Wyngaarden, *The Future of the Kingdom* (Grand Rapids, Mich.: Baker, 1955), p. 85.

[15]Hamilton, *Basis of Millennial Faith*, p. 53.

[16]Wyngaarden, *Future of the Kingdom*, pp. 175-78.

[17]For example, Hughes, *New Heaven and New Earth*, pp. 46-48.

[18]For a defense of the assertion that the church is the New Israel, see Thomas R. Schreiner, "The Church as the New Israel and the Future of Ethnic Israel in Paul," *Studia Biblica et Theologica* 13/1 (April 1983): 17-38.

[19]William Hendricksen, *Israel in Prophecy* (Grand Rapids, Mich.: Baker, 1968), p. 54.

[20]Ibid., p. 55-56.

[21]Hamilton, *Basis of Millennial Faith*, pp. 55-56.

[22]Hendricksen, *Israel in Prophecy*, p. 56.

[23]For detailed discussions of Old Testament prophecies applied to the church, see Wyngaarden, *Future of the Kingdom*, pp. 88-142; Allis, *Prophecy and the Church*, pp. 134-59.

[24]Hendricksen, *Israel in Prophecy*, p. 57.

[25]See, for example, ibid., pp. 16-32.

[26]Ibid., pp. 32-52.

[27]See, for example, Hoekema, *Bible and the Future*, p. 140, who cites Herman Bavinck, Louis Berkhof, William Hendricksen, G. C. Berkouwer and Herman Ridderbos as advocates of this view. See also O. Palmer Robertson, "Is There a Distinctive Future for Ethnic Israel in Romans 11?" in *Perspectives on Evangelical Theology*, ed. Kenneth S. Kantzer and Stanley N. Gundry (Grand Rapids, Mich.: Baker, 1979), pp. 217-27.

[28]Hughes, *New Heaven and New Earth*, p. 50; see also Hendricksen, *Israel in Prophecy*, p. 51.

[29]For a discussion of this development, see Mark L. Karlberg, "Legitimate Discontinuities between the Testaments," *Journal of the Evangelical Theological Society* 28/1 (1985): 15-18.

[30]Willem A. VanGemeren, "Israel as the Hermeneutical Crux in the Interpretation of Prophecy (II)," *Westminster Journal of Theology* 46/2 (Fall 1984): 269-97.

[31]For the use of similar terminology by a progressive dispensationalist, see Kenneth L. Barker, "The Scope and Center of Old and New Testament Theology and Hope," in *Israel and the Church: Essays in Contemporary Dispensational Thought*, ed. Craig A. Blaising and Darrell L. Bock (Grand Rapids, Mich.: Zondervan, 1992), pp. 293-328.

[32]Van Gemeren, "Israel as the Hermeneutical Crux (II)," pp. 284-85.

[33]Ibid., p. 277.

[34]Ibid., pp. 291-92.

[35]This is the position of the Dutch theologian C. Graafland as described by Willem A. VanGemeren, "Israel as the Hermeneutical Crux in the Interpretation of Prophecy," *Westminster Journal of Theology* 45 (1983): 143.

[36]Ibid.

[37]Karlberg, "Legitimate Discontinuities between the Testaments," p. 18.

[38]VanGemeren, "Israel as the Hermeneutical Crux (II)," p. 288.

[39]Ibid., p. 289.

[40]This is Schreiner's judgment in "Church as the New Israel," p. 27.

[41]See, for example, Krister Stendahl, *Paul Among Jews and Gentiles and Other Essays* (Philadelphia: Fortress, 1976), p. 4.

[42]Schreiner, "Church as the New Israel," pp. 32-38. See also Dan G. Johnson, "The Structure and Meaning of Romans 11," *Catholic Biblical Quarterly* 46/1 (January 1984): 101-3.

[43]Cox, *These Last Days,* p. 41.

[44]See, for example, the discussion in ibid., pp. 12-16.

[45]Hamilton, *Basis of Millennial Faith,* pp. 53-54.

[46]Hoekema, *Bible and the Future,* pp. 240-43; Cox, *These Last Days,* pp. 72-74.

[47]Cox, *These Last Days,* pp. 74-77.

[48]Hoekema, *Bible and the Future,* p. 243; Cox, *These Last Days,* pp. 77-78.

[49]For the connection between the Apocalypse and Paul's writings, see, for example, Sydney H. T. Page, "Revelation 20 and Pauline Eschatology," *Journal of the Evangelical Theological Society* 23/1 (March 1980): 31-43.

[50]See, for example, Meredith G. Kline, "The First Resurrection," *Westminster Theological Journal* 37/3 (Spring 1975): 366-71.

[51]Hamilton, *Basis of Millennial Faith,* p. 123. See also Ray Summers, "Revelation 20: An Interpretation," *Review and Expositor* 57/2 (April 1960): 181-82.

[52]Cox, *These Last Days,* pp. 68-71.

[53]Norman Shepherd, "The Resurrections of Revelation 20," *Westminster Theological Journal* 37/1 (Fall 1974): 34-43.

[54]Cox, *These Last Days,* pp. 70-71; Hamilton, *Basis of Millennial Faith,* p. 130.

[55]The location of the reign is the subject of the short study by Roman Catholic scholar Michel Gourgues, "The Thousand Year Reign (Rev. 20:1-6): Terrestrial or Celestial," *Catholic Biblical Quarterly* 47/4 (October 1985): 676-81.

[56]Benjamin B. Warfield, *Biblical Doctrines* (Edinburgh: Banner of Truth, 1988), p. 649.

[57]See, for example, Hughes, *New Heaven and New Earth,* pp. 58-59; Summers, "Revelation 20," p. 180. See also William Hendricksen, *More Than Conquerors: An Interpretation of the Book of Revelation* (Grand Rapids, Mich.: Baker, 1973), p. 229.

[58]Kline, "First Resurrection," p. 372-75.

[59]Hoekema, *Bible and the Future,* pp. 234-35.

[60]James A. Hughes, "Revelation 20:4-6 and the Question of the Millennium," *Westminster Theological Journal* 35/3 (Spring 1973): 288.

[61]Hendricksen, *More Than Conquerors,* pp. 230-31.

[62]Hoekema, *Bible and the Future,* p. 230.

[63]See Hughes, "Revelation 20:4-6," pp. 289-91.

[64]Hamilton, *Basis of Millennial Faith,* p. 119.

[65]Hughes, "Revelation 20:4-6," pp. 299-302.

[66]See also Hoekema, *Bible and the Future,* p. 236.

[67]For example, Hughes, *New Heaven and New Earth,* p. 56; Hoekema, *Bible and the Future,* pp. 228-29; Hamilton, *Basis of Millennial Faith,* pp. 132-33. R. Fowler White hints at a possible alternative view in "Reexamining the Evidence for Recapitulation in Revelation 20:1-10," *Westminster Theological Journal* 51 (1989): 342-43.

[68]Hendricksen, *More Than Conquerors,* p. 226.

[69]See Hughes, *New Heaven and New Earth,* p. 57.

[70]Hamilton, *Basis of Millennial Faith,* p. 132; Hughes, *New Heaven and New Earth,* p. 57; Hendricksen, *More Than Conquerors,* pp. 226-28; Hoekema, *Bible and the Future,* pp. 228-29.

[71]See, for example, Hughes, *New Heaven and New Earth,* p. 61.

[72]For a summary statement concerning the exegesis involved in this assertion, see White, "Reexamining the Evidence," pp. 325-36.

[73]Hamilton, *Basis of Millennial Faith,* pp. 136-38.

[74]White argues for recapitulation as well from the motif of the angelic ascent and descent in the book of Revelation ("Reexamining the Evidence," pp. 336-43).

[75]Hendricksen, *More Than Conquerors,* pp. 44-48. See also Hoekema, *Bible and the Future,* pp. 223-26.

[76]Warfield, *Biblical Doctrines,* p. 645.

[77]Kline argues theologically as well as exegetically for the amillennial view. In contrast to it, the two millenarian alternatives conflict with the terms of the covenant of grace. See Meredith G. Kline, "The First Resurrection: A Reaffirmation," *Westminster Theological Journal* 39/1 (Fall 1976): 117-19.

[78]For example, Loraine Boettner, "A Postmillennial Response to Amillennialism," in *The Meaning of the Millennium: Four Views,* ed. Robert G. Clouse (Downers Grove: InterVarsity Press, 1977), p. 200.

[79]Jay Adams, *The Time Is at Hand* (Philadelphia: Presbyterian and Reformed, 1974).

[80]For example, Hamilton, *Basis of Millennial Faith,* p. 38.

[81]Charles Ryrie, *Dispensationalism Today* (Chicago: Moody, 1965), pp. 91, 94.

[82]George N. H. Peters, *The Theocratic Kingdom* (Grand Rapids, Mich.: Kregel, 1952), 1:167-68.

[83]See, for example, Ladd, "A Historic Premillennial Response," pp. 189-91; Hoyt, "A Dispensational Premillennial Response," in *Meaning of the Millennium,* pp. 192-98.

[84]For example, Bruce Milne, *What the Bible Says about the End of the World* (Lottbridge Drove, Great Britain: Kingsway, 1979), pp. 84-85.

[85]For example, David L. Turner, "The New Jerusalem in Revelation 21:1—22:15: Consummation of a Biblical Continuum," in *Israel and the Church,* pp. 275-77.

[86]Hamilton, *Basis of Millennial Faith,* p. 129.

[87]Ladd, "Historic Premillennial Response," p. 189. See also Hoyt, "Dispensational Premillennial Response," pp. 195-96.

[88]See, for example, Erickson, *Contemporary Options in Eschatology,* pp. 86-89.

[89]Ladd, "Historic Premillennial Response," p. 190.

[90]Hoyt, "Dispensational Premillennial Response," p. 195.

[91]Some exegetes argue for the extension of millennial participation to all believers on the basis of mention in the text of two groups of saints: (1) the martyrs and (2) all others who did not worship the beast, that is, "who died in their faith." Hendricksen, *More Than Conquerors,* p. 232. See also Hamilton, *Basis of Millennial Faith,* p. 52.

[92]For a recent discussion of this text, see Paul S. Minear, "Far as the Curse is Found: the Point of Revelation 12:15-16," *Novum Testamentum* 33/1 (January 1991): 71-77.

[93]See, for example, Hoyt, "Dispensational Premillennial Response," pp. 193-94.

[94]White, "Reexamining the Evidence," p. 326.

[95]White insightfully challenges the millenarian alternative and similarly finds it to present an incoherent picture; ibid., pp. 321-25.

[96]See, for example, Hoekema's treatment in *Bible and the Future,* pp. 41-54.

[97]Allis, *Prophecy and the Church,* pp. 83-84.

[98]For example, Hamilton, *Basis of Millennial Faith,* pp. 16-17. See also Travis, *I Believe in the Second Coming,* who employs the term "hope" in each of the seven chapters of his book.

[99]Hamilton, *Basis of Millennial Faith,* p. 13.

[100]For example, ibid., p. 34.

[101]Hoekema, *Bible and the Future,* pp. 36-37.

Chapter 7: Optimism—Pessimism—Realism

[1]David L. Turner pinpoints three hermeneutical issues in the debates over eschatology. See his "The Continuity of Scripture and Eschatology: Key Hermeneutical Issues," *Grace Theological Journal* 6/2 (1985): 275-87.

[2]For a concise discussion of these views, see Merrill C. Tenney, *Interpreting Revelation* (Grand Rapids, Mich.: Eerdmans, 1957), pp. 134-46.

[3]This thesis is set forth in D. M. Kromminga, *The Millennium in the Church* (Grand Rapids, Mich.: Eerdmans, 1945), pp. 313-14.

[4]See, for example, Ernest R. Sandeen, *The Roots of Fundamentalism: British and American Millenarianism, 1800—1930* (Chicago: University of Chicago Press, 1970), pp. 36-37.

[5]Tenney erroneously chastizes the preterist view for failing to account adequately for the claim of Revelation to be a prediction of the future *(Interpreting Revelation,* p. 137). Preterists indeed find a future reference in the book to the extent that it is a prophecy of the coming victory over the forces of evil.

[6]For the Jewish background to this theological problem, see the short treatment by T. Francis Glasson, "The Temporary Messianic Kingdom and the Kingdom of God," *Journal of Theological Studies* 41/2 (October 1990): 517-25.

[7]Marcus J. Berg, "Jesus and the Kingdom of God," *Christian Century* 102/13 (April 22, 1987): 378-80.

[8]Bruce D. Chilton, *God in Strength: Jesus' Announcement of the Kingdom* (1978; reprint, Sheffield, England: JSOT, 1987), pp. 287-88.

[9]Bruce D. Chilton, "Introduction," in *The Kingdom of God in the Teachings of Jesus,* ed. Bruce Chilton, Issues in Religion and Theology, number 5 (Philadelphia: Fortress, 1984), p. 25.

[10]See Joel Marcus, "Entering into the Kingly Power of God," *Journal of Biblical Literature* 107/4 (1988): 663-75.

[11]Ibid., p. 674.

[12]See, for example, the discussion of Puritan missions in Iain H. Murray, *The Puritan Hope* (London: Banner of Truth Trust, 1971), pp. 131-83, esp. pp. 149-51, 178. See also John Jefferson Davis, *Christ's Victorious Kingdom* (Grand Rapids, Mich.: Baker, 1986), pp. 118-19.

[13]H. Richard Niebuhr, *The Kingdom of God in America,* Harper Torchbook edition (1937; reprint, New York: Harper and Row, 1959), p. 194.

[14]Murray, *Puritan Hope,* p. xv.

[15]See, for example, Reinhold Niebuhr, "Intellectual Autobiography," in *Reinhold Niebuhr: His Religious, Social and Political Thought,* vol. 2 of the Library of Living Theology, ed. Charles W. Kegley and Robert W. Bretall (New York: Macmillan, 1961), p. 15.

[16]For example, Reinhold Niebuhr, *An Interpretation of Christian Ethics,* Living Age Edition (New York: Meridian Books, 1956), pp. 97-123.

[17]See, for example, his discussion in Reinhold Niebuhr, *The Nature and Destiny of Man,* Scribner Library edition (New York: Charles Scribner's Sons, 1964), 2:287-98.

[18]Ibid., 2:320.

[19]Jürgen Moltmann, *The Experiment Hope,* trans. M. Douglas Meeks (Philadelphia: Fortress, 1975), p. 45.

[20]Ibid.

[21]Ibid., p. 49.

[22]Ibid., p. 52.

[23]Ibid., p. 49.

[24]Ibid.

[25]Ibid., p. 51.

[26]Jürgen Moltmann, "Hope and History," *Theology Today* 25/3 (October 1968): 385.

[27]Moltman, *Experiment Hope*, p. 59.

[28]See William Dean Ferm, *Contemporary American Theologies* (New York: Seabury, 1981), p. 62.

Chapter 8: Our Present in the Light of God's Future

[1]The thesis that eschatology focuses on Christ is ably defended in Adrio König, *The Eclipse of Christ in Eschatology: Toward a Christ-Centered Approach* (Grand Rapids, Mich.: Eerdmans, 1989).

[2]G. C. Berkouwer, *The Return of Christ* (Grand Rapids, Mich.: Eerdmans, 1972), p. 19.

[3]See Stanley J. Grenz, *Prayer: The Cry for the Kingdom* (Peabody, Mass.: Hendrickson, 1988).

[4]George E. Ladd, "The Revival of Apocalyptic in the Churches," *Review and Expositor* 72/3 (Summer 1975): 267-68.

[5]See, for example, Michael D. Williams, "Where's the Church? The Church as the Unfinished Business of Dispensational Theology," *Grace Theological Journal* 10/2 (1989): 165-82; Kenneth L. Barker, "False Dichotomies between the Testaments," *Journal of the Evangelical Theological Society* 25/1 (March 1982): 3-16.

[6]For a discussion of the Christian Zionist movement from a critical perspective, see O. Kelly Ingram, "Christian Zionism," *The Link* 16/4 (November 1983): 1-13.

[7]Central to the newer outlook in Christian theology is the work of Paul Van Buren. His position is articulated in *Discerning the Way* (New York: Seabury, 1980); *A Christian Theology of the People of Israel* (New York: Seabury, 1983); and *Christ in Context* (San Francisco: Harper and Row, 1988). Important as well are the efforts of Jürgen Moltmann. See, for example, his "Christian Hope: Messianic or Transcendent?" *Horizon* 12/2 (1985): 328-48; "Israel's No: Jews and Jesus in an Unredeemed World," *Christian Century* 107/32 (November 7, 1990): 1021-24. See also Walter Riggans, "Toward an Evangelical Doctrine of the Church: The Church and Israel," *Churchman* 103/2 (1989): 129-35.

[8]For a discussion of the major contemporary attitudes toward Israel, see Paul R. Dekar, "Does the State of Israel Have Theological Significance?" reprinted in *Conrad Grebel Review* 2/1 (Winter 1984): 31-46. See also Gabriel Fackre, "Perspectives on the Place of Israel in Christian Faith," *Andover-Newton Review* 1/2 (Winter 1990): 7-17.

[9]For a discussion of this, see Mark L. Karlberg, "Legitimate Discontinuities between the Testaments," *Journal of the Evangelical Theological Society* 28/1 (March 1985): 15-17.

[10]Stanley H. Gundry, "Hermeneutics or *Zeitgeist* as the Determining Factor in the History of Eschatologies," *Journal of the Evangelical Theological Society* 20/1 (1977): 50.

[11]John Jefferson Davis, *Christ's Victorious Kingdom* (Grand Rapids, Mich.: Baker, 1986), p. 127.

[12]This is the consensus reached by the newer research into the kingdom of God in the teaching of Jesus. See Bruce Chilton, "Introduction," in *The Kingdom of God in the Teaching of Jesus*, ed. Bruce Chilton, Issues in Religion and Theology, number 5 (Philadelphia: Fortress, 1984), pp. 25-26.

[13]Edgar Young Mullins, *The Christian Religion in Its Doctrinal Expression* (Philadelphia: Roger Williams, 1917), pp. 471-72.